FROM SUN TO SUN

From Sun to Sun

Daily Obligations and Community Structure in the Lives of Employed Women and Their Families

WILLIAM MICHELSON
Professor of Sociology
University of Toronto

ROWMAN & ALLANHELD
PUBLISHERS

ROWMAN & ALLANHELD

Published in the United States of America in 1985
by Rowman & Allanheld, Publishers
(a division of Littlefield, Adams & Company)
81 Adams Drive, Totowa, New Jersey 07512

Copyright © 1985 by William Michelson

All rights reserved. No part of this publication
may be reproduced, stored in a retrieval system, or
transmitted in any form or by any means, electronic,
mechanical, photocopying, recording, or otherwise,
without the prior permission of the publisher.

Library of Congress Cataloging in Publication Data

Michelson, William M., 1940–
　From sun to sun.

　Bibliography: p.
　Includes index.
　1. Mothers—Employment—Ontario—Toronto Metropolitan
Area.　2. Children of working mothers—Ontario—Toronto
Metropolitan Area.　I. Title.
HD6055.2.C22T676　1985　　305.4'2'09713541　　84-18245
ISBN 0-86598-149-3

85　86　87　/　10　9　8　7　6　5　4　3　2　1
Printed in the United States of America

This book is gratefully dedicated to the memories of Linda Hagarty and Alexander Szalai, whose uplifting and creative contributions, in unique ways, were inspiring influences on the content and form of the research reported.

Contents

List of Tables		ix
List of Figures		xiii
Preface		xv
Chapter 1	Maternal Employment in Perspective	1
Chapter 2	Measuring Daily Life: Its Objective and Subjective Aspects	14
Chapter 3	Why Women "Work"	32
Chapter 4	Employment Status and the Daily Routine	43
Chapter 5	The Immediate Context: Household Division of Labor	60
Chapter 6	Outcomes of Maternal Employment	72
Chapter 7	Single Parenthood: How Special?	89
Chapter 8	Implications for Children of Maternal Employment	101
Chapter 9	The External Context: How Supportive?	116
Chapter 10	Summer Vacation: How Free (and for Whom)?	145
Chapter 11	Emergent Implications for Policy and Practice	154
References		165
Appendix	The Survey Instrument	171
Index		205

List of Tables

2.1 Means and Standard Deviations of Minutes in Three Types of Parent-Child Contact as Coded from Observation and from a Time-Budget Survey.   22

2.2 Pearson Product-Moment Correlations of Minutes in Three Types of Parent-Child Contact as Observed and as Recorded by Time-Budget Self-Reports.   23

3.1 Median Income by Employment and Marital Status of Female Head of Household.   39

3.2 Reasons for Taking Outside Employment by Contentment with the Decision to Have Done So.   40

3.3 Husband's Income and Contentment with the Decision to Take Outside Employment.   41

4.1 Mean Number of Minutes Devoted to Major Activities by Married Women on a Weekday by Employment Status.   51

4.2 Children's Accompaniment on Excursions During Previous Six Months by Employment Status of Wife.   54

4.3 Mean Number of Minutes Devoted to Employment, Housework, and Child Care by Husbands and Wives by Employment Status of Wife.   55

4.4 Correlations of Daily Minutes of Work to Minutes in Other Activities (Men and Women).   55

4.5	Mean Number of Hours in Each Behavior Setting on Weekend for Wives by Employment Status.	57
4.6	Mean Number of Hours Women are at Home with Children During Weekend in Absence of Husband, by Wife's Employment Status.	57
4.7	Mean Number of Minutes Devoted by Women to Selected Activities, by Age of Children.	58
5.1	Correlations of Time Devoted by Husbands and Wives to Activities on a Weekday by Employment Status of Wife.	68
6.1	Correlations of Women's Perceived Time Pressure for Average Week with Perceived Time Pressure for Particular Activities.	77
6.2	Percentage of Wives Reporting a Lot or a Great Deal of Worry about Being Too Busy for Particular Activities by Employment Status.	79
6.3	Correlations between Minutes Devoted to Specific Activities and Women's Perceived Time Pressure "Yesterday."	80
6.4	Mean Tension in Selected Daily Activities (Men and Women).	82
6.5	Typical "Conflicts" Among Employed Mothers by Employment Status.	84
7.1	Forms of Nonspousal Assistance Received during Past Month by Employment and Marital Status.	92
7.2	Mean Minutes Devoted by Women to Major Activities on a Weekday, by Employment and Marital Status.	93
7.3	General Happiness Among Women by Employment and Marital Status.	98
7.4	Self-Characterizations Among Women by Employment and Marital Status.	99

7.5	Women's Specific Concerns by Employment and Marital Status.	100
8.1	Selected Aspects of Time Usage by Children, by Employment Status of Mother (2-Parent Families Only) and Age of Child.	105
8.2	Mean Number of Minutes Children Devote to Selected Activities on a Weekday, by Age and Sex.	109
8.3	Mother's Characterization of Children by Their Age and Her Marital and Employment Status.	112
9.1	Mean Time Pressure Scores for Women by Type of Child Care Services Used.	118
9.2	Company on Trips from Home by Married Women.	123
9.3	Destination of Married Women's Trips from Home by Employment Status.	124
9.4	Company and Mode of Travel in Trips by Married Women by Employment Status.	124
9.5	Mode of Travel Used for Married Women's Trips Home, by Selected Trip Origins and Employment Status.	125
9.6	Mean Minutes a Weekday in Travel by Mode of Transportation and Employment Status of Married Women, for Husbands and Wives.	126
9.7	Time Pressure Yesterday by Mode of Travel to Work, by Sex.	132
9.8	Tension in Employed Women's Travel by Selected Types of Distance (Correlation Coefficients).	135
9.9	Mean Number of Household Responsibilities by Employed Mothers, by Type of Employment Hours and Flexibility of Job Structure.	139
9.10	Differences in the Percentage of Female Respondents Responsible for Specific Household Chores by Degree of Workplace Flexibility.	140

9.11	Mean Time Pressure Scores by Kinds and Degree of Flexibility in Employment.	141
10.1	Average Minutes on a Summer Weekday a Subsample of Children Spend on Selected Activities (and Differences from School Term Time Distributions for the Same Children), by Age.	146
10.2	Correlation Coefficients Describing Relationship of the Amount of Time Individual Respondents Spent on Specific Categories of Activity During the Weekdays Sampled in the School Term and Summer Surveys.	149
10.3	Mean Minutes on a Summer Weekday a Subsample of Husbands and Wives Spend on Selected Activities (Differences from School-Term Time Distributions for the Same Respondents) by Wives' Employment Status.	150
10.4	Mean Weekday Time in Minutes Children Spend with Their Mother and Father During the Summer, by Age of Child and Mother's Employment Status.	151
10.5	Married Women's Perceived Time Pressures for "Last Week" (During Summer) and the Average Week, by Employment Status.	153
11.1	Women's Hours of Employment a Week and Contentment with Decision to Work.	157

List of Figures

1.1	A Social-Ecological Perspective on Maternal Employment.	11
3.1	Historical Increases in Selected Consumer Price Indices and in the Percentage of Married Women, with Children under 6, in the Labor Force.	36
4.1	Andy Capp on Household Chores.	46
4.2	Sally Forth on Quality Time.	49
5.1	Dennis the Menace on Household Division of Labor.	61
5.2	Minutes a Weekday Husbands and Wives in Two-Parent Families Devote to Housework and Child Care by Wives' Employment Status.	66
6.1	Mean Time Pressures for Married Women by Employment Status.	75
7.1	Frequency of Use of Restaurants and Take-out Food for Dinner, by Women's Marital and Employment Status.	95
7.2	Perceived Time Pressures for Women, by Employment and Marital Status.	96
8.1	Cumulative Chart of Mean Minutes in Specific Modes of Travel per Day, by Age Category of Child.	107
9.1	Distances between Women's Homes, Child Care Locations, and Places of Employment.	134
9.2	Distance from Home to Three Child Care Alternatives.	134

Preface

In 1977, I was part of an interdisciplinary research team at the University of Toronto working on *The Child in the City*. This team's objective was to create and complete a program of research on how recent changes in urban areas had affected the lives and well-being of children. A number of aspects of urban areas were examined: the environment, intergroup relations, social-service systems, legal and political structures, and more. One was child rearing. Who brings up children in urban society? What difference does it make whether children are at home or in various forms of external child-care arrangement?

As part of our attempt to assess what was already known on the subject and to identify what required attention,* we came across what appeared to be a major gap in research knowledge. Virtually nothing was available as to how children's lives are altered by increasingly frequent decisions on the part of mothers to hold outside employment. Psychologists had focused attention on the importance and effects of particular types of child care and on such particular concepts as parent-child separation, but the general question was unanswered: What kinds of lives children do lead when their parents themselves make this critical life-style decision?

Children's lives can not be viewed in isolation from the objective and subjective situation of their parents. Therefore, we had to design research that could link an important "structural" commitment on the part of mothers, i.e., to take outside employment, to major dimensions of the lives of their children. (We took into consideration another growing trend, that many mothers are single parents.) We sought to do this by understanding what maternal employment means in the daily lives, challenges, and pressures of women. Insofar as women and children function within the interactive system we know as the family, this required studying behavior, interaction, and outcomes among the various members of families, viewed in terms of women's employment and marital status.

---

*This is the subject of William Michelson et al., *The Child in the City: Changes and Challenges,* University of Toronto Press, 1979.

Families and family members, moreover, do not exist in a vacuum. When they respond to the responsibilities taken on by a given family member, such as the wife/mother, the ease or difficulty of what they do and hence the personal outcomes are based also on whether the outside world is set up to facilitate or hinder their actions. The community is made up of practices, services, facilities, locations, opening and closing hours, and travel needs, which, in their presence or absence, convenience or inconvenience, can influence whether maternal-employment options are viable.

With a financial contribution from Canada's Ministry of National Health and Welfare, National Welfare Grants Programme, a survey of 544 Metropolitan Toronto families with children was held as part of a multiphase research project in 1980. This research was created to assess, in as great detail as possible, the linkages among women's everyday commitments, their resultant pattern of activities, what others in their families do and experience in consequence, and what personal outcomes and problems occur in given contexts. As part of the picture, we sought to assess how such potential external supports as child-care alternatives, transportation options, and flexibility in work and other structures function logistically and contribute to ease or pressure.*

This book, then, is intended to present maternal employment, a widespread contemporary phenomenon that concerns many participants, in a perspective that makes it easier to understand what problems and outcomes can arise. It is intended to illustrate how empirical research that links structural, contextual, behavioral, and subjective phenomena can be applied within such a perspective. It is intended also to add to our knowledge, with the results of the research effort in Toronto, of how and under what conditions maternal employment affects women and their children. Some lessons for policy and practice are drawn from these results.

The book therefore begins with an attempt to identify relevant aspects of concern about maternal employment and to integrate them into a useful explanatory perspective. This perspective treats maternal employment in social-ecological terms, linking macro factors to personal outcomes through a variety of mutually interacting, contextually relevant factors. The latter factors include family-system dynamics and a chronogeographic view of community.

Chapter 2 deals with the innovations and major decisions that had to be made to implement this wide-ranging, complex perspective. It provides the methodological details for the data drawn upon subsequently. Considerable attention is given the time-budget technique, especially experimental work on

---

*The U.S. Department of Transportation, Urban Mass Transportation Administration, made a grant, CA-11-0024, which facilitated the analysis of such considerations.

increasing its relevance concerning parent-child activities, subjective aspects of time-use, and coverage of all family members.

Results from the survey, which bear on a number of questions pertinent to maternal employment, form a complex step-by-step argument in the following eight chapters. Chapter 3 looks at why women "work," as a background to understanding what they pay as a price for being employed.

Chapter 4 turns to what is different in everyday life when women with children have full-time, part-time, or no employment. It focuses on people's use of time and their trade-offs among activities. Differences by employment status are shown and are analyzed in terms of competing explanations. Such considerations as obligatory activity, quality time, and the overall reality of days and weekends are examined in greater detail. The chapter indicates the role of a major responsibility like employment in shaping typical daily activity.

How a woman's daily round fits the demands on her is in part a matter of a family's division of labor. When women have outside jobs, do husbands fill the gap at home? What do husbands and wives take responsibility for and under what conditions? Where do children fit into the division of labor at home? These matters are treated in Chapter 5.

Chapter 6 covers a number of personal outcomes. Among these are amounts and sources of time pressure, actual vs. ideal time pressures, and the relationships between time pressures and degree of worry, actual daily activity, and household responsibility. This chapter assesses how tension reflects both the complete daily round of activity and its components. The analysis evaluates the pros and cons of outside employment, as well as how everyday hassle relates to other life concerns, self-concepts, and general happiness.

Single parents presumably face the same problems and logistical difficulties as married women, but with lesser financial resources and no spouse to share the chores. Chapter 7 compares the responsibilities, activities, and feelings of single and married parents, tracing the role of employment in both these groups.

The focus changes to children in Chapter 8. How are their lives altered by their mothers' employment status and accompanying child-care arrangements? Data on activity, contact, and location are explored, according to children's age and sex. The effects of different child-care arrangements are assessed, and some trade-offs of cost and benefits in child development are discussed. Chapter 8 ends with mothers' assessments of how their child-care practices become pressured, and with what result.

Families and individuals alike are thought to get some logistical help from parts of the urban infrastructure. In Chapter 9, some of these are examined to see how much support — and difficulty — they offer to the employed mother. These include child-care arrangements, complex transportation considerations, flexibility in employment, land-use, and timetabling.

Conditions for both parents and children change when school closes for the summer. Is this more or less of a problem for the employed mother? Chapter 10 looks at how children's lives are altered during the summer. Then the focus turns to employment-related differences in what parents do in response.

A number of the results noted in the previous eight chapters are pertinent to public policies and practices. Chapter 11 discusses selected directions toward improvement. The main research instrument appears as an appendix.

The research benefited from the resources, skills, and support of many persons and institutions. In appreciation of the depth of these contributions, I shall attempt to recognize their extent and nature.

First, the University of Toronto's Child in the City Programme was supported by a sustaining grant from the Hospital for Sick Children Foundation. The project could not have been formulated or launched without this grant. Colleagues in The Child in the City who collaborated in the design of the project and who were Coinvestigators at various stages of the data collection, processing, and analysis include Linda Hagarty, Susan Hodgson, and Suzanne Ziegler. Many of the details of the study originated from individual colleagues and from our joint interaction; specific credits are given in the text. As the Principal Investigator, I am also grateful to the Department of Sociology, University of Toronto, for released time to serve as Director of The Child in the City Programme and for an extended leave of absence and sabbatical leave, during which the analysis was conducted and the first drafts were written. A grant from the Humanities and Social Sciences Committee of the University of Toronto's Research Board helped facilitate the final draft.

I am indebted to J.E. Theriault of the Ministry of National Health and Welfare (Government of Canada), National Welfare Grants Programme, for his stewardship and support of this project.

The Institute for Transportation Studies, University of California, Irvine, supported some of the analysis and literature with a small grant and I.T.S. administered the work conducted with the Urban Mass Transit Administration grant described on p. xvi. I am extremely grateful to Gordon J. (Pete) Fielding, Al Hollinden, Will Recker, Genevieve Giuliano, Esther Francke, Nancy Jahr, and Lyn Long. The Program in Social Ecology, University of California, Irvine, cosponsored this U.M.T.A. grant and contributed vital computer funds, a second institutional home for the Principal Investigator, and a one-quarter study leave.

The data were gathered at the University of Toronto and analyzed largely at the University of California, Irvine. In addition, the Principal Investigator is grateful to The Institute of Cultural Geography, University of Lund, Sweden, and particularly to Professor Olof Wärneryd, for a quiet but stimulating setting, where most of the initial draft was written and discussed.

Tommy Carlstein, Torsten Hägerstrand, Bo Lenntorp, and Solveig Mårtensson made especially helpful suggestions.

In Toronto, Suzanne Ziegler directed the first phase of the study. Catherine Rivers supervised the complex task of sampling and interviewing on a day-to-day basis for the second-phase survey. Linda Hagarty directed the coding operations, with later assistance by Suzanne Ziegler and Ethan Phillips. A large corps of interviewers and coders deserves grateful acknowledgment, however anonymously. Les Cseh organized and cleaned the data for analysis. Sue Ray did an enormous amount of typing for this research. Martha Friendly and Judith Kjellberg made useful contributions near the completion of the study.

In Irvine, the data analysis benefited from extensive commitments and outstanding efforts by Sherry Ahrentzen, Joan Campbell, Doug Levine, and Linda Naiditch. Danny Sun and Jim Hayes did computer programming, the latter facilitated by cooperation from The Public Policy Research Organization, U.C.I. A number of undergraduates helped with bibliographic and analytic aspects as part of research "internships"; I am particularly grateful in this regard to Alfonso Amezcua, Jessica Bernstein, Theresa Foley, George Rojo, Felecia Tarnol, and Julia Wesley.

Not least, I am grateful to Marcia Bell, Joan Gordon, Jill Vidas, and particularly Carol Wyatt for secretarial support during repeated drafts.

Rowman & Allanheld made the publication process surprisingly smooth. The efficient, professional contributions of Spencer Carr, Toby Dicker Hopstone, Dan Kirklin, and Toby Krutt are happily acknowledged.

As Principal Investigator, I am deeply appreciative of the benefits of working with so many first-rate colleagues. Nonetheless, when tactical decisions had to be made and inevitable conflicts of time, resources, and priorities arose during the course of the study, I took the responsibility for resolving them. I orchestrated the design and operation of the study, organized the analysis, and wrote the book. Hence, while so many of the ideas and so much of the effort came from my collaborators, responsibility for shortcomings lies with me.

One common strand bound researchers and respondents. This was the hope that the data and our conclusions would prove illuminating and helpful in dealing with phenomena that pertain to so many persons. This report is meant less as a critique than as a stepping-stone to societal adaptation to maternal employment. We hope that you, the reader, will treat these materials accordingly, asking what you yourself can do to help enable men, women, and children optimize the quality of their everyday lives.

1
Maternal Employment in Perspective

Formally and substantially, this is a book about the contextual dimensions and personal implications of maternal employment.

At heart, this is a book about everyday hassle. The noun *hassle* refers to situations. Hassle-filled situations are neither random nor inescapable. People have responsibilities that make demands on them. Logistics help determine the extent of the hassle they encounter in meeting these demands. Hence, this is also a book about everyday responsibilities and logistics.

This body of research did not start out of a concern with feminist issues. The original focus was on urban children. Moreover, the lessons learned apply to the vast majority of people. But, in between, there is no missing what confronts employed mothers. Their activities set the stage for the lives of their children—and illustrate, in accentuated form, phenomena with which others as well must grapple.

Employed mothers typically spend their days and find their responsibilities and logistics in families, workplaces, and communities, so this book is about these as well. Hassle in everyday life reflects the logistics of families, workplaces, and communities, as they affect what the individual has to do in a 24-hour day.

The dimensions and implications of maternal employment are many and complex. This first chapter spells them out and puts them in order.

Maternal Employment – a "Problematique"

Why is there so much interest today in maternal employment? It is hardly new. Women have been in the labor force since prehistory. What we are now experiencing is a broad trend in Western societies away from fairly recent cultural prescriptions that woman's place is in the home, spending essentially all her time on activities that nurture husband, family, and dwelling place. Of course, even this prescription did not keep all women out of the world of employment. Women who were poor, single, or widowed or who were unusually highly trained usually worked outside the home. There is no reason to think they had it any easier than today's employed women—quite the contrary. However, our awareness of maternal employment, an awareness that comes from widespread exposure to this phenomenon, has grown.

Numbers can make this point clearer. Somewhat over half of all married women in the United States and Canada, representing all social and demographic divisions, now have outside jobs. This includes married women with children. Whereas, as recently as 1950, only 11.9% of American women with children under six years of age held jobs, this percentage rose steadily to 18.6% in 1960, 30.3% in 1970, and 45.1% in 1980 (United States Department of Commerce, 1975, part 1, p. 210). By 1981, 47.8% of mothers of children under six were employed in the United States, and 47.2% in Canada. In Canada, 55.1% of mothers of school-age children were employed at that time, about 5% under the comparable U.S. level (U.S. Department of Commerce, 1982–83, p. 382; Statistics Canada, 1982, p. 25; Mortimer and London, 1984, p. 27). This trend is large, widespread, and growing.

The traditional cultural pattern for North American women has been eroded in another way as well. In the United States, one in five families with minor children is now headed by a single parent, as is one in seven such Canadian families. This is nearly twice the percentage of just ten years before (U.S. Department of Commerce, 1982–83, p. 43; Statistics Canada, 1982, p. 25). In both countries, women head the great majority of these families: nine times more than men in Canada. In response to economic necessity at least, single mothers are more likely than their married counterparts to be in the labor force.

One writer estimates that only 31% of American families with children now fit the traditional cultural stereotype (Hayghe, 1982, p. 29). This means that the vast majority of mothers is now in a situation for which their culture and probably their upbringing did not prepare them.

Thus, in North America and elsewhere, maternal employment is new and poorly understood. But does that make it a problem for women? According to my dictionary, a *problem* is "a question raised for inquiry, consideration, or solution [and alternatively] a source of perplexity, distress, or vexation" (Webster's New Collegiate Dictionary, 1981, p. 910).

According to the former definition, maternal employment is indeed a "problem." It is a novel phenomenon, all of whose implications are not known. It is a typical example of cultural lag (Ogburn, 1964). An innovation in one aspect of society (often but not necessarily in technology) occasions unexpected changes in other aspects of life. Once these are recognized, practice and policy must adapt to the new situation.

This view is affectively neutral: a problem is a puzzle, a challenge.

But those in the midst of such trends find it difficult to be affectively neutral about the uncertainties in their own lives. As the second definition of *problem* suggests, perplexity turns to distress or vexation. This does not necessarily mean that there is something wrong with maternal employment. It is quite possible that the problem is not maternal employment itself, but rather the welter of employment-related considerations, traditional rules, and societal assumptions.

Yet, despite the precision and neutrality of most of these definitions, we generally interpret a problem not only as if the main phenomenon itself were wrong but as if relatively straightforward cause-and-effect processes were in operation. Thus, a problem should have a solution (both in the singular). In this sense, I do not view maternal employment as a problem at all.

The French have a word, *problematique,* that serves my point of view better. A noun, unlike our adjective *problematic,* its most literal translation is probably "problem set." This implies a plurality of conditions, though the English *problem* still implies that something is wrong. A problematique is a question or phenomenon of public interest or concern that requires explanation, usually through analysis of the interrelationships of several different factors. One can talk about a problematique without casting aspersion on the phenomenon itself. This book therefore views maternal employment as a problematique, not as a problem.

What, then, makes up this problematique? In the next section, I shall sketch some of the factors that have arisen through research and public debate. After that, I shall try to link them more explicitly and dynamically. The relative emphasis I place on any aspect reflects my assessment both of how much present need there is to explicate it and of how central it is to my overall focus on the logistics and outcomes of everyday routines and activities. Specific discussions of the literature, hypotheses about major areas of concern, and the objectives and details of the original research are reserved for chapters which follow.

Contributions to the Problematique

Different observers put the spotlight on different aspects and implications of maternal employment. Each can be highly demanding and thought-provoking, and hence it is not surprising that these typically have been examined one by one, rather than in terms of their interconnectedness.

LABOR-FORCE EQUITY

Inequitable practices within the labor force have placed a doubtful cast on maternal employment. A number of concerns have been recognized and documented. Are women hired on the same basis as men, according to qualifications, for all jobs? Do women get equal pay for equal work? To what extent do women have equal opportunity for promotion? To what degree are women sexually harassed?

Women's positions on such matters have largely been in favor of equality—that one's sex should not matter at the workplace, only qualifications and performance. Nonetheless, women can take on the appearance of requesting gender-specific treatment when asking for various forms of employment-related flexibility and support, to reflect such pressures as child care, which fall most heavily on women. The contradiction is more apparent than real, however, in that this flexibility could as easily benefit men as women, breaking precedents more than budgets.

CHILD-CARE AVAILABILITY AND QUALITY

A special challenge to mothers of young children and a requirement for most outside employment is child care. Are there sufficient child-care places to meet demand? Do the various child-care alternatives fit the needs of different employment situations? Are these affordable? Accessible? Is the care adequate? How positive is the environment in which the children spend this time? How different is it from the experience they would have had with their mothers at home—and in what ways?

Child care is a sine qua non for employment when children are young, but mothers' concerns about employment extend well beyond whether they can get good child care. Many worry that they are depriving their children and themselves of an experience for which there may be no substitute. Others, in contrast, believe that trained child-care providers improve on what mothers can personally provide their children. Furthermore, even assuming sufficient places and stimulating experiences in child care, women have to fit the temporal organization and spatial location of child care into everything else they have to do during the day.

When children are of school age but still not yet autonomous, care is still needed in interim periods when children are supervised by neither parents nor teachers: before and after school, lunch hours, and the like. Responses to these needs have arisen both in and out of school buildings, and the number of so-called latch-key children, who go home to an empty house or apartment after school, has also increased.

Even assuming that sufficient high-quality child-care arrangements are available and that children are treated humanely and positively, what kind of new life style are children increasingly assuming, in activity, social contact, place, and travel?

EXTERNAL CONTEXTS

Some observers have looked at factors outside the employed mother and her family, including and beyond the role each plays as an constraint or support in her life. This view does not, for example, take the usual structure of employment hours as given, but rather asks how they square with those of other activities in the community and with particular demands on the individual worker. How could alternative ways of organizing employment affect loads on other institutions in the community? How does the interaction of employment with other parts of the employed mother's *community context* affect the nature and intensity of her daily life? The same questions have been asked about child-care institutions.

Transportation is an example of a community context. It is necessary for the accomplishment of many daily activities. There is concern that women lack the flexibility of men because they do not have access to the same forms of transportation. Does maternal employment create travel demands that are not recognized? Is women's experience of travel different from men's?

The traditional mother met certain important responsibilities, such as school liaison and preventative health care for children, during the business day, when these were and are most readily available. How well have the institutions that provide such services adapted to maternal-employment trends and the obligations involved? What absolute constraints are placed on employed women, regardless of how willing they are to organize their own lives efficiently?

BEHAVIORAL IMPLICATIONS

Many observers have explored how employed women's typical weekday activities differ from those of housewives. Much concern about women's roles focuses on the formerly dominant household role; attention therefore is on the nature and extent of the employed woman's commitment to household tasks. Intrafamilial division of labor becomes a main point of concern. Do employed mothers' external commitments change the balance of what gets done, or do these women carry a double load? Does a change in the division of labor at home compensate for any cutbacks in women's domestic contributions? Do machines or outsiders take over certain tasks? Are things done at different times of the day or week? On the other hand, do intrafamilial adjustments — or their absence — affect what else, beyond employment and domestic tasks, employed women find themselves able to do?

There has been some interest in differences full-time and part-time employment make on various kinds of everyday behavior outside the job. How, also, do the logistics of the external context affect daily activities?

In short, what behavioral trade-offs accompany maternal employment, in view of women's external and intrafamilial contexts? Are the behavioral dynamics of taking employment the same for women as for men?

PERSONAL OUTCOMES

Still other observers have turned directly to the search for what appear to be direct outcomes of maternal employment. For example, many who are interested in women's free and equal access to the world of employment have looked for the positive self-conceptions and types of interaction that typically accompany successful participation in adult affairs, making encouraging prognoses. Others, to see whether maternal employment strains traditional spousal relationships, have pursued such outcomes as marital harmony. Still others have explored outcomes of maternal employment for other family members, including role-model effects for children, the personal sensibilities of husbands, and the care of sick or aging relatives.

As I indicated at the outset, explicit or implied hassle is usually involved, either as a cost of derived benefits or as a factor in undesirable outcomes.

The absence of some of the other factors just listed from many discussions of outcomes is surprising and disappointing. Anyone deeply concerned with maternal employment wants to know just what circumstances make the difference in the positive or negative personal implications. Conversely, some recent assessments that include considerations of interactions among the factors in this complex problematique provide reasons for optimism.

Let us therefore turn to a more connected view of factors that enter the problematique of maternal employment.

A Social Ecology of Maternal Employment

It is useful to think of the fit among different parts of this problematique as a "social ecology." In one sense, *ecology* is an explanation of the state of an entity in relation to the other entities in its environment. At the same time, it is also the study of how a given environment or context functions in terms of the interrelationships of the entities within it. In other words, it deals both with the many factors involved and with the interaction among them. It is not a theory, nor is it devoted to any one field. Although used originally by natural scientists in such fields as botany and zoology, it is a perspective that helps us deal with real-world problematiques, in contrast to the testing of theories, which are abstracted from the complexities of the real world and whose influence is always on an "all else equal" basis. *Social ecology* extends the ecological perspective to explicitly include the personal, interpersonal, structural, and cultural factors of problematiques involving human health, welfare, safety, and similar concerns. As with biological ecology, it is a way of looking at a situation in light of all the factors that bear upon it and which need be addressed for improvement (see Catalano, 1979).

Bronfenbrenner (1979) has fruitfully applied such a perspective to child development. He shows how one can understand more fully the forces that combine in explaining the development of children, by referring first to proximate and then to increasingly distant systems of interaction with and concern to children. This gives researchers a conceptual apparatus with which to describe children's situations, for explanation and improvement.

We saw in the previous section that researchers and the lay public alike have delineated many aspects of maternal employment one by one, but less typically in combination. Yet there is a need to understand the various components of daily life, as well as how people react to them, in terms of their context and the interactions among them. Calling something a social-ecology perspective provides no guarantee of a perfect operational model, which is always a mirage. However, for an issue like maternal employment, it points us in the right direction and makes a fruitful outcome more likely.

Before turning to the actual interconnection of factors, it is necessary to look at several theoretical paradigms that serve as a basis for bringing them together.

INTEGRATING THEORETICAL PERSPECTIVES

Structural Antecedents

In previous work (Michelson, 1976, epilogue), I indicated my belief that the road to amelioration lies not only in knowing what is happening and what the consequences are, but also in learning why the particular practice is occurring and not something else. This involves going back to considerations that precede the action in question. It involves understanding the various interests that were brought to bear and the structural conditions (such as economics, law, governmental and private sector procedures, and normative dictums) that affect these interests.

For example, before we can really understand maternal employment, we first need to know something about why so many mothers of young children now have outside jobs. It is difficult to fully understand what people do and what outcomes arise from it without knowing *why* they are doing it.

The Family as a Complex System

It is now commonly accepted by psychologists, sociologists, and therapists that what happens to one member of a family affects the others. The various members of so tight a group form a system, with regularized actions and expectations — similar to other kinds of systems, such as ecosystems and complex machinery. Because the interlinkages are so close, when one part changes its operation or fails, the activity or outcome of the other parts is inevitably affected. There may be no intent to change more than one entity in a system, but the relationships between this entity and each of the others make an isolated change (or intervention) almost impossible.

Scientists typically view systems as operating in an equilibrium, which can be altered in evolutionary ways, with mutual readjustments, or broken down entirely. Change in systems is not necessarily bad. The point is to observe what a change in any one part means both for the other interacting parts and for the system as a whole.

In the case of maternal employment, the family system is undergoing a change from the traditional set of relationships, in which the wife was expected to provide unfaltering support to husband, children, relatives, most aspects of household work, and community institutions. In return, the husband was expected to provide economic support, physical strength, and protection. The wife was frequently considered essential to the husband's career — and vice versa. Now that major changes in the total set of obligations facing women have occurred, with employment, the men in the system are directly involved. There may be changes in the nature and division of household activities, in spousal relationships, and in the functions of women in men's careers, at least. Men may find adapting to these changes emotionally difficult. Children are an obvious part of the same system. The need for sufficient and suitable child care to permit employment is obvious. However, other outcomes of this complex relationship for children are relatively poorly understood or documented — a reason for the study described in later chapters. What happens when women's traditional volunteer roles, not least in caring for the older generation, other relatives, and the handicapped, conflict with the demands of paid employment?

Hence, regardless of the reasons employment is undertaken, the daily routine and its outcomes must also be understood in terms of systematic interactions within the family.

Temporal and Spatial Dimensions of Local Community

Although people's external community context may be highly varied in content, its time and space characteristics typically affect their daily routines logistically. All aspects of the community have important dimensions in time and space. They are open or accessible, a lot or a little. They are effectively there or not at certain times of the day and night.[1] They temporally coincide or diverge. They are close or distant from each other and from users or potential users. Travel relates space to time: the available means, speeds, and routes of transportation translate distances into time. Of course, time-use is clearly determined by more than proximity and available transportation, just as use of space reflects more than its temporal qualities. But time and space are nonetheless closely linked as they reflect local communities.

Temporal and spatial dimensions of local community are logistically relevant in everyday life because the day and its routine are inescapable aspects of time management. Everyone's day has 24 hours. The external context's time and space characteristics have permissive or restrictive influences. These must be fit and balanced within the 24-hour day. As Staikov formulated this view (1973), the day is a zero-sum game. It is a fixed resource. Anyone wishing to do something new or different or to do more of an existing activity must do so at the expense of something else. This is fine when the replaced activity is considered inconsequential or when somebody else can do it instead, but not when trade-offs must be made among highly important activities. Time pressures come from inescapable conflicts within our time boundaries, to which the timing and spacing of relevant aspects of our external context contribute heavily. Not all communities are alike in this regard. Their contributions are variable but subject to organization and planning, once the desirability of this is seen. Reference to the temporal and spatial dimensions of the community is an important step in going beyond "blaming the victim" for his or her own time pressures.

Hence, time-use and its spatial underpinnings have been examined by those interested in the behavioral considerations and implications of various forms of planning (e.g., Gutenschwager, 1973; Michelson, 1975, forthcoming 1985). But even with a common theoretical perspective on how external phenomena affect the logistics of time-management, there are different theoretical outlooks on time-use.

One view takes time as a resource to be consumed, much like money (Becker, 1965; Chapin, 1974; Reed, 1976). Time-consumption is seen as an expression of cultural, group, or individual priorities and values. According to this view, one would plan external context to more closely reflect what people choose to spend time on.

Yet people do not have perfect freedom, and there are possibly many occasions when demonstrated behaviors reflect constraint, not choice. The length of time spent in traffic jams can be related only indirectly to choice. Therefore, others tend to relate observed behavior to logistical constraints. Cullen (1978), for example, notes that much of everyday behavior is relatively routine, not requiring ongoing decision making but rather reflecting habits. These habits, however, are said to reflect ambient possibilities, given the spatial and temporal dimensions of the community, and are neither necessarily optimal nor viewed as such.

A school of thought called time geography (or chronogeography) attempts to explain behavior by studying the potential provided in the external contexts of communities, regions, and even nations (see Carlstein, Parkes, and Thrift, 1978; Parkes and Thrift, 1980). Its founder, Torsten Hägerstrand, conceptualizes each individual as on a path through space within a time frame—ultimately a lifetime but, for practical urban applications, a day (Hägerstrand, 1963). Hägerstrand looks at what a person does in terms of what a person can do. What a person can do is limited but not determined by three kinds of constraints:

1. capability constraints—limits to what a person can get into his or her schedule on a given day, under the conditions in which he or she lives and works
2. coupling constraints—whether sufficient numbers and appropriate

types of people can get together within existing temporal and spatial conditions to make an activity possible

3. authority constraints — aspects of the organization of activities, such as opening and closing hours, which potentially narrow what a person can do (Hägerstrand, 1970)

As one of Hägerstrand's colleagues, Mårtensson, put it, people's biographies reflect their external contexts more than we customarily acknowledge (1979). Felson (1981, p. 226) enlarges the relevant picture: "One might see the events of the world as consisting largely of systematic accidents, whether pleasant or perverse, which occur because of socio-temporal limits of everyday life."

Temporal and spatial dimensions of local community alter our view of maternal employment. Rather than looking only at specific details of employment per se or work trips and child care as particular events to be managed, we focus on the overall pattern of daily activity and the external factors that come to bear on it. The nature and feasibility of particular parts of the whole are best understood within the whole picture. Palm and Pred (1974), for example, made a useful application of this perspective to the situation of women, in which transportation is very central.

FROM MACRO FORCES TO PERSONAL OUTCOMES

In an article entitled "The Next Generation in Dual-Earner Family Research," Rapoport and Rapoport (1982) identify three levels of previous research on this topic. They call them the *macroscopic level,* which includes what I call structural antecedents, as well as the trend to maternal employment itself, *middle level,* which covers various workplace and community factors, and *grass-roots levels,* including both intrafamilial considerations and outcomes. They note the need to examine interaction between these levels.

Such an approach is necessary not only to learn more but to understand what is actually happening and for what reasons, prerequisites for subsequent adaptive actions. For example, it is difficult to comprehend the outcomes of maternal employment without first understanding an individual's preexisting motivations to undertake it. The nature and degree of constraints and opportunities arising from external and intrafamilial situations of the everyday routine also provide indispensable insight.

Figure 1.1 puts together a number of these considerations from the problematique, in view of the theoretical perspectives. This highly simplified figure lacks the many feedback loops of the sophisticated systems or ecological model. My intention is to suggest some of the most important ways in which the constituent parts fit into the total picture of maternal employment.

Maternal Employment in Perspective 11

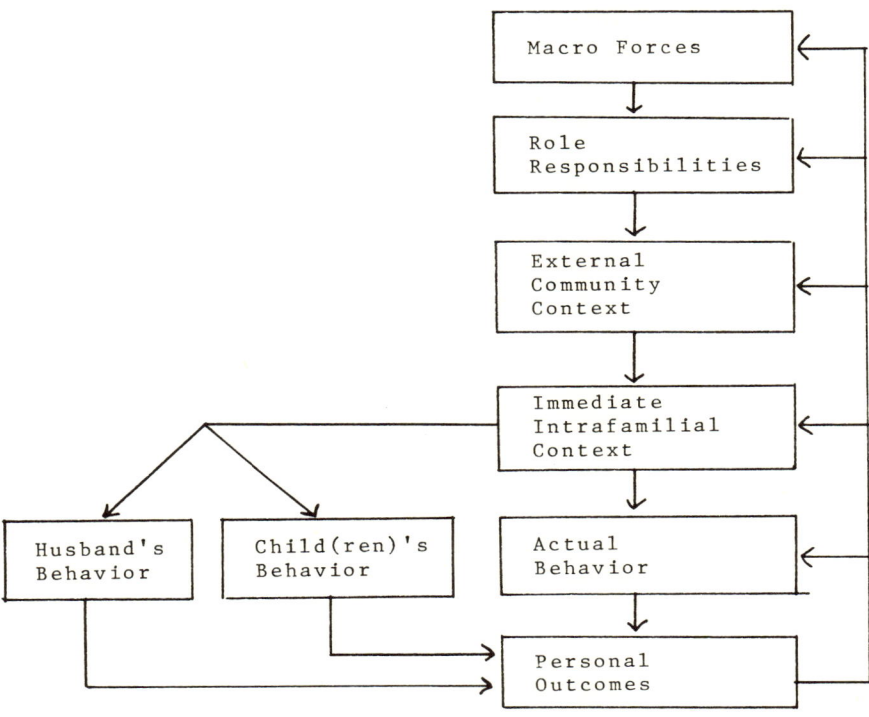

FIGURE 1.1.--A Social-Ecological Perspective on Maternal Employment

The fact that arrows point from one box to another implies a precedence among the considerations, but they have to be viewed conjointly.

The macro forces include what Chapin called *predisposing* and *preconditioning* influences on behavior (1974). These include people's personal motivations and orientations, on the one hand, and societal conditions (e.g., inflation, economic expansion, conservatism), on the other, which influence so much of the former type of influences. In the case of maternal employment, these include labor-force trends, economic pressures on families, and greater societal emphasis on equality between the sexes.

From among combinations of these two macro forces, people select and, to some extent, receive a combination of roles: in or out of the work force, marriage, parenthood, and more. Each role carries with it expected sets of behaviors. Some behavioral demands are more explicit and deterministic than others. The translation, however, from expectation to actual behavior requires organization within the confines of the 24-hour day, in view of the particular person's environment. The external context that mediates between ideal and actual role-related behaviors includes such considerations as the nature and degree of flexibility on the job, distances a person must go for various needs and wants, availability and efficiency of means of travel, childcare possibilities, and the timetabling and spatial relationships of commercial, professional, and institutional services of many kinds.

The intrafamilial context specifies exactly how general role expectations are to be viewed and realized within a particular household. A traditional wife's role may be maintained or cut back. The presence of many or very young children may intensify certain demands. The husband's background or characteristics may reinforce or modify expectations. Although the intrafamilial context is very influential because of its physical and affective immediacy, what happens there is nonetheless contingent on external constraints, which are generally at least one step beyond the control of the family involved.

For the employed mother, actual behavior or activity reflects, in highly simplified form, how the expected behaviors of the roles women take on are filtered through external and intrafamilial contexts. Some behaviors (e.g., employment) may come through in full measure; others, such as some nurturative activities, may be curtailed by time conflicts.

We would, moreover, expect the other members of the family also to undergo modifications in their behaviors as a consequence of changes the wife and mother encounters. Some of these changes are intended and appreciated; others are not.

Kenneth Burke once wrote:

> ... any complete statement ... will offer some kind of answers to these five questions: what was done (act), when or where it was done (scene), who did it (agent), and how he did it (agency), and why (purpose). [Cited by Asplund, 1979, p. 12]

But behavioral outcomes are not the final step. Behavior is a link between demands and conditions, on the one hand, and personal outcomes, on the other. How women feel about their jobs and possibly their lives is formed not in the abstract but as a result of a behavior pattern fashioned from many sources and conditions. A woman's view may reflect what happens not only to her but also to her husband and children, which in turn feeds back to the family system. Regardless of the desirability of any one source, such as the job itself or a husband or a child, the total pattern may be frustrating or exhausting—or more exhilarating than any component alone. Furthermore, the interaction among considerations may mean that the outcomes are positive, notwithstanding demonstrated hassle, if the macro forces are strong enough. Similarly, outcomes may be negative, despite strong motivating forces.

Societal trends have to be connected with personal outcomes, not in the abstract, but with specific reference to pertinent contexts and emergent behaviors. Only through understanding these complex interactions can we intervene in appropriate ways, for outcomes those affected will find better. In this process, everyday behavior is the central focus, as consequence of logistics and as cause of hassle.

The remaining chapters of this book examine maternal employment with respect to the components and dynamics of the perspective described here. Considerations are taken up one by one, each adding to the previous degree of complexity and interaction built from the perspective in Figure 1.1. The final chapter treats implications for policy and practice. Nonetheless, it is first necessary to detail how the demands of this perspective had to be met within a particular study, through a series of research decisions and procedures, some necessarily innovative.

Notes

1 For a stimulating discussion of the liberating aspects of extending opportunities into the "frontier" of the hours of the night, see Melbin (1978).

2
Measuring Daily Life: Its Objective and Subjective Aspects

If the content of our everyday lives and its subjective effects on us reflect our external circumstances and contexts, situations related to family structure and organization, and individual responsibilities, yet consist of a wide range of activities and lead to highly varying and idiosyncratic outcomes, measuring these aspects of daily life is a challenge of coverage, detail, and sensitivity. It is necessary to gather and integrate information about a family's structural context and responsibilities, its urban and institutional contexts, its internal composition and organization, its complex of activities and movements, its interpersonal daily life, and appropriate outcome measures. Fortunately, there are precedents for the study of many of these factors. Nonetheless, the art of optimizing breadth and depth, while interrelating the different levels of data, remains difficult to master.

In this chapter, I discuss a particularly synoptic method for assembling information on the content, dynamics, and interpersonal structure of daily life, with ways to expand this method's reach. Then I explore broader considerations on sampling, field methods, analysis, and interpretation, as part of a description of how my colleagues and I designed and implemented our study. Although this chapter serves the conventional purpose of outlining a study's methodology, our focus is on innovative procedure, which may be necessary to capture the realities of the lives of employed mothers and their families.

The Time-Budget: Precedents and Potential

The perspective introduced in Chapter 1 requires a wide range of factors and information to be assessed. However, the medium of everyday activity is a critical link between macroscopic structures and forces and microscopic considerations. Time-use studies have made significant contributions to the literature on the effects of maternal employment. Typically, these studies have used a research method called the time-budget. A methodological challenge to researchers generally and to our own study in particular is how to use the time-budget in a systematic yet sensitive way to link time-use to other important aspects of the problematique. Linking objective time-use information to people's subjective feelings about their activities and pattern of activities was a particular challenge.

The time-budget itself is a record of what a person has done during a specified period of time, usually a 24-hour day or a multiple. This record is detailed: it lists a person's activities in chronological order and usually states when each activity began and terminated. For each activity, time-budgets usually record what other persons were involved, where the activity took place, and whether there were other simultaneous activities. Time-budgets also allow for other time and activity-specific data, depending on the researcher's special interests and the degree that researcher and respondent are willing to persevere in a compulsively detailed and exact accounting of a period of the respondent's life. (For a more detailed methodological discussion of time-budgets, see Michelson, 1985.)

The results of time-budget procedures can take various forms. The time devoted to each activity is observed, reflecting a coding scheme that categorizes responses. Such schemes typically divide behavior into from ten to several hundred categories of varying generality. One popular and widely used scheme has ninety-nine categories (Szalai et al. 1972). For example, one may report the average time devoted to each of the activities coded by members of the whole aggregate of respondents or, on the other hand, compare average activity times by subgroup (e.g., men vs. women, employed vs. nonemployed, young vs. old).

The other information gathered is typically analyzed in a parallel way. This yields results on the mean time members of aggregates or subgroups spend with particular persons, in particular locations, and in secondary activities.

Two-way and three-way analyses can deal with more complex considerations, such as how much time is devoted to certain activities with which other people, and in what locations. Such complex analyses are relatively rare in the literature, which is devoted more to descriptive and comparative time-use analyses.

One can also assess not how long an activity takes but rather *when* it occurs. Researchers on housework, for example have been interested in the question of when particular housework activities are performed (Berk and Berk, 1979). Others with an interest in city planning and transportation have arranged these data to learn about sequencing (Hemmens, 1966).

The complexity of such analyses becomes even greater when attempting to include a subjective dimension of the fabric of everyday life. Although there are few examples blending the various objective sides of time-budget analysis with subjective elements, the experimental work of several researchers demonstrates the feasibility and promise of doing so (Cullen & Phelps, 1978; Patrushev, 1982).

The time-budget is an increasingly popular way of measuring important parts of everyday life that vary as a function of other forces and factors and in turn can have a bearing on subjective outcomes for the persons involved. The variety and complexity of potential analyses suggest that what any analyst actually does will be only part of what is possible. The extent and precise nature of information gathered episode by episode will reflect the goals of a study. In addition, the items of information to be linked to time-use and to each other will reflect a larger perspective or model for explanation of the problematique under investigation.

Our initial focus in this chapter was the challenge to the methodology in general and the time-budget in particular by our perspective on maternal employment. The methodological developments to be reported occurred in our specific research project. Although the perspective of Chapter 1 provides a roadmap, our methodological decisions and developments were a response to our specific goals.

A research project entitled "Child Care under Constraint" was designed by researchers associated with The Child in the City Programme, University of Toronto, with the support of a contribution by the Welfare Grants Directorate of Canada's Ministry of National Health and Welfare. The goals of this project were threefold:

a. First, the project was intended to document a wide range of logistical aspects of daily life in the families of employed and single mothers, each in comparison to more traditional comparison groups. Data would indicate, in terms of the daily round and its various activities, consequences of assuming the responsibilities of employment and single parenthood, respectively. The project would detail the difficulty of managing this daily round and fulfilling its responsibilities, while also noting typical forms of adaptation women use to carry out such efforts.

b. A second goal was to assess, both objectively and subjectively, outcomes of women's growing responsibilities, primarily for women and the children in their families and to some extent for male heads of household as well (where present).

c. A third goal was to assess policies and practices bearing on the everyday lives of employed and single mothers. Among these were family division of labor, child-care structures, the timetabling and land-use pattern of public- and private-sector facilities, transportation, and employment structures and practices.

These goals served as the basis for the selection of variables to be studied and pointed to ways our study would differ from most others. Some of the methodological requirements are as follows:

a. Analyses of daily time-use should delineate the activities of single mothers, employed and not.

b. Data should include not only what people do but also the accompanying logistical considerations.

c. Data on various family members should be taken for the same time periods and within the same families, so as to assess interactive effects, rather than randomized between families and days.

d. Taken as a contribution to role responsibilities, employment should be broken down by its extent, for assessment for the implications of part-time employment and other factors.

e. Children's life styles should be assessed by the same methodology and viewed as a potential function of their parent's daily routines.

f. Subjective outcomes should be assessed and, wherever possible, linked to specific aspects of the daily routine.

g. The effects of external institutions, practices, and contexts on daily life should be assessed, linking them as far as possible to each other and to individual outcomes.

The many methodological requirements of our overall perspective and specific project goals meant a need for the expansion of research tools and for innovation. This had an immediate effect on our use of time-budgets and also on other aspects of substance and procedure. Let us first look at time-budget considerations and then turn to other selected developments.

SIMULTANEOUS COVERAGE OF ALL FAMILY MEMBERS

The time-budget may be self-administered in diary form or obtained by interviewers. In the former case, respondents typically record the activities of the day as they transpire, updating their entries every few hours. In interviews, they usually report what happened the day before. If no greater recall is required, the two methods are considered equally valid. However, even when an interviewer distributes and then collects diaries, people are less likely to complete a diary than an interview. Because we wished to solicit time-use information for all family members on the same day, interviewing appeared to ensure optimal cooperation and quality of coverage. Sequential interviewing of family members, however, would be extremely time-consuming, as the typical time-budget takes at least a half hour to complete. Sequential interviewing would also be difficult to organize and would make confidential answers difficult, if not impossible. It was important to lose neither persons nor information as a result of the research procedures.

The solution was to arrange a time-budget session with eligible, consenting families at a time when all members could be present. The session was always on a Tuesday through Saturday, to follow a weekday. At this session, the interviewer presented every member of the family ten years old or over a time-use protocol, to be filled out in her presence. She gave them common instructions and then circulated among them while they filled out the protocols, to help ensure the adequacy of the responses. In this way, simultaneous records were obtained from all able to give them, in virtually the time it would have taken to interview one person and with the quality control of the interviewer.

Children under ten were included by another procedure. Time-budgets on these children were solicited in the first part of a subsequent personal interview with the female heads of households. The women were encouraged to fill any gaps in their children's day by referring back to the children, who were still present after the family time-budget session.

In this way, time-use information was gathered from all family members, relatives, boarders, and anyone else resident as part of the household. Only on occasion would it prove impossible to assemble all family members. Then one person, usually the female head, would be asked to solicit the necessary cooperation later the same day from the missing person(s), usually the male head or a teenager. Time-use protocols were completed by both husbands and wives in 91% of the 434 two-parent families interviewed in our survey phase.

A different technique was formulated to deal with the previous weekend, always somewhat more removed than the immediately previous weekday and hence remembered in less detail. Work by Swedish researchers (Carlstein et al., 1968) helped point to our procedure. We adopted the unit of one hour as the minimum time to be considered (compared to however little time a weekday activity would consume, often as little as a couple of minutes). Only information on respondent's behavior settings, such as home, work, and stores, (see Barker, 1968, on behavior settings) was gathered. The protocol is question 37 in the interview schedule in the Appendix. It covers all the hours of the previous weekend. Each family member is accorded a line of a different color or texture. Behavior settings are the rows, and hours are the columns. Each person's line extends from left to right through the requisite hours and varies up and down according to the behavior settings utilized. When such a chart is completed, the observer can immediately see the degree of togetherness, travel, home-use, external recreation, use of outside space, and so forth of any family. The chart can also be broken down for statistical analysis.

LINKING OBJECTIVE AND SUBJECTIVE ASPECTS OF TIME-USE

In Chapter 1, I said that researchers make interpretations about daily life from objective time-use data. For example, if an individual gives evidence of little time devoted to leisure or sleep, this is characteristically interpreted as denoting a difficult life. But this may not be the case. The meaning and intent of an activity or its absence are never self-evident; some degree of inference is always necessary. Giving much time to an activity like work or commuting can reflect choice or compulsion. Therefore, it is desirable to build subjective interpretation into time-budget techniques in as integral fashion as possible.

The University of Michigan's Survey Research Center did this by inserting an extra column on the time-diary. For each episode, the respondent was asked to check one box on a five-point scale in answer to the question "When you were doing this, how did you feel?" (Michelson and Reed, 1975, p. 196). More recently, a Soviet researcher, Patrushev (1982), applied a similar scale to leisure time in particular.

Cullen and Phelps (1978) found in their work that respondents are more able to identify negative than positive aspects of time-use. They found that stress and annoyance in an activity are associated most with unpleasant or difficult conditions (46%), followed by disruptions (19%), greater than expected difficulty (17%), interference with subsequently planned activity (10%), and difficulty in fitting it in (8%). They also measured the degree that individual activities were routinized, from specifically arranged or planned, on the one hand, to time-filling, on the other.

With reference to these experimental efforts, we decided to add two specific subjective dimensions, in the form of columns, to the traditional time-budget protocol. Both were to be answered on a seven-point scale, so as to increase the likelihood of variation. The first column measured the degree that an activity was tense or relaxed. The second measured how much it was felt to have involved choice.

The tension dimension was intended to assess the degree of tension or relaxation associated with specific activities, contacts, locations, or combinations. It permitted as well the creation of a full-day measure of tension or relaxation, based on weighting the values for individual episodes according to the time devoted to them.

The same operations were intended for the scale of choice. We were interested in how women regarded the degree of compulsion associated with specific activities, parallel to observing the tension from certain activities.

Such a procedure makes more explicit the respondents' interpretations of how they experience their activities than do summary measures relating to the day or even more remote indices like marital-happiness and similarly used outcome measures.

SUPPLEMENTARY CHECKLIST ON PARENT-CHILD ACTIVITIES

People often wonder if time-use studies produce valid and complete pictures of what respondents do during the period under study. The research community has provided a qualified yes. Validity studies indicate that, provided recall does not extend beyond the previous day, people have indeed come and gone as they have reported. The major dimensions of the day are reported with reasonable accuracy, and hence the inferences analysts draw about how daily life differs among different subgroups or nations should be correct. Nonetheless, no one argues that *all* details are reported correctly in time-budget approaches. One would not turn to the time-budget as a means of getting sensitive information about sexual or other extremely personal activities. Furthermore, short or passive activities are likely to be submerged in the reporting of longer, more active behaviors at about the same time.

Coding schemes are two-edged swords. Even if respondents list their activities in an extremely precise, detailed way, schemes long enough to include fine distinctions of behavior become dysfunctional, because many categories are mentioned only infrequently. Respondent descriptions of their activities may not always be so specific as a detailed breakdown of categories. On the other hand, if only few categories are used in the coding scheme, researchers' inquiries on specialized interests are stymied. In the present study, we asked for information on all aspects of the daily round, including household, employment, child-care, social, leisure, and travel activities. But with our special concerns about the nature of parent-child contact under different degrees of maternal employment (e.g., "quality-time" hypotheses, among others), we were anxious to get an even greater level of detail about this one area of daily activity from the same survey source of data.

During a pilot study that preceded the main survey, which will subsequently be described in more detail, we examined the validity of "yesterday" time-budget interviews and experimented with the use of a supplementary checklist on parent-child activities.[1]

Thirty-seven respondent families were interviewed on three different days, the latter two consecutive. The first day we asked questions about a family's objective circumstances, including its employment situation and child-care arrangements. The session terminated with the selection of a typical weekday the interviewer could return and conduct systematic observation of a family's activities at a time when most family members would be home. Normally, this was from late afternoon through early evening, two to three hours. On this second day, only systematic observation would take place. The interviewer/observer would record detailed activity information, as on a time-budget, as well as her assessment of the degree of involvement in the parent-child contact. She used the same scale as Goldberg (1977), making distinctions among direct contact (that is, common activity in the same place), indirect contact (together but in dissimilar activities), and available contact (at home but neither together nor in similar activities).

On the very next day, the third contact involved an interview that included a "yesterday" time-budget for all family members, collected as described above. This put us in a position to evaluate the validity of time-budget data for a period of the day in view of observational data for that same period.

Following the traditional time-budgets on the third day, the female head of household was asked at the beginning of a longer personal interview to specify whether "you or anyone else in the family did certain activities for or with your children yesterday that might not have been long enough to put on your sheets or which did not occur to you to mention." A list of thirty possible activities was read, and information about which such activities had occurred and the timing and persons involved was recorded in an extra column in the time-budget pages.

The validity study indicated, first, that respondents did not claim on the time-budgets to have done activities which they were not seen to do.

Second, the female heads of households, the focus of our analysis, were found to fail to report more than half (58.6%) of what they had been seen to do. Nonetheless, the activities they did report occupied three-quarters of the time observed, suggesting that respondents remember the more time-consuming activities. The supplementary checklist increased the number of activities by about a third of those previously unmentioned, or to about 55% of potential. This addition of about 14% in number of activities accounted for a time increment of only about 5%, showing the short duration of typical forgotten activities. With the use of the supplementary checklist, survey methods could be shown to account accurately for about 80% of time expenditure.

An analysis of the nature of activities reported with and without the supplementary checklist confirmed expectations of the kind of selective reporting in which respondents engage. It also underlined the value of such a checklist to ascertain the incidence of certain types of activities. Active, time-consuming activities are well-reported. In the present context, these include eating (100%), television viewing (85%), preparing meals (77%), cleaning up afterwards (81%), talking to children about social activities and things that they are going to do (76%), and playing with or teaching children (60%).

The checklist is helpful, though, in gaining some other activities people typically fail to mention on their own. These include kidding around with children (20% before the checklist; increased to 45% thereafter), showing affection to them (10%; 44%), checking up on them (14%; 40%), giving them support (3%; 39%), and listening to them (0%; 31%). Positive but largely passive aspects of child care are not customarily remembered without probing. The same is true of activities, whether active or passive, that are generally considered negative. The latter include making demands on children (21%; 42%), punishing them (5%; 37%), and stating disapproval (16%; 35%).

A final analysis of retrospective time-budgets in comparison to what was observed assesses the validity of conclusions made from the former approach. How exact are inferences made from time-budgets, given the qualitative and quantitative forms of selectivity of response? This cannot be answered in the absolute but must reflect the subject of any particular analysis.

We analyzed this question, using Goldberg's scheme for categorizing parent-child contact, mentioned above. How different are the conclusions drawn through survey and observational methods for the same family at the same period of time?

Table 2.1 indicates the means and standard deviations of the minutes independent coders classified the thirty-seven families as devoting to the three types of contact, according to survey and observational methods. The observer coded the types of contact as they occurred; survey material was coded *post hoc* from the more detailed categories of activity and location. Both the means and the rather substantial standard deviations, including interfamilial variations, are virtually identical from the two methods.

The logical next question is whether what you learn about any particular family is consistent across the two methods, apart from variations between families. Correlational analysis provides this assessment. Pearson correlations were computed and are reported in Table 2.2. These are very high and statistically significant relationships, indicating that the time-budget picture of parent-child contact according to Goldberg's scheme is highly valid on the basis of observation.

TABLE 2.1

Means and Standard Deviations of Minutes in Three Types of Parent-Child Contact as Coded from Observation and from a Time-Budget Survey

	Observations		Time-Budget Survey	
	Means	Standard Deviations	Means	Standard Deviations
Direct Contact	55.8	32.2	55.2	31.2
Indirect Contact	67.4	42.7	70.2	38.3
Available Contact	27.0	27.6	25.1	31.7

n = 37

TABLE 2.2

Pearson Product-Moment Correlations of Minutes in Three Types of Parent-Child Contact as Observed and as Recorded by Time-Budget Self-Reports

Direct contact:	$r = +.80$
Indirect contact:	$r = +.75$
Available contact:	$r = +.78$

As a consequence of these analyses, we incorporated a supplementary checklist of more specific parent-child activities than most coding lists provide (see question 6 in the Appendix). We also felt more confident in the use of the time-budget approach as a central tool in meeting the research objectives sketched.

Although the place of the time-budget in the study of maternal employment deserves explicit attention, and the development of the time-budget must be expanded and described, one research tool does not a study make. The analyses and inferences in subsequent chapters become clear only when our central tool is placed in the greater perspective of study design and linkages with other information. Let us turn to these, focusing in a similar way on developments and innovations.

Survey Strategy and Structure

It was taken as given that an empirical study that attempted to deal systematically and thoroughly with the subject matter and perspective sketched in Chapter 1 would have to include time-use procedures, and so we tailored them accordingly. It was similarly taken as given that a study that incorporated these procedures would be a survey. As stated, the pilot involved systematic observation in part. It also included considerable focused interviewing, without standardized response formats. These last-named procedures, however, become unnecessarily time-consuming and expensive when applied to the large numbers of families necessary to provide a representative view of different situations, family structures, and experiences. They were used to confirm or secure appropriate and effective questions to be given to a larger number of respondent families.

Nevertheless, the choice of a survey approach does not mean that our moves were traditional and well-charted. A number of developments and innovations had to be made in formulating our study. These fall roughly into three divisions: sampling, content (beyond the time-budget), and field procedures.

SAMPLING FOR RANGE, DEPTH, AND REPRESENTATIVENESS

The sampling process was intended to select, without interpersonal bias on the part of interviewers, families for study who are representative of families in Metropolitan Toronto, but who represent important subgroups in sufficient numbers for analysis. For example, it was considered essential to be able to analyze the data in terms of women's different employment situations, the effects of single parenthood, the different ages of children, and different types of child care. The sample was drawn in several stages, utilizing geographic clusters, stratification on selected variables, and random selection of families for contact.

First, a random sample of census tracts in Metropolitan Toronto was selected. Forty tracts were picked, one by one, out of a hat. The representativeness of the first twenty tracts and of the full forty, representing 5% and 10% samples of tracts, was compared to the characteristics of all families in Metropolitan Toronto. On all major socio-economic and demographic variables, such as income, ethnicity, and percentage of single-parent families, the 5% sample of twenty tracts was within 1% of the whole population of families, little different from the 10% sample. Since it was more economical to concentrate on fewer clusters, the 5% sample was retained.

The next step was random sampling of addresses for contact within each of the twenty tracts selected. Because we had access to no reliable source listing the names and addresses of families relevant for study, screening in the field was the basis for finding eligible families. Before the field screening, every household address within each of the tracts was listed from appropriate directories and then serially numbered. The order in which addresses would be visited for screening for eligibility was determined by a random-numbers table.

Interviewers were then sent out to concentrate on individual neighborhoods and, in the preselected order, to find out if the family at any given address had any children up to and including the age of fourteen living there. The total number of interviews required within a tract was proportionate to the population of the tract.

Nonetheless, other requirements were placed on the interviewers. So as to get a sufficiently large and diverse subcategory of single-parent families, interviewers had to gather data from minimum numbers of these families within each tract, representing their percentage of the population (approximately 20%). Interviewers could exceed such a minimum if sufficient numbers of single-parent families appeared naturally in the preselected order of addresses visited. On the other hand, if the requisite number within a tract did not appear normally within the flow of screening interviews, interviewers ceased accepting two-parent families into the sample at the point when their acceptance would preclude having the minimum number of single-parent families within the target sample for the tract. There was "oversampling" to achieve sufficient numbers of diverse single-parent families. This procedure yielded 103 families headed by single mothers, 19% of the eventual total of 544 families interviewed. An additional 6 families were headed by single fathers; altough interviews were held with them, coded, and analyzed informally, the results were too meagre to include in our formal analyses and results, reducing the effective sample to 538 families.

During the screening, the interviewers were instructed to stratify for age of children within families and for types of child care. Approximately equal numbers of families having at least one child within the ages of 0-3, 4-6, and 7-14 were chosen. This assured that the implications of outside employment and single parenthood could be explored for various ages of children. A family could potentially satisfy more than one category of children's age, and an equitable distribution of children by age was easily assured.

Beyond that, small quotas were established within each tract to ensure that sufficient numbers of families utilizing at least one of six different child-care alternatives would be interviewed, so that a comparison among users of these services over the whole sample could be made. As a result, at least twenty children, usually more, were cared for by

a. a parent at home,
b. a day-care center,
c. home day care,
d. siblings, grandparents, or other relatives,
e. before- or after-school program, and/or
f. no one at all (i.e., so-called latch-key children).

There was stratification according to whether the mother was employed. This was expected to be well distributed throughout the population, giving no need to make the sampling process even more complex. Such an assumption was upheld in the resultant sample. Among the two-parent families, 247 of the wives were employed and 188 were not; 68 of the single mothers had outside employment and 35 did not.

The sampling process was extremely time-consuming and costly, but the sample represents an appropriately wide spectrum of families and situations in numbers suitable for analysis. Indeed, as might be expected in Metropolitan Toronto, interviews were held in approximately twenty different languages, from English and French through a variety of European languages, as well as several different dialects of various Asian languages.

Because there were several stages of sampling and because of the need for expressed cooperation at the outset from diverse family members, it is difficult to calculate a firm, standard response rate. Taking a base of families eligible for study, the response rate was between 56 and 60%. Although not optimal, this rate is consistent with that of another recent study that treated a similar set of concerns with a comparably complex set of research protocols (Berk and Berk, 1979). Although there were some initial differences in response rates between interviewers (leading to the replacement of some interviewers), there were no consistent differences in response rates between sections of the city or segments of the population that would a priori bias the results. A review of response rates in various time-budget studies shows great variation—from 46.2 to 100%. This review comments that "The cumulative consequence [of many different difficulties] is a generally low response rate." (Altergott, 1982, p. 252).

CONTENT BEYOND TIME-USE

Time-use information was collected as indicated previously from all members of the household. As an addendum to his or her time-budget protocol, each person over ten years of age also had a reasonably simple scale on self-characterizations of mental health and happiness. The scale, taken from the Canada Health Survey, was to serve as an additional, more general, subjective-outcome measure. Once the initial, group-oriented section of the survey was completed, the interviewer continued with a more detailed interview with the female head of household, the central person in our theoretical scheme. Ideally, but not always actually, she was interviewed in the privacy of a separate room.

The questions complementing time-use data covered a variety of phenomena. They are, once again, found in the Appendix.

Some of these complementary questions were objective and factual, covering family circumstances, socio-economic characteristics, employment and travel patterns, child care and other supportive arrangements, and information about how the family deals with such situations as illness and vacations. Most of these questions are straightforward and traditional in their approach.

Other questions aimed at more subjective dimensions of the daily routine and required more original development. The most evident of these was a series of time-pressure measures,[2] called "busy scales".[3] Found as questions 7, 8, 10, 11, and 13 in the Appendix, these aim to provide an assessment, independent of that provided in activity-associated tensions, of the general perception of time pressures respondents associated with time periods and particular sectors of life. Questions 10, 11, and 13 in particular deal with a 21-point scale, extending from +10 to −10. The equilibrium point of 0 represents exactly enough time for a respondent to do what she needs or wants. Positive values represent increasing amounts of activity for the time available, i.e., higher time pressure. Negative values represent more time than activity to fill it, i.e., time on one's hands. In questions 10 and 11, degrees of time pressure associated with stated periods of time—"yesterday," "last week", "the average week"—are considered. In question 13, the perceived time pressures in such sectors of life as employment, household work, and child care are assessed. These questions were prominent in the analysis of subjective outcomes, reported in Chapter 6, both as individual factors and in multivariate analyses.

Other, more conventional subjective measures, taken from the literature, included other life stressors, and questions focused on some of the common dilemmas facing mothers of young children who do and do not choose outside employment. These include evaluations of their satisfaction with the courses chosen.

Additional questions let respondents state what they saw as the source of their pressures and problems and to elaborate on solutions they personally use or would advise others to implement. Yet other questions attempted to assess certain aspects of behavior within the family. One set of questions, for example, addressed family division of labor in terms of customary responsibility, rather than just the time logged in the time-budgets. Because this alternative approach to measurement of intrafamilial division of labor has been used by some others (e.g., Geerken and Gove, 1983), the empirical approaches of two methodological schools can be compared within the one current study; time-budget data can be compared with responsibility-based answers. Another set of questions deals with how family members alter their behaviors under pressure.

In addition, mothers were asked to make some evaluations of their children, for analysis in view of their daily routines. Data about external community context were elicited from direct questions; such data were also drawn from relating additional information about transit accessibility, for example, to information about home locations. In considerations of urban context, we gathered exact locational data about trip destinations, places of work, child care, and the like. This enabled the eventual use of geocodes and the ability to deal with contextual phenomena more precisely.

The main survey took place in March through June 1980. These months ran the gamut of weather conditions, from blizzards to near summer weather. School-holiday periods were eliminated. Every day covered by a time-budget was a regular school day. To ascertain differences in daily logistics and child care during a period school was not in session, a much shorter follow-up study of 78 respondent families selected randomly from the major survey was conducted during July and August 1980. The summer substudy provided time-budget data that could be compared with that obtained during the school term from the same persons. A small number of additional questions about changes in children's and parents' activities from the school year to summer vacation was also asked. Although time-use studies are typically scrupulous about equalizing coverage on different days of the week (e.g., Szalai, 1972), they seldom assess how periods of the year that directly affect some family members bear on the day-to-day activities of others. All times of the year are not equal in their implications for behavior (see Michelson, 1971).

FIELD STRATEGIES

The sampling plan, with its screening requirements, was carried out more or less as anticipated. As in similar studies (e.g., Johnson, 1977), the necessity to screen in the absence of comprehensive, current registries of households and their characteristics led to onerous and expensive searching for eligible households. On the other hand, our data needs placed a potential burden on respondent families as well.

The typical interview, first with all family members and then with the female head of household, took close to three hours. A few took five to seven hours. Respondents and interviewers alike saw the interviews as grueling, although many of the women interviewed also found them therapeutic or functional in terms of future planning. After pretesting, many of the interviewers were ambivalent about their own role in securing such extensive data with only intangible benefits to offer their hard-working respondents. In consequence, respondents were offered $10 per family as a token acknowledgment of the time and effort involved in their participation. A small percentage of respondents expressed no interest in personal compensation, preferring that the funds be donated to the Hospital for Sick Children Foundation.[4]

No one could pretend that our payment was commensurate to the task at hand. The task itself was of variable length, and there is no standard wage-rate for responding to interviews. The individuals' own normal wage rates were highly variable. Nonetheless, a tangible exchange beyond assistance to long-range policy making or personal catharsis appeared to interviewers to be an effective, pragmatic aspect of the collaboration of respondents. It had the additional benefit of releasing interviewers from their own doubts, encouraging them to obtain information as systematically as possible.

ANALYTIC PERSPECTIVES

The general strategy of analysis is to examine the various parts of our problematique in as sensitive detail as possible. This involves disaggregating the sample and relevant data in many ways, with the aim of illuminating specific points with as rich data as possible. Optimally, each point could be examined in the perspective of more than one question or type of information.

An alternative to this could have been the creation of a single model, artificially transforming various data scales into continuous variables interrelated by an algorithm, such as path analysis. My personal observation of work in this tradition is that the meanings of the contributory considerations tend to become obscured if they are not first analyzed in ways that are close to their original format and if assumptions are forced in the transformation of highly selected variables for use in a synoptic analytic method.

I prefer to construct an assessment of the larger scene by analyzing the individual component parts in their idiosyncratic detail and increasingly observing interconnections through data and logic. Therefore, as in a previous study (Michelson, 1977), subsequent chapters will deal with particular subjects of the data, each, however, in view of preceding analyses.

In such a disaggregated analysis, different assessments call for analyzing different segments of the total sample. For example, in analyses that call for observation of differences in daily life according to sex, within families, the logical comparison is between men and women in two-parent families, excluding single mothers. This leads to frequent differences in the number of respondents contributing to tables.

In addition, in a study of this length and complexity, there are random omissions of answers. Rather than reduce the sample for analysis to only a single subset with totally complete information, we report the fullest information available on any question. Fluctuations among respondents by question are minor. The numbers upon which analyses are conducted are given at the outset in the text, in terms of basic characteristics of the sample, and in major tables. In some cases, n's are omitted, because including them would compound the complexity of already large arrays of data. With a single exception, the sampling design was such that all analyses represent adequate numbers of respondents in the most specific cross-classificatory category (i.e. cell sizes). The only category that did not permit this is the breakdown to single mothers with part-time jobs; these respondents are excluded from tables where their numbers would make such analyses unwarranted. Significance-test results are reported where justified.

In a few analyses, there is double counting of families. A family might, for example, have children in more than one age category or might utilize more than one form of child care. We chose to assess the effects of caring for children of particular ages and the effects of use of certain child-care arrangements through a comparison of families in each given situation. (An initial analysis of all possible combinatorial categories proved far less insightful and operationally fruitful than simply comparing families who fit individual categories.) In such cases, there is no pretense of division of the whole sample into watertight categories; the comparison is between families with specific situations, and some families report more than one situation and are counted more than once.[5]

Thus, disaggregated analysis has its complexities and inconsistencies, both in the structure of the data and in the completeness of its reporting. Nonetheless, our major concern, as stated at the outset, is to extract a meaningful picture from the data collected.

In this regard, we designed and carried out a postanalytic phase to our project, to assist our interpretation of the validity, meaning, and implications of the data.

After initial tabulations and analyses had been completed, we held group discussions with respondent women and the occasional husband. One of the final questions of the survey had asked, "Would you be interested in hearing the results of this study in about six months, together with other persons who have helped us—and saying what you think about these results?" Every respondent answering that question positively was invited in writing and, when possible, by telephone to attend one of seven meetings scheduled throughout Metropolitan Toronto at different times of the day and week. These meetings, held in September 1981, were attended by approximately 7% of the female heads of households in the major survey.

One purpose of these meetings was to provide feedback to respondents. But more pertinent to the results was the opportunity to get respondents' opinions of the accuracy of the initial results and interpretations. The prevailing opinion was that most of the findings and conclusions (all the important ones) indeed represented respondent situations as they understood them, although respondents disagreed with one or two minor findings. Furthermore, respondent discussion proved extremely valuable in testing the interpretation of the results. Elaboration in the discussions made much clearer what various relatively factual results actually meant. A number of the points in subsequent chapters incorporate interpretations and elaborations gained through these discussions.

Such open-ended follow-up techniques are fruitful in our experience of such studies. Nonetheless, there is no reason to expect widespread participation in postanalysis discussion sessions. There is undoubtedly a biasing selectivity in the subgroup of respondents who actually participate, regardless of the nearly unanimous agreement in principle to such participation during a survey. All insights must be considered with this in mind.

In the current follow-up phase, it is evident that relatively few attended, even though the scheduling of meetings attempted to reflect different life situations. Those who came reflected the spectrum of situations in our sample. But, on ethical grounds, we did not precisely measure selective bias by matching this input to earlier data. We had promised respondents confidentiality and anonymity, and we did not feel it consistent to investigate individual-level data with the persons we had come to meet.

The substance of arguments, counterarguments, agreements and disagreements is a tangible supplement to survey data, regardless of how selective its source.

Discussions along quite different lines also inform the chapters to follow. A policy workshop involving approximately fifteen representatives of federal, provincial, municipal, and private-sector interests was held in Toronto in March 1982, under the sponsorship of The Child in the City Programme and the Ministry of National Health and Welfare. We presented an updated description of the study and its findings, with extensive discussion of the implications for policy and practice. These discussions also helped guide the content to follow, though it should be made clear that the group did not reach consensus on anything but the need for varying, flexible and culturally sensitive approaches to policy concerning maternal employment and child care.

The foregoing provides a basis for understanding the chapters which follow. In some cases, nontraditional developments and innovations were necessary to secure or report our data. Now let us turn to the many issues that surround the problematique of maternal employment.

Notes

1 Suzanne Ziegler took the lead in this part of the study. Results are presented in greater detail in Ziegler and Michelson (1981).

2 Linda Hagarty and Susan Hodgson were active in the conception of these scales.

3 Linda Naiditch gave them this name during her analyses of these data.

4 This was the body which provided basic funding to The Child in the City Programme. When we were attempting to elicit respondents' cooperation, it was of interest to note that the indirect relationship of the project to this foundation meant more to the respondents than did the more direct funding relationship to a government ministry.

5 It is recognized that families are typically categorized by age of youngest child, so as to reflect the greater legal degree of care the youngest generally requires. There are nonetheless characteristic demands from children in other age brackets, which our results should indicate — not just if the youngest child falls in that bracket.

3
Why Women "Work"

A classified ad in a California newspaper (*The South Coast Shopper,* 1980) addresses itself to "Ladies/Housewives," as if these terms were mutually exclusive. Our language betrays itself in a similar way when we refer to those with paid employment as "working." It conveys the implicit hypothesis that those who do not have paid employment do less of whatever it is that *work* suggests.

We know from experience that no such dichotomy exists. Many people like employment-related activities, just as others dislike some. On the other hand, some employment-unrelated activities are dreaded, even at the same time that others are pleasurable. Some employment situations are relatively flexible, closely reflecting individual dispositions and interests. Some nonemployment activities are uncomfortable and obligatory, consuming great periods of the day and night. In the days of totally segmented sex roles, it was said, "Man may work from sun to sun, but woman's work is never done."

Scholars are reluctant to make hard and fast boundaries between work and leisure (e.g., Dumazedier, 1974; Aas, 1982). How people regard activities is highly variable, depending on a variety of factors in the context of these activities. Thus, while not all "work" is necessarily negative or involuntary, the stereotype extends well beyond paid employment. More neutrally, the variety of activities that are expected of and hence performed by a person, pleasantly and willingly or not, might be called *role responsibilities.*

Paid employment is a major role responsibility. When people commit themselves to an employer or contract, they establish a new commitment to other persons or collectivities. Many of the daily activities of housewives are also role responsibilities, given some form of division of labor within households. Education is a role responsibility for children of school age.

Rather than implying fruitless and invidious comparisons through use of the common term *work,* we shall explore a wide variety of activities associated with different role responsibilities. We will examine their nature, extent, and personal interpretation. Paid employment, nevertheless, is a phenomenon of considerable magnitude and current interest. As Chapter 1 suggested, maternal employment is the main focus of this and a plethora of other works, not least because of its potential affects on other daily activities, many of which are also role responsibilities.

Paid employment potentially adds to or interferes with other demanding commitments. It is important to understand at the outset what combination of reasons for undertaking it the individual has. The explanation also clarifies women's subjective feelings about their routines. If paid outside employment is undertaken for largely intrinsic reasons, for what Maslow (1954) called self-actualization, at the top of his hierarchy of values (far from those needed for survival), reflecting the employee's personal desires and interests, one would expect it to be experienced more benignly than if undertaken relatively involuntarily.

This chapter therefore begins the empirical section of the book by examining the conditions under which mothers of young children have taken paid outside employment. It examines as well some signs of why their orientation to employment is worth considering in subsequent chapters.

In principle, one could ask with equal validity why men "work." Surely some of the same dynamics apply to men. Nonetheless, history tells us that men have long been expected to work, that work is a foregone conclusion. The trends we have cited show that employment among a broad spectrum of women is relatively recent and growing. Therefore, our question has particular salience for women, who must justify to themselves why they have broken from role patterns that only recently were accorded near-universal approval. It has been noted with irony: "It is the *unemployed man* who was seen as a social problem, [while] it was the *employed woman* who was seen in *virtually the same ways*" (Kanter, 1977, p. 61).

The Context of Increased Maternal Employment

Our survey was not designed for the purpose of assessing historical trends. It has to do with what people do, for what reasons, and with what impacts. Survey findings nonetheless assume more meaning when viewed within the context of societal change. Several factors emerge in literature and statistics about the trend to increased maternal employment that lend credence to what individuals now say about their situations.

As with other phenomena, such as residential mobility, maternal employment can be understood as a function of *push* (predisposing) and *pull* (preconditioning) factors. Push factors are those motivating an individual to undertake employment. Pull factors are those of the external demand for women to fill work-force positions.

As we noted previously, some mothers of young children held jobs even when there was no cultural support for this in North America. Several writers state that subsequent increases in maternal employment reflected demands for additional categories of workers. The employers attracted women according to categories of societal approval of employment (Ross, Mirowsky, and Huber, 1983; Oppenheimer, 1982; Fox and Hesse-Biber, 1984).

World War II, for example, saw the opening of many industrial jobs for women, given the need for production and the conflicting demands for male labor. Previously it was acceptable for a woman to work if young and single or childless, but the factory door now opened to women whose children were in school or even older. After the war, particularly in the 1950s, the huge growth in service jobs swelled the general demand in the economy for women to fill so-called pink-collar jobs. The demand was greater than could be filled by existing "acceptable" categories of women, so the conceptions of acceptability gradually changed to include mothers of young children. As one review of trends put it, "In recent years, increases in maternal employment have been greatest among women who previously had very low rates of employment: that is, among mothers with very young children." (Mortimer and London, 1984, p. 27)

A "rachet effect" has occurred: once a woman decides to enter the work force, she continues in it (Ross, Mirowsky, and Huber, 1983). Growing demand, deemed acceptability, and experience in the labor force have combined to stimulate a major trend. Hayghe (1982) notes that, between 1968 and 1980, the number of married women in the U.S. labor force rose by 600,000 a year.

Opportunity alone can not account for this trend. If women had been truly satisfied with homemaker status, it is not a foregone conclusion that so many would have entered the work force. In previous eras, increased demand for certain occupations was satisfied through immigration, without altering traditional sex roles. Thus, some degree of push had to accompany the pull of the economy.

One such push came from the experience of regular employment by women during World War II. If the experience was successful then, why not later, too? This push was joined by a large increase in the percentage of women receiving higher education and the emergence, particularly among this cohort, of the women's liberation movement. Equality between the sexes in the workplace and elsewhere was emphasized; spouses and society would simply have to adapt to women's right to control their situations in their own interests. There was a growing acceptance that, if women received intrinsic benefits from employment, it was their prerogative to be in the labor force—marital status, family demands, or not. If fathers could have jobs that contributed to their self-esteem and satisfaction, so could mothers. Ross, Mirowsky, and Huber, for example, note polls indicating a change in the percentage approving employment by married women (even if their husbands could support them) from 21% in 1938 to 60% in 1970 and to 72% in 1978 (1983, p. 810).

Furthermore, employment during the admittedly difficult years of child rearing may be undertaken more readily today because the length of this period in a woman's life has been decreasing. The average interval between the birth of the first and last babies has declined to about seven years (Fox and Hesse-Biber, 1984, p. 31).

When mothers of young children take outside employment, however, self-gratification is a minor factor. As the figures on increasing single-parent families show, separation and divorce have become common. Although at present the majority of families still remain intact, the marital breakup observed in others adds to the pressures on married women for income and workplace experience. Such pressures are of course real and present among women who head single-parent households.

Moreover, economics is a push factor even without the threat or reality of single parenthood. Following the lead of previous observers (e.g., Rapaport & Rapaport, 1971; Holmstrom, 1972; Howell, 1973a), Ross, Mirowsky, and Huber claim unequivocally, "On the whole, wives enter the labor market for economic reasons" (1983, p. 810). During the last twenty years, the rate of inflation has been high, particularly with respect to such costly crucial commodities as housing. Even among women in traditional two-parent families, there is a growing feeling that a second income has become essential to maintain the desired standard of living.

Figure 3.1 indicates the similarity in the curves of increases in labor-force participation by married women with one or more children under six and in the costs of living generally and of housing specifically. It is suprising that, until the late 1970s, the increase in maternal employment *leads* cost of living increases, dispelling potential assertions that inflation alone "caused" increased maternal employment. Nonetheless, the parallel growth of the curves supports popular observations and experiences of the perceived economic necessity of maternal employment.

Fox and Hess-Biber (1984) cite a 1980 Roper poll on why women have jobs. Roper asked, "Are you working primarily to support yourself, to support your family, to bring in extra money, or for something interesting to do?" All but 15% answered in economic terms, about half of these reflecting the need for basic support and half for bringing in extra money (p. 30). In a recent study by Kamerman, 75% of respondents replied that they worked "for the money," including 60% of white married professional women and 90% of working-class women (1980, p. 87).

Several researchers, though, have concluded that, among married women, economic reasons for taking jobs are more pronounced among women whose husbands have relatively low incomes. (Cochran and Bronfenbrenner, 1979; Hayghe, 1982; Mortimer and London, 1984). By inference, self-actualization is more of a factor behind a wife's employment when the husband brings home a greater than average income.

Benenson (1984) issues some confirming facts from recent U.S. sources in

36 Why Women "Work"

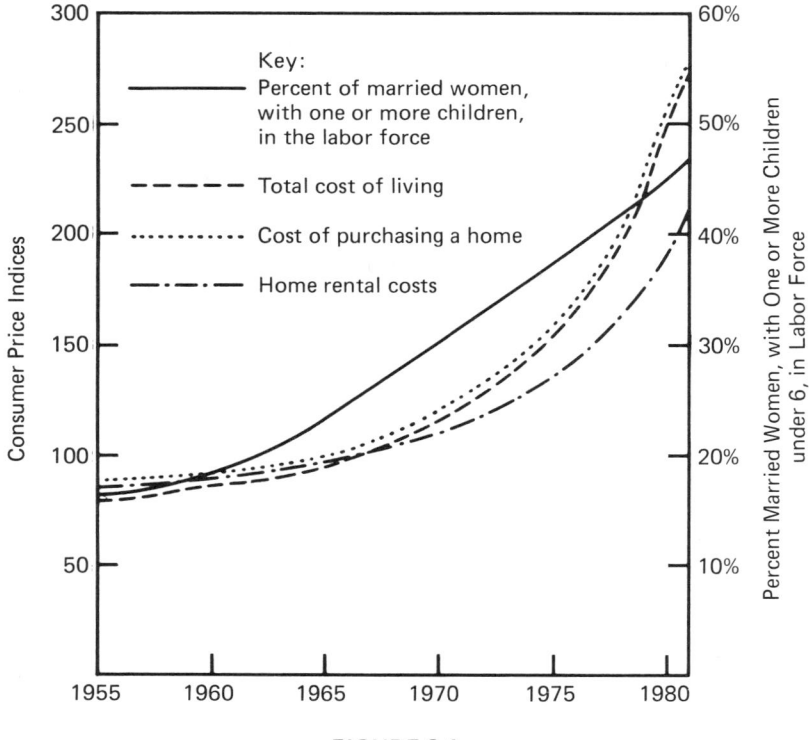

FIGURE 3.1.
Historical Increases in Selected Consumer Price Indices and in the Percentage of Married Women, with Children Under 6, in the Labor Force.

Sources: U.S. Department of Commerce, Bureau of the Census, *Historical Statistics of the United States,* Part 1, 1975, p. 134 (Series D63-74), p. 210 (Series E135-166) and *Statistical Abstract of the United States,* 103rd ed., 1982-83, p. 382 (Table 638) and p. 461 (Table 757).

this regard. He notes that the percentage of women who have prestigious professional careers is still extremely small. In addition, while women whose husbands earn large salaries ($50,000) are well represented in the labor force, they lag in percentage of participation considerably behind those whose husbands earn modest salaries, regardless of the level of their own education.

Married women's income is not all available for consumption, however. Extra expenses are usually incurred for child care, for transportation, and for convenience goods and services due to a shortage of time. Hayghe (1982) indicates that, after meeting these expenses and those for desired consumer items, "dual-earner families tend to save less than their traditional counterparts" (p. 37). Nonetheless, both Hayghe and Oppenheimer (1982) conclude that the wife's income under these circumstances does compensate successfully for the deficiencies of the income earned by the husband. In the words of the latter, "wives' earnings, low as they were, provided a functional substitute for upward occupational mobility of the husband" (p. 349).

These arguments and data suggest that, even though the economy has come to depend increasingly on women and the culture is more supportive of maternal employment, participation on the part of many women reflects a perceived economic need. The positive messages of women's liberation are reflected in the primary motivation of some—but possibly a clear minority of—mothers with jobs. Knowledge of why women "work" is one key to understanding how they react to their emerging daily routines. We hypothesize more negative reactions and outcomes for those whose employment is relatively involuntary than for those working primarily for the interest and stimulation.

With this background, let us turn to data from our Toronto sample. These should be examined first for their consistency with what has been learned elsewhere and then for their contribution to linking orientations about employment to outcomes.

Dynamics of Employment Status

Just as the definition of the word *work* has fuzzy bounds, all jobs are not the same in quality or quantity. The women sampled varied greatly in the extent of their employment and in the kind of jobs held.

The extent of employment, subsequently called *employment status,* is a central independent variable in our perspective. It refers to a set of potentially great role responsibilities, which, alone or in combination with others, create parameters around which other activities must be fit. Employment, however, is not an all-or-nothing proposition. Jobs are either full-time or part-time. Hence, when examining the dynamics of employment, we shall keep a distinction between mothers of young children with

1. full-time,
2. part-time, and
3. no outside employment.[1]

Respondents were asked, "Do you have full-time, part-time, or no paid employment?" (Question 23). They were also asked the number of hours a week a job required. In accord with Statistics Canada's practice of defining employment status according to the respondent's own categorization (Statistics Canada, 1983, p. 56), direct answers to the above question were the basis for classification by employment status. Data on weekly hours of employment are, in any case, consistent.

Within two-parent families, 161 women were employed full-time, 86 part-time, and 188 did not have paid outside employment. Among the single mothers, a somewhat higher percentage had full-time employment; 55 were employed full-time, 13 part-time, and 35 were housewives.

As might be expected, the percentage of part-time employees in our sample of women with children under 15 years old (31.4%) is somewhat greater than census reports for all women in about the same age range (15-44). Statistics Canada reported this figure at 27% both nationwide and in Ontario in May 1983 (p. 56); Hayghe reports American figures of 24% for 1978 (1982, p. 28).

If employment status, as thus derived, is to be used throughout this analysis, it is important to learn the extent that it masks important underlying characteristics and orientations of respondents — conditions that potentially precipitate the extent of employment. We have already suggested that not all respondents would necessarily have the same orientation toward their work and its potential daily hassle. Do full-time and part-time employees reflect different degrees of economic and noneconomic reasons for paid employment? Do they vary demographically or in the kinds of jobs they hold? In other words, what, if anything, do employed mothers bring with them into their employment status which helps explain their daily situations and the implications thereof?

Contrary to our expectations, women with full-time positions did not differ in the qualitative nature of their jobs from those working part-time. The distribution of women with professional, managerial, white-collar, and the various service and blue-collar positions was not only relatively even in the sample but, more important, did not differ according to full-time or part-time status. This is not to argue that on-the-job tasks, wage rates, fringe benefits, or continuity of employment are necessarily similar. Part-time jobs are often deficient in many of these respects, but no information from our survey shed light on them.

Several demographic factors failed to vary with employment status as might have been expected. One might, for example, have hypothesized that degree of outside employment would vary inversely with family size. No such variation was found among the employment-status categories of the married women.[2]

The families did not differ by employment status in the distribution of ages of children, even though one might expect outside employment to be more pronounced among parents with older children. Although the sampling process roughly equalized the percentage of families who would have children in the age brackets 0-3, 4-6, and 7-14, nothing in the sampling would have equalized this distribution within employment status categories, for which there was no stratification in the sampling.

The mean ages of the women in the three categories — full-time, part-time, and no employment — were an almost identical 34.7, 34.9, and 33.5 years. Their husbands were, on the average, three years older, representing the same essential similarity.

Consistent with the literature, the single major socio-demographic factor that does differentiate the three categories of women's employment status is income. The data from the Toronto sample not only support previous findings that women are more likely to take jobs if their husbands are relatively low earners, but also indicate that such women are more likely to take full-time jobs. The median income for the men whose wives have full-time jobs was $18,240, compared to $21,842 for husbands of part-time employees, and $22,273 for husbands who are the sole breadwinners. Such differences in husbands' incomes, as indicated more broadly in Table 3.1, provides some factual grounding for the hypothesis that economic motivations may be prominent in the decisions to take employment, particularly full-time, by mothers of young children.

As Hayghe (1982) suggests, adding women's incomes to those of their husbands turns the picture around entirely. Full-time work by women whose husbands have the lowest median incomes produces a comparatively high median family income, $29,000, compared to $26,100 for families with part-time employment by women and of course the same $22,200 when the wife does not have a job.

The differential income figures for husbands do not mask unemployment, a potential but not actual antecedent variable. Unemployment was not prevalent in the (1980) Toronto sample. Moreover, data gathered in 1981 by Statistics Canada suggests that husbands of employed women are less likely to be unemployed than are those of housewives. Only 7.4% of the former lacked jobs, compared to 11.2% of the latter (Statistics Canada, 1982, p. 25).

In Table 3.1, further examination of family income among the sufficiently large categories of single mothers, those employed full-time and those not employed, supports the familiar, lamented picture that female heads of household are relatively poor. Those employed full-time had median incomes of $13,250; those without employment had median incomes of $4,473.

TABLE 3.1

Median Income by Employment and Marital
Status of Female Head of Household

Employment and Marital Status	Husband's Income	Family Income
Married, full-time job	$18,240	$29,000
Married, part-time job	$21,842	$26,100
Married, not employed	$22,200	$22,200
Single, full-time job	——	$13,250
Single, not employed	——	$4,473

Examining family incomes by mode, rather than by median, shows the previous conclusions even more strongly. The income categories fitting the greatest number within each category of families ranges downward from $30,000–$39,999 in the two-career families to $25,000–$29,999 in two-parent families where the woman works part-time and to $20,000–$24,999 in two-parent families with a male wage earner alone. Single-parent modes directly reflect the medians.

More direct assessment of the economic orientation toward maternal employment was provided by answers to the question, "In the case of yourself and your family, what kinds of things did you consider when you decided to go out to work full-time or part-time?" Monetary considerations were given by about 70% of the employed women in the sample. Among the married women, money was mentioned significantly more by those with full-time jobs (68%) than by those employed part-time (49%). It is not surprising that this figure is even higher (78%) among the employed single mothers, who do not have a spouse's income in the picture.

Therefore, we must pay attention to differential income as a factor in maternal employment and its implications. Income is clearly a precipitant of employment. What we must ask as well is whether economic reasons for taking a job are in any way related to affective reactions to the role responsibilities thus created.

Most women report contentment with their decision to undertake outside employment, as do other women with the decision not to take jobs. Neverthe-

TABLE 3.2

Reasons for Taking Outside Employment by Contentment With the Decision to Have Done So.

Contentment with Employment Decision	Monetary Reasons	Entirely Nonmonetary Reasons
Very content	26.8%	58.6%
Content	27.4	19.8
Neutral	33.5	13.5
Discontent	5.0	1.8
Very discontent	5.0	3.6
Other	2.3	2.7
	100.0%	100.0%
n =	(179)	(111)

less, the degree of satisfaction with this decision is very much higher among those citing only nonmonetary considerations in taking jobs. Table 3.2 indicates that 58.6% of this latter group are very content with the decision to work as compared to less than half that percentage (26.8%) among those citing monetary reasons. An analysis of variance of the differing degree of contentment with the decision to "work" among the groups defined by financial and only nonfinancial rationales for holding jobs shows that the chance that these two groups are equally satisfied is less than .001.[3]

The reflection of the husband's income in the relationship between reasons for working and contentment with the decision to work is shown in Table 3.3. The contentment of employed women with their decision to take a job is shown according to their husbands' incomes. This table indicates clearly that the less a husband earns, the less satisfied a woman is with being in the labor force. These women have decided to seek outside employment out of perceived necessity, rather than as a positive choice reflecting intrinsic interests in the job, more often than have women with affluent husbands.

Our role is not to make or substantiate claims about absolute need for any particular level or increment in income in a family. Nonetheless, the feeling that the income brought home by the employed mother is actually needed in the majority of cases was captured in the words of one of the respondents during the final phase of the study:

> For a long time I think women went to work to have the extra things: new furniture, an extra car, a vacation, extended vacation. . . . but as time has gone by, the economy has almost demanded that women go to work, just to keep up the standard of living. Of course, . . . you feel guilty about being away, you know. . . ."

TABLE 3.3

Husband's Income and Contentment with the Decision to Take Outside Employment

Contentment with Decision to Take Outside Employment	Husband's Income		
	Under $20,000	$20,000 $24,999	$25,000 and over
Content	56.9	76.7%	81.8%
Neutral	35.0	18.6	12.7
Discontent	8.1	4.7	5.5
	100.0%	100.0%	100.0%
n =	(123)	(43)	(55)

A minority point of view of the true need for additional income was that sufficient room remained between material goods and nonmaterial considerations. That is, sufficient concern for traditional sex roles and child-rearing practices justified trade-offs in housing quality, personal possessions, and holiday trips.

These arguments suggest that outside employment, among single mothers and mothers with full-time jobs in two-parent families, is based in large part upon perceived economic need, that such employment, though viable for most, nonetheless entails trade-offs and costs, and they are therefore less likely to view it benignly. Let us now turn to more detailed consideration of these trade-offs and costs and under what conditions they appear.

Notes

1 Other important dimensions in extent of employment revolve around variations in how a given commitment of time is scheduled or administered. These include shifts, flex-time, and more. They will be considered in Chapter 9, as part of flexibility in employment.

2 Single-parent families, were, on the average, 1½ persons smaller than two-parent families, i.e., all lacking a spouse and, in every second case, one child.

3 $F = 19.72$; d.f. $= 1$.

4
Employment Status and the Daily Routine

Time is a finite resource: its use for our purpose lessens its availability for another. Time on the job is spent at the expense of something else. The importance of the activities traded off varies, but the total length of the day does not. Furthermore, the greater the amount of time spent working, the greater these trade-offs must be.

A worldwide literature has documented many aspects of how women's employment affects everyday behavior. These studies provide strong expectations for what the Toronto data should show but inevitably leave additional aspects unclear. Our analysis will address these aspects.

Expected Patterns

LEISURE AND SLEEP

The consensus from previous studies is that married women who take on outside employment have less leisure and get less sleep. Such free-time activities may be valuable, indeed essential, but their length is not explicitly regulated by external collectivities or authorities. Hence, when the daily routine gets tight, employed wives transfer time from their sleep and personal recreation.

For example, in their 1965 comparison of time-use in twelve nations both in Eastern and Western Europe and in the U.S.A., Szalai and his colleagues (1972) found that one of the most consistent and striking findings across nations was less sleep on the part of employed women. They averaged from 6 to 60 minutes less than nonemployed women, depending on their location (p. 130). Stone calculated the differences in sleep between nonemployed and employed mothers among Eastern European and Western European/American samples; in the former countries employed mothers slept 58 minutes a night less, compared to 24 minutes less in the latter (Stone, 1978, p. 120).

Furthermore, in the aggregate, employed women devoted 10% fewer of their waking hours to free-time activity than did housewives (Szalai et al., 1972, p. 131). A more specific analysis of the same data shows that married women with both jobs and children have 66 minutes a weekday less free time than do nonemployed married women with children (Harvey, 1983).

More recent studies show the same pattern. A Norwegian study (Central Bureau of Statistics of Norway, 1983, p. 42) shows that employed women get 48 minutes less time for sleep and other personal needs per day than housewives. The former spend more than an hour less time in leisure activities, as well. Moreover, both discrepancies had increased since a similar survey nine years before.

Japanese data run parallel to European and North American data. Employed wives were seen in 1975 to get marginally less sleep than their nonemployed counterparts (about seven minutes a night), but had almost three hours a day less leisure time (Matsushima, 1982, pp. 206-7). These differences had also increased from previous studies in 1956 and 1967.

Data amassed for the whole week would hide weekday differentials if people caught up on weekends for what they can't do on weekdays. Nonetheless, studies that assess weekly time-use confirm daily trends. Stone (1978), for example, shows that both employed and nonemployed mothers sleep much more on Sundays, their day off, or both (p. 121). A 1979 study of Finnish time-use (Niemi et al., 1981) shows that, on a weekly basis, employed women still get about a hundred minutes less sleep than do housewives (pp. 25, 29). The former also have about five hundred minutes less free time.

American data are highly similar. An urban sample taken in 1975 (Robinson, 1977) indicates a difference of 102 minutes a week in sleep between the two categories of women, all married. The discrepancy in weekly free time was even greater than in the Finnish sample — 762 minutes.

The impact of the extent of employment (i.e., full-time vs. part-time jobs) can not be determined from these studies.

HOUSEWORK

A second area of consensus in previous studies is that employed women spend less daily time in housekeeping activities. Staines and Pleck (1983), for example, cite numerous studies that found negative correlations between women's hours spent at their jobs and the hours they devoted to various kinds of housework (pp. 17-18). Vanek (1984, p. 98) interprets this to suggest that women are forced to "cut corners" under the pressures of employment responsibilities.

The previously cited twelve-nation study produced evidence of similar differences across all the countries. Although women do more housework in some countries than in others (for example, 72% more in Yugoslavia than in

Bulgaria), in the aggregate, housewives spent almost 75% more time on household chores on the average day than did married women with jobs: 429 minutes to 249 minutes (Szalai et al., 1972, p. 126).

More recent studies in additional countries uphold these conclusions and suggest how they apply to particular housekeeping activities. A nonrandom sample of more than seven hundred families in Toronto, taken during 1969-71, shows nonemployed wives spending exactly twice the time in housework as their employed counterparts, 256 minutes to 128 (Derow, 1977, p. 423). Japanese data from 1975 (Matsushima, 1982, p. 202) indicate nearly triple the housework investment by housewives (311 minutes to 107). The aforementioned 1979 Finnish data show less extreme but nonetheless comparable differences (265 minutes to 184).

Most household activities are cut back, though the studies suggest that none are eliminated. Most studies show that the amount of time spent cooking, ironing, and household cleaning varies greatly by employment status. For example, data from Halifax, in Canada, indicate a regular cutback in time for various household chores; cooking, from 84 minutes per day down to 40 minutes; housecleaning and repairs, 128 minutes to 63 minutes; laundry, 43 to 18; and marketing 27 to 23. (Clark, 1977, p. 810; see also Harper and Richards, 1979). However, the Japanese study (Matsushima, 1982) shows the greatest cutback in the time devoted to sewing and knitting; on which the average Japanese housewife spent 63 minutes per day, compared to only 2 minutes for employed women. In that study, differences in daily cleaning time were nearly as great—64 minutes to 8 minutes.

Another dimension of housework is when it is performed. In a highly detailed description of who does what kind of housework at what time of day, Berk and Berk (1979) provide empirical support for the logical expectation that employed women typically do housework at a different time of day than housewives do. Once employed women leave for their job, they must postpone additional household chores until their return, usually the evening, if they choose to do them at all that day.

A second form of time transfer is from the weekday to the weekend. Fox's analysis (1978) of the 1965 U.S. sample used in the 12-nation study shows that, while employed married women with children spent 189 minutes in household activities on weekends, compared to 330 for nonemployed mothers, the former spent somewhat more time in these activities during the weekend, 297 minutes to 243. This does not make up for the discrepancies during the five weekdays, but it does represent more of a balance on the part of employed mothers toward household work. Derow (1977) and Matsushima (1982) support with their Canadian and Japanese data the same devotion to household by employed mothers on the days when they have fewer employment-role responsibilities. In contrast, however, these studies show near *equality* in this regard on weekend days. Indeed, the similarity of

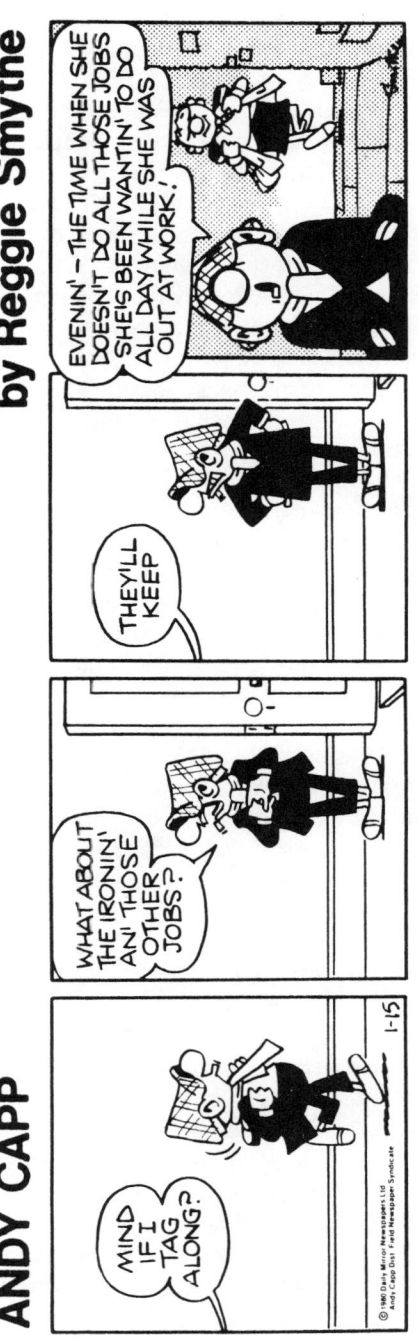

FIGURE 4.1 *Andy Capp on Household Chores* (ANDY CAPP by Reggie Smythe © 1980 Daily Mirror Newspapers, Ltd. Courtesy of News America Syndicate)

activities during the weekend underscores the potent effects of employment on other role responsibilities during weekdays.

CONTACT WITH CHILDREN

Time spent with one's own children appears from the literature to be still another trade-off with time on the job. The twelve-nation survey found that housewives spent 128 minutes a day on average in primary child-care activities, compared to 72 minutes for employed mothers (Szalai et al., 1972, p. 127). The 1975 Japanese sample indicates a difference of 66 minutes to 12 minutes (Matsushima, 1982, p. 202).

The 1979 Finnish survey not only supports the general picture but indicates that these differences in child-care time hold regardless of the ages of the children involved. The mean for housewives was 80 minutes of contact in primary activities with children, compared to 32 for employed mothers. Younger children take more time, but the difference in contact by employment status remains: 182 minutes to 132 minutes when the youngest child is three years of age or younger. Where the youngest child is four to six, the figures narrow to 72 minutes vs. 60 minutes, and they narrow even more, 9 minutes to 7 minutes, when this child is seven or older.

Derow (1977, p. 59) recalculates American data from Walker and Woods (1976, p. 132–33) that show the same conclusions: on differences by employment status, on consistency in the direction of these differences across age categories, and on a distinct lessening of both child-care time and employment-status differences as children grow. In addition, she shows that direct physical care of children, though given in greatest quantity to young children, is customarily viewed as a primary activity, while nonphysical forms of contact, which extend more evenly across ages of children, are typically seen as secondary activities (i.e., done simultaneously with other forms of activity) and amount to more than twice again the amount of time devoted to primary child-care activities. Nonetheless, these secondary child-care activities vary by employment status exactly as do primary activities.

In her sample from Toronto, Derow (1977) goes on to show that not only does the expected difference in primary child-care time by employment status occur on weekdays (129 minutes per day vs. 63 minutes), but it occurs on the Sunday surveyed as well. Then the difference is a somewhat narrower 89 minutes to 59 minutes. Fox's analysis of the 1965 U.S. time-budget survey (1978, p. 134) suggests that these Sunday differences extend to both physical and nonphysical forms of child care.

Parents are more sensitive about variations in child-care devotion than about, for example, housework. Having less time to be with children is a source of concern and sometimes guilt. In this regard, many parents feel that the total amount of time they spend with their children does not matter as much as does the quality of the time they spend. Hence the term *quality time* (e.g., Howell, 1973a; Portner, 1983, p. 171), has entered public consciousness.

Employed mothers typically attempt to make time in their routines available for direct, stimulating contact with their children (e.g., Rutter, 1981). They hope that this effort can provide as much or even more quality time than the children would receive under other circumstances. The children would thus not be personally deprived as a consequence of their mothers' employment.

The subjectivity of a term like *quality time* makes it difficult to measure, however suitable an objective. That employed parents provide as much or more "quality" time for their children is currently an hypothesis, without the weight of evidence that is behind the various trade-offs documented to this point.

TRAVEL

Differences in amount of daily travel according to women's employment status are not as clear-cut or as linear as differences in time devoted to the types of activity discussed previously. Most women with outside employment commute, which housewives do not. On the other hand, time employed women lack because of their employment can be channeled by housewives into other activities, many requiring travel. For example, Derow's analysis (1977, p. 425) shows that housewives devoted twice the mean time to travel for shopping on a weekday as did employed women.

The twelve-nation study indicated much more travel by employed women (an average of 70 minutes, compared to 39 for housewives), but this difference was more than accounted for by a mean of 43 minutes in commuting to work. Moreover, not all housewives take trips away from home on weekdays; the percentage of housewives going out during the day varied from 33% in the Federal Republic of Germany to 91% in Hungary (Szalai et al., 1972, pp. 587, 591–92).

Many recent studies confirm these differences in the balance of total travel and specify the differences in trip purpose (Chumak and Braaksma, 1981; Hanson and Hanson, 1981; McGinnis, 1978; Pickup, 1981; Studenmund, Kerpelman, and Ott, 1978). Others, however, do not find differences in travel time related to women's employment status (Bayes et al., 1982; Sen, 1978; Matsushima, 1982).

At least two studies suggest that the nonwork trips that employed women are less likely to take during the workweek are postponed to weekends (Hanson and Hanson, 1981; Pant and Bullen, 1980).

Thus, on balance, previous research makes us expect that employed women spend more of their daily time in travel, even though the purposes of

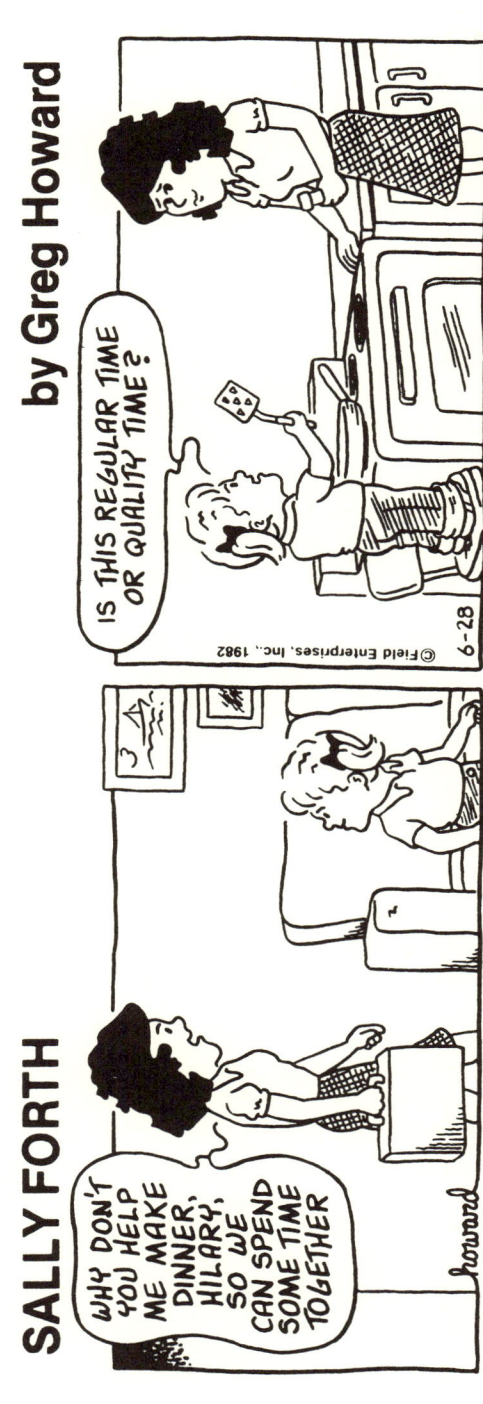

FIGURE 4.2 *Sally Forth on Quality Time* (SALLY FORTH by Greg Howard © 1982 Field Enterprises, Inc. Courtesy of News America Syndicate)

their trips are clearly different from those of their nonemployed counterparts. Quite another consideration is how *mode* of travel, its circumstances and consequences, compares to men's situations; this will be taken up in Chapter 9.

Additional Concerns

It is evident that the literature gives us much to expect about how the everyday activities of employed mothers in Toronto should differ from those of housewives. There are, however, many concerns on which this literature is either inconclusive or silent, which deserve our attention:

1. Surprising little attention has been paid to the degree of women's employment. Most conclusions reflect only whether women have jobs or do not. In some cases, those with part-time employment are placed in the same category as housewives. Part-time employment requires analysis in its own right.

2. While it is clear that various activities are traded off because of the need for time on the job, the literature does not compare the degrees that these activities are cut into.

3. Although there is a sizable literature comparing women's use of time to men's, which will be examind in Chapter 5, little work has been reported on whether women's pattern of trade-offs is similar to or different from men's. Part of that question is the total time obligation created by a man's or woman's full set of role responsibilities.

4. We have argued that employment should be a highly significant factor in explaining daily time-use by women. Nevertheless, such other factors as the age of children might be thought to explain time-use more fully. How important is employment status in comparison to other factors?

Let us thus turn to the Toronto data. Part of our purpose will be to examine the patterns that have emerged from other studies with data "custom-made" for these questions. I shall also attempt to shed light on some of the questions extending beyond most of the research to date.

Daily Life and Employment Status among Toronto Families

Time-budget data help assess daily-activity differences associated with the employment status of the married women. Table 4.1 summarizes these data within eleven aggregate categories.

The results are consistent with expectations. The columns make clear that mothers with part-time jobs are most frequently between the extremes of full-time and no employment, in regard to their nonemployment-related activities.

TABLE 4.1

Mean Number of Minutes Devoted to Major Activities
by Married Women on a Weekday by Employment Status

	Employment Status		
	Full-Time	Part-Time	Not Employed
Activity			
Employment	392	126	–
Housework	128	251	302
Child Care	64	105	134
Active Leisure	13	31	28
Education	9	7	4
Passive Leisure	93	127	171
Personal Care, Sleep	570	601	611
Shopping	33	49	48
Civic, Organized Activity	8	16	12
Social Activity	34	28	45
Travel	81	66	44
n =	(160)	(86)	(188)

Not surprisingly, employed women spend less time in housework, child care, passive leisure, personal care and sleep, shopping (full-time only), and social activity. These women spend more time traveling, depending on the extent of their job commitment: those with full-time jobs spend 81 minutes a day traveling, compared to 66 minutes for part-time workers and 44 minutes for housewives.[1]

Let us turn from broad categories to more specific considerations. Sleep, for example, had received considerable interest in the literature. Consistent with these studies, the women in Toronto with full-time jobs slept an average of 431 minutes a weeknight, compared to 455 minutes for housewives. Women with part-time jobs were in between, averaging 444 minutes.

Of all the individual leisure activities, the most time goes to television viewing. Observers customarily hypothesize that women without jobs watch a lot of television. This hypothesis appears borne out by the current data, insofar as housewives average 100 minutes a weekday watching television as a primary activity, compared to 56 minutes among those with part-time jobs and 48 minutes for full-time. The interpretation as to how housewives spend the day is not at all obvious, however, in that their husbands watch only 2 minutes less television per weekday. The data suggest that, by doing household chores during the daytime, housewives clear time to watch TV with their husbands in the evening. Employed women are more likey to do some chores in the evening while their husbands are watching television alone (Figure 4.1 to the contrary notwithstanding).

The figures for individual household chores vary similarly to the aggregate figures. Thus, the differences are divided relatively equally among such activities as food preparation, dishwashing, indoor cleaning, laundry, gardening, and animal care. Nevertheless, women who have full-time jobs perform many household responsibilities at different times of the day and week than do part-time employees and housewives, whose patterns are roughly similar to each other. The mother with a full-time job outside the home tends to use evenings and weekends for laundry, ironing, indoor cleaning, grocery shopping, and, when possible, medical and dental care for the children. The other categories of mothers are more likely to fit these tasks into the actual workday.

Like the other aggregate categories, child care is made up of many specific activities. Included among these is the difficult matter of quality time.

Operationalizing (i.e., defining and then measuring) quality time is extremely slippery, if only because the term itself is so value-laden. Most activities uniting parents and children potentially can be of high quality if imbued with meaning and affection. Objectively assessing and measuring them are not tasks to be taken lightly.

Attempting to provide some type of pertinent information, we differentiated child-care activities as logically as possible as *discretionary* and *nondiscretionary*. We deemed discretionary those activities that required common participation of parents and children and that were not typically part of the everyday "survival" routine. Such discretionary activities, taken from approximately twenty-five that form the general category of child care, include reading to children, indoor games, outdoor games, instructional communication, social communication, joking and other unstructured contact, listening to children, showing affection, and making plans with children. Nondiscretionary activities, on the other hand, include such standard activities as baby and child care, getting medical attention, waking the child and putting him or her to bed, and getting the child ready.

Of the total time for child care during the average weekday, about a quarter is devoted to discretionary activity. Between categories of employment status, the difference in minutes of discretionary activity is the same as in the total devotion of time to child care; the absolute differences between categories are relatively narrow, though. Among those with full-time jobs, 17 minutes is devoted to such discretionary activity; among those with part-time jobs, 20 minutes; among housewives, 32 minutes.

The belief of many employed mothers that they give as much or more of this kind of time to their children as do housewives is not objectively supported in terms of absolute duration. Their commitment is, however, reflected somewhat by the fact that these time allocations represent a slightly higher percentage of total child-care time. Employed mothers devote 26% of their child-care time to discretionary activities, compared to 19% and 24%, respectively, for those with part-time jobs and none.

Such discretionary activities are often of short duration and easily forgotten. There was evidence in our pilot study that they are not as well represented in traditional time-budget information as are the longer, obligatory activities. For this reason, as part of the interview with the female head of household, we included the supplementary checklist discussed in Chapter 2. As a consequence, we could tally the *number* of specific child-care activities reported as primary or secondary activities on the time-budget or on the follow-up checklist.

The picture that emerges resembles that from just the duration of primary activities. Mothers with full-time jobs average 7.07 episodes of discretionary activity on the average weekday, compared to 9.30 for housewives.

The discretionary time of part-time employees is an anomaly, with the least amount and the greatest number of episodes (9.85). Women with part-time employment are usually found between the two extremes of employment status, though in many instances they are closer to housewives than to full-time employees.

Excursions are a form of what people consider quality time, when parents take their children out personally. Respondents were asked about six typical types of excursion: to movies, swimming, skating, museums, clothes shopping, and outside Toronto. We asked whether their children had gone on each type of excursion during the preceding six months and, if so, with whom (question 36). This provided a basis for assessing whether women's employment status makes a difference in whether parents take their children on such excursions and, if so, what effect that has on children's opportunities.

Table 4.2 indicates only marginal and inconsistent effects of maternal employment on parental accompaniment on excursions. Much more consistent, however, is the trend of children to have experienced this type of activity during the previous six months if their mothers are in the labor force. Employed parents, while not always able to go themselves, appear to make arrangements that result in some of the opportunities they desire for their children.

At any single point of time, employment, housework, and child care activities are considered obligatory. (Over a period of time, they are potentially negotiable.) Table 4.3 therefore combines the daily time wives and husbands devote to these activities. The specific activities making up the more general categories include both traditionally male- and female-oriented tasks around the house. Among the wives, time in obligatory activities is highest for those with full-time jobs; they devote an average of 584 minutes to obligatory activities, compared to 482 for those with part-time jobs and 434 for those without employment. Furthermore, wives with full-time jobs not only put in more time in such activities than other women, they devote almost an hour

TABLE 4.2

Children's Accompaniment on Excursions During Previous Six Months by Employment Status of Wife*

Activity	Employment Status	Who Took Children on Excursions During Previous Six Months		
		Parents	Other than Parents	Children Didn't Go
Movies	Full-time	32.9%	34.9	32.2
	Part-time	36.1%	27.9	36.0
	Not employed	36.2%	23.4	40.4
Swimming	Full-time	18.3%	34.0	47.7
	Part-time	22.1%	32.6	45.3
	Not employed	19.6%	25.6	54.8
Skating	Full-time	26.2%	38.3	35.1
	Part-time	35.3%	28.2	36.5
	Not employed	30.3%	24.5	45.5
Museum	Full-time	23.5%	26.2	50.3
	Part-time	27.1%	21.1	51.8
	Not employed	12.3%	18.0	69.7
Out of Toronto	Full-time	63.4%	8.4	28.2
	Part-time	72.1%	11.6	16.3
	Not employed	60.4%	14.1	33.2
Clothes Shopping	Full-time	87.1%	3.9	9.0
	Part-time	91.8%	2.4	5.8
	Not employed	80.3%	3.7	16.0

*For married couples only

more than their own husbands to these tasks. In other words, they work the most! In contrast, in families in which the wife has a part-time job or is a full-time homemaker, it is the husband who spends relatively more time in obligatory activity.[2]

Another view of the trade-offs comes from answers to a direct question (#14), "Do you have any special ways to save time, when you are busy or pressed?" Almost all respondents (94%) claim to give up a certain amount of sleep when overloaded. As for housekeeping reductions, 55% answer that they reduce indoor cleaning. Another 28% reduce food preparation time by using convenience items, and 29% prepare food in advance.

These assertions are reinforced by data on eating out. About 30% of women with full-time jobs say that they and their families eat dinner out four or more times a month, compared to 22% of those with part-time jobs and

TABLE 4.3

Mean Number of Minutes Devoted to Employment, Housework and Child Care by Husbands and Wives, by Employment Status of Wife

	Wife's Employment Status		
	Full-Time	Part-Time	Not Employed
Wives	584	482	436
Husbands	529	556	554

20% of housewives. Similarly, 25%, 15%, and 17% utilize take-out food outlets four or more times a month. These differences are not dramatic, but they are in the expected direction.

Table 4.4 views directly the trade-offs of time by individuals, as contrasted to the category averages in Table 4.1. Table 4.4 reports the correlation coefficients linking employment time to the other categories of activity with which it competes. The coefficients for women are all in the directions suggested by the literature. They are also at high significance levels. Time women devote to employment, for example, is inversely correlated with time they devote to housework (−.51), passive leisure (−.34), and child care (−.33). Given the size of the sample, only the trade-off with time devoted to educational activity (−.06) fails to achieve statistical significance. Nonetheless, as Table 4.4

TABLE 4.4

Correlations of Daily Minutes of Work to Minutes in Other Activities (Men and Women)

Correlation of Worktime With	Women	Men
Housework	−.51	−.32
Child Care	−.33	−.14
Active Leisure	−.17	−.17
Education	−.06*	−.15
Passive Leisure	−.34	−.27
Personal Care, Sleep	−.23	−.36
Shopping	−.22	−.31
Civic, Organizational Activity	−.11	−.15
Social Activity	−.15	−.19
Travel	+.26	−.22

*Not significant

indicates, these trade-offs are of different magnitude. Housework is by far the greatest trade-off with employment time.

The sole time-use that varies positively with employment time for women is travel—consistent with the previous research.

Table 4.4 has similar data for husbands' trade-offs with their own employment time. These help address the question of whether wives and husbands make the same trade-offs with their jobs. The men's data do not have the same meaning as that of their wives, though. Virtually all the men are employed full-time, so variations in their daily work time are marginal in comparison to those of women, which range from none at all to more than eight hours. For example, among women, an increase in work time from a zero base to a positive value brings with it the need to travel to work and hence also an increase in daily travel. In contrast, a man who works longer during a particular day than another is likely to devote less time to travel that day, probably having less time left for a leisure activity trip. He will have commuted in any case. For these reasons, women's travel varies positively with time on the job, and men's varies negatively.

Nonetheless, men have inverse relationships of work time to all other activities, just as do women. While these are all statistically significant, none has the magnitude of women's trade-off of housework for paid employment. Employed women thus make different trade-offs than do men: employment occurs in a different context for women.

Do employed mothers catch up during weekends? Data on weekend time-use present fewer clear-cut differences by employment status. Table 4.5 shows that those with full-time jobs, who had spent less time shopping during the week, take about three-quarters of an hour more time shopping on weekends. As might be expected, some but not all employed women are shown to be on the job. But, beyond that, there is rough equality in terms of such disparate phenomena as sleep (more than eight hours a night for all), church, recreation, and socializing.

Table 4.6 shows that there is also essentially equality among the categories of women in weekend child-care responsibilities, in contrast to the weekends. Employed mothers are no less likely to be home alone with some or all of their children for a substantial number of the waking hours of the weekend.

The three categories of employment status have reasonably equal distributions of children by age. Mean time-use for each category therefore reflects the same blend of children's ages, effectively neutralizing whatever effects the age factor has on mothers' everyday activities. One would still expect that differential demands are placed upon mothers according to the ages of their children. In that age of children is independent of the employment status of the respondents, this former factor could be of equal or greater explanatory value regarding time expenditure than the latter.

Time devoted to selected activities is broken down by both age of children and employment status in Table 4.7. Not surprisingly, age of child is most po-

TABLE 4.5

Mean Number of Hours in Each Behavior Setting
on Weekend for Wives by Employment Status

	Employment Status		
Behavior Setting	Full-Time	Part-Time	Not Employed
Sleep	16.9	16.4	17.0
Workplace	1.5	2.2	—
Shopping, Commercial	2.8	2.1	2.0
Public Offices	.1	.3	.2
Outside, Near Home	.7	.5	.5
At Home (But Not Sleeping)	19.8	20.2	21.0
Place of Worship	.6	.7	.7
Recreation	2.8	2.7	3.0
Others' Home	2.7	2.9	3.3
School, Day-Care	.1	.0	.1
n =	(149)	(78)	(178)

tent in the explanation of minutes devoted to child care. The younger children demand more time, and marginally less time is given in turn to housework and passive leisure. Having a young child also curtails daily travel for housewives, but not for mothers with jobs, who have to go out anyway. The increase in travel with children's age probably reflects both increased freedom for the mothers and chauffeuring needs of the children.

Regardless of these logical relationships, Table 4.7 also shows that employment status is highly pervasive and strong in its effects. Age of child has

TABLE 4.6

Mean Number of Hours Women are at Home with Children During Weekend
in Absence of Husband, by Wife's Employment Status

	Women at Home Alone During Weekend	
	With All Children	With Some Children
Wife's Employment Status		
Full-time	4.66	5.40
Part-time	4.21	5.45
Not Employed	4.31	5.21

58 Employment Status and the Daily Routine

TABLE 4.7

Mean Number of Minutes Devoted by Women to Selected
Activities, by Age of Children*

	0-3 years		4-6 years		7-14 years	
1. Employment						
wife with full-time job	385	(n=53)	379	(44)	392	(108)
wife with part-time job	112	(39)	128	(24)	129	(54)
wife with no employment	–	(85)	–	(75)	–	(108)
2. Housework						
wife with full-time job	125		144		129	
wife with part-time job	221		222		272	
wife with no employment	286		304		331	
3. Child Care						
wife with full-time job	109		74		41	
wife with part-time job	162		121		88	
wife with no employment	218		151		81	
Total Obligatory Activities						
wife with full-time job	619		597		562	
wife with part-time job	495		471		489	
wife with no employment	504		455		412	
4. Passive Leisure						
wife with full-time job	87		94		93	
wife with part-time job	121		143		139	
wife with no employment	157		171		172	
5. Total Travel						
wife with full-time job	76		65		81	
wife with part-time job	65		56		60	
wife with no employment	34		41		47	

*Time-use for mothers listed under each age category relevant to her family

an obvious influence, but employment creates a de jure demand for a large, finite number of hours per day that is simply imposed on the daily timetable. However prominent other influences may be, the employed mother has relatively little time within which to maneuver, particularly if employment is full-time.

The conjoint effects of several influences on activity are impressive. The box within Table 4.7 on total obligatory activities, broken down by both employment status and age of child, shows not only that women with full-time jobs have the heaviest daily workloads, but that having a child under four years of age makes this load significantly higher. All women with full-time jobs have greater loads than other women who have infants; among the former, there is an inverse linear relationship between their obligatory work time and the age of their children.

Women's total obligatory activities could also be explained by their family incomes or their ethnic backgrounds. A high family income could lead to a reduction in household work and child care done personally. Recent immigrant groups are said to expect more domestic labor from women than do those who have become acculturated over a longer period of time. An ANCOVA statistical routine based on Multiple Classification Analysis was run to examine the effects of ethnicity and family income on the obligatory activity of female heads of household, taking into consideration their marital and employment status. This analysis showed that employment status remains a highly significant explanation of obligatory activity ($p < .001$).[3] Ethnicity has some degree of explanatory power independent of employment status, though not as strong ($p = .053$). Obligatory activity beyond that explained by employment status required approximately 41 minutes a day less of female respondents classified as of no identifiable ethnic background other than Canadian for two generations than it did of those with clear ethnic identities. Family income, however, has found to be unrelated to obligatory activity ($p = .27$).

In sum, women's daily routines are clearly affected by outside employment. They do less of everything except their jobs and travel, and the total load adds up measurably despite whatever reductions they make in other activities, particularly when the children are young.

From these results, we still do not know anything about the immediate context in which these trade-offs are made. If employed mothers do less at home, for example, do others in the family come to their support and do more? What is the relationship between women's routines and those of their husbands and children, particularly with respect to domestic needs? Let us turn to Chapter 5 to address such questions.

Notes

1 The columns of minutes per day do not add up to 1440, because we collected information on a day that was not necessarily exactly 24 hours long. The time-budgets commenced at the time people woke up on the weekday in question. However, to measure accurately the amount of sleep respondents enjoyed, the time-budget concluded at whatever time they arose the next day—not necessarily the same time as on the original day. In any case, the time-use figures are consistent with those gathered in other studies.

2 These conclusions have been independently confirmed by recent analyses in England and France, according to personal communications from J. Gershuny and C. Roy, respectively, in October 1983. See also Geerken and Gove (1983, p. 91) for estimates of these phenomena for families with employed and nonemployed women; in that work, however, the data on husbands and wives do not come from the same families.

3 Marital status was not significantly related to the amount of daily time devoted to obligatory activities.

5
The Immediate Context: Household Division of Labor

The preceding chapter makes it clear that outside employment is a role responsibility that, depending on its extent, presents mothers with time-consuming obligations that crowd many or even most other activities in the weekday timetable. Although weekends typically allow more time for sleeping, shopping, and socializing, among other activities, nonemployment-related pursuits still are not in the weekly time-use pattern distributed evenly among those with and without jobs.

One possible result is that employed women, especially if working full-time, fill the same domestic role responsibilities more efficiently or under greater pressure. Another is that they make do with fewer domestic activities (e.g., simpler meals, permanent-press instead of ironing, less frequent dusting). Still another alternative is that some other person or persons take up the slack.

When one member of a small system like the family has to trade off time for specific chores, the most direct, logical expectation is for another member to make complementary adjustments. In the nuclear family, the husband, as another adult, is the first candidate to make supportive trade-offs when his wife is employed. Depending on their ages, children can also step into the breach. Persons from outside the family can be hired to substitute for family members, to clean, garden, shovel snow, and more. For example, we noted in Chapter 4 a slightly greater reliance on restaurants and fast food when women are employed.

Given the inelasticity of time, trade-offs are made whether women like them or not. Whether others can personally compensate for what women once might have been expected to do themselves would seem to make a difference in how women feel about their routines. A recent study (Ross, Mirowsky, and Huber, 1983) indicates that employed women are less depressed if their husbands help with the housework. The authors go on to say,

The Immediate Context: Household Division of Labor 61

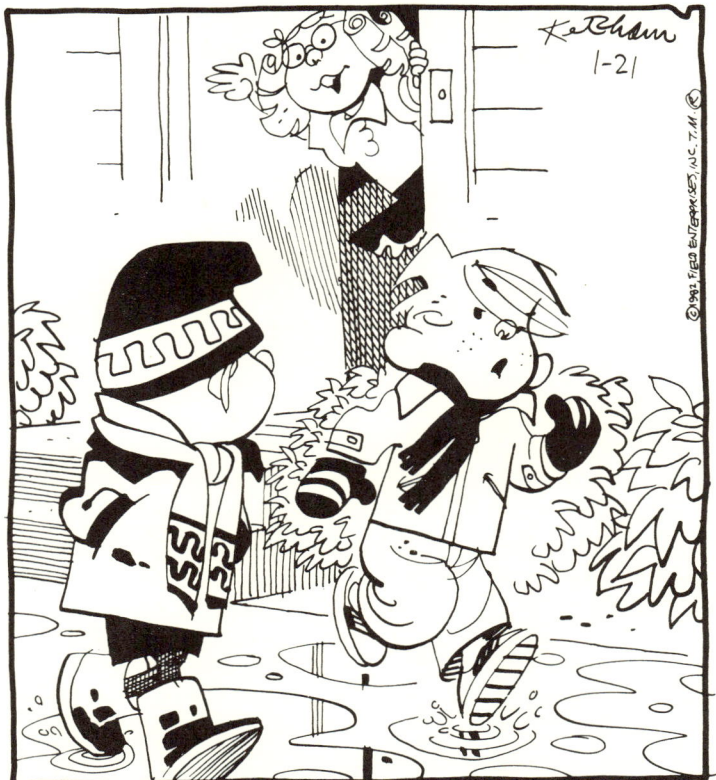

FIGURE 5.1 *Dennis the Menace on Household Division of Labor: Amusing but is it Accurate?* (DENNIS THE MENACE ® used by permission of Hank Ketcham and © by News Group Chicago, Inc.)

". . . there is reason to think that a trend toward married women's employment may eventually reduce sex typing in the division of household chores, since there tends to be a more egalitarian division of labor in the home if the wife is employed . . ." (p. 810).

The specific literature on the subject is not so hopeful about the spread of sexual egalitarianism. Let us therefore temper what logic might lead us to expect about our findings with a short look at the experience of other studies.

Accumulated Evidence

One clear finding from the accumulated evidence is that women, even if employed, still do the greatest share of household and child-care activities. While the time they devote to these activities is diminished, it still is much more than the time anyone else gives. In general, traditional household sex roles appear to have stayed the same in the great majority of families. The change has been in how much time employed women are able to invest in these traditional role responsibilities, not in the balance of commitments within families.

The 1965 cross-national study showed that, when both spouses are employed, the amount of time women devote to household obligations, marketing, and child care during the weekday comes to three to five times as much as their husbands do. In North America and Western Europe, employed married women spend about 300 minutes a day in these activities, compared to just an hour by their spouses. In the Eastern European samples, these figures were 270 and 101 minutes, respectively (Stone, 1978, pp. 126-27).

American data have produced similar conclusions. A recent review of studies by Vanek (1984)[1] concludes, "The recent findings indicate that housekeeping continues to be women's responsibility in the division of labor in marriage. With paid employment, wives take on a second job and compress their housekeeping into fewer hours" (p. 101). Derow's findings in Toronto are similar (1977).

There is somewhat more controversy over whether husbands do in fact contribute more when their wives are employed, even if this falls substantially short of equality. Vanek's review (1984, p. 207) notes that two studies suggested a significantly greater likelihood of spousal sharing of tasks but then criticizes them on methodological grounds and cites contrary results from Walker and Woods (1976) and from her own work (1973). New data by Geerken and Gove (1983, p. 90), though derived from estimates rather than time-budgets, are consistent with those of Walker and Woods in their emphasis on traditional household role behavior.

The 1979 Finnish data (Niemi et al., 1981, pp. 41-42) show that the percentage of domestic work contributed by men increases from 22% to 33% when their wives have jobs. But this reflects a mean increase of only three minutes in the time contributed, from twelve to fifteen minutes a day.

In nearby Norway, data gathered in 1980-81 show the minimal differences in men's contributions to housekeeping and child care according to their wives' employment status. While the wive's times for these decrease from 6.8 daily hours for housewives to 5.6 for those with part-time jobs and to 4.2 with full-time jobs, their husbands devote 2.5, 2.6, and 2.6 hours, respectively (Central Bureau of Statistics of Norway, 1983, p. 105).

In still a different culture, these gender differences are even more pronounced. The 1976 Japanese figures (Matsushima, 1982, p. 200) show that, in families with children, husbands devoted five minutes a day to housework and child care, compared to over six hours by their wives, if the latter were not employed. If, however, the wives had jobs, reducing their domestic workload to about three and a half hours, the men averaged four minutes — surely no evidence of compensation.

In Sweden, where an extremely high percentage of women is employed and where public-support services are more accessible than in many other countries, women between 25 and 44 years old still spend 33 hours a week in household work, compared to 13 hours for men in the same age bracket (Nordenstam, 1984, p. 11).

The various pieces of evidence are summed up by Norwegian observers: "Sex roles in unpaid household work seem to be more difficult to change than sex roles in paid employment. In all urbanized and industrialized societies, we find a growing female participation in the labor force, but no accompanying growth in men's household work" (Grønmo & Lingsom, cited in Nordenstam, p. 11). This is surely evidence of what Ogburn meant by a cultural lag (Ogburn, 1964).

Staines and Pleck conducted a sophisticated analysis of the effects of the work schedules of husbands and wives on their families (1983). They found that such phenomena as the relationship of spousal work shifts had more effect on women's time-use than on men's. Such a finding is made understandable by men's relative inflexibility about performing domestic activities.

The argument has also been made that, although men have not been found to accommodate to maternal employment to any marked degree, women have customarily accommodated to men's employment. Only in recent years has there been significant opposition to the assumption that the whole family must move to a different city when the husband's employer says to do so, regardless of the wife's local activities. The concept of the two-person career, in which the wife, through entertaining and personal accommodation, is expected to be a major factor in her husband's occupational performance, is by no means dead. The politician's, clergyman's, organization man's wife is still considered an obligatory but unpaid part of the team. When the appointment of a new president of a major university was announced, for example, one news article mentioned that his employed wife would be cutting her workload to meet the social obligations of the office. The reciprocal form of this support has not been institutionalized, however. Although the facts of the preceding case are not known, there is less likelihood that he cut back his job commitments when she undertook her employment. This book does not deal specifically with the two-person career, but it is noted as part of the significance of how little intrafamilial division of labor has changed to reflect maternal employment.

There is less in the literature on how children contribute to household work when their mothers are employed. Time-budget studies have rarely considered children, partly because of the difficulties in eliciting such information, partly because of the extra costs and potential analytic complications, and partly because of the adult focus of much policy-oriented survey research. Walker and Woods (1976), however, found that children contributed 5% of household labor time when their mothers were not in the labor force. This increased to 10% when the mothers had jobs. As the data on husbands indicate, these figures undoubtedly represented an increase but not a doubling of children's support, since the total amount of household work done normally decreases. Howell (1973b) and Propper (1972) found that adolescents take a larger amount of responsibility for household tasks when their mothers are employed. Van Vliet found increased participation by girls in particular (1980). If these findings are representative, we would expect the Toronto data to show that children are a real but subsidiary source of support for household work in families and that their contributions increase under certain circumstances. One might, for example, hypothesize an increase within families headed by single mothers in particular.

What about support from outside the family? One obvious and unambiguous form of support is child care. Without child care, most mothers are unable to undertake outside employment, and of course this is an absolute necessity when children are young. Thus, the question addressed here is not whether people have it but the logistical implications and outcomes of alternate forms. Such considerations are taken up in Chapters 8 and 9.

Less clear is how much employed mothers rely on outside persons for some of the other household tasks, such as cleaning and gardening. Surely the occupations of cleaning woman and gardener are well known, but it is not certain that their contributions are central to the typical employed mother's trade-offs.

Derow's review of help from outside the family (1977, pp. 76-77) suggests that this may vary by culture and by socio-economic class within a culture. For women in professional occupations, paid help for drudge work around the house may be more common. But the most representative study cited, Vanek's analysis of the 1965 U.S. time-budget survey (1973), is extremely cautious. Among employed women, 14% used outside help, only 3% more than the percentage of housewives who do the same. This suggests that, while a certain segment of the population may have outside help for certain jobs, it is not necessarily a special compensating support for employed women. In view of the percentage of women who take jobs out of need for additional money, this should not be surprising. Economic logic says that they would not be willing to turn a set part of this over to others unless necessary, as in the case of child care, which can be expensive enough. Where money is less of an object in the employment decision, outside help is more plausible; but such help is not uncommon in affluent households in any case.

Another way to look at intrafamilial division of labor is to study statements about responsibilities rather than about time expenditures. It is possible to view supports and trade-offs in terms of responsibility for necessary tasks, rather than in terms of duration, which has been shown to be relatively elastic. From this methodological perspective, the literature has been more encouraging about a possible spousal adjustment to maternal employment (e.g., Kamerman, 1980), though this can be criticized on grounds that survey responses may reflect ideology more than do studies of time-use (cf. Vanek, 1984).

A recent study with this approach (Geerken and Gove, 1983) indicates that the percentage of husbands participating in most of the selected household activities examined is relatively high — from slightly under 50% doing some housecleaning, dishwashing, and cooking, to about 80% doing home and yard maintenance, child care, and bill paying. However, husbands take major responsibility only for the maintenance activities, and there is a relatively even division by sex of who is in charge of paying bills. The wives take the paramount responsibilities for all other domestic activities. Employment-status differences among the wives account for marginal differences in participation by the husbands but not for differences of any mentionable magnitude in responsibility (p. 93).

Harper and Richards (1979) analyze this question by looking at frequency of participation in domestic activities by husbands and wives, reaching identical conclusions (p. 293).

The Toronto data can clarify the above points, since systematic time-budget data were taken from husbands, wives, and children in the same families and for the same days. Furthermore, a question on degree of responsibility in various household tasks (question 29) not only enables a comparison with such results as those by Kamerman (1980) and Geerken and Gove (1983) but enables some examination of the relationship between time budgets and answers to responsibility questions.

Intrafamilial Dynamics

Results from the Toronto data confirm the major tenets established in the literature. Despite maternal variations in time devoted to housework and child care according to her employment status, the wife still devotes more time to these activities than does her husband, within each employment status category. For example, women who have full-time employment still devote approximately three times as much time to these functions. In families where the wife has a part-time job, this ratio is approximately 5 to 1, and it increases to 6.7 to 1 when the wife is not employed. See Figure 5.2.

Nevertheless, there is evidence that men devote somewhat more time to housework when their wives have full-time jobs. For example, men whose wives have full-time employment average 57 minutes a day in housework,

66 The Immediate Context: Household Division of Labor

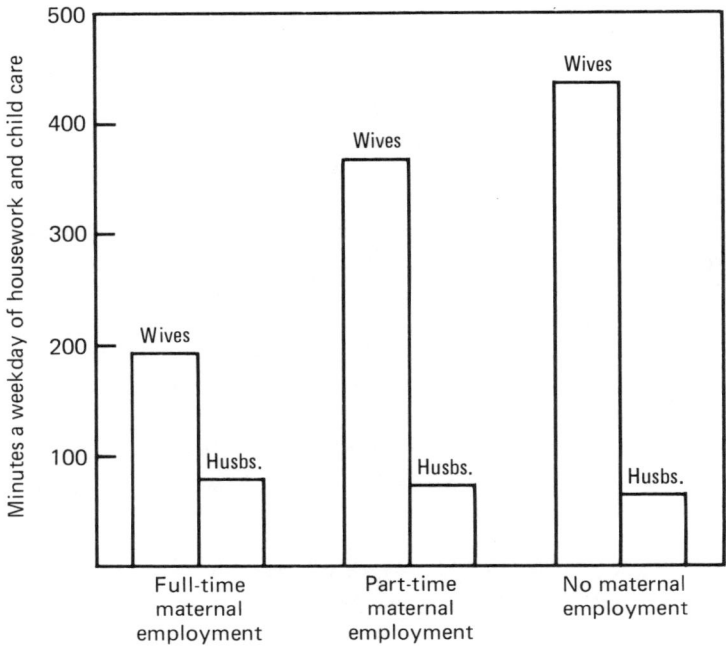

FIGURE 5.2.
Minutes a Weekday Husbands and Wives in Two-Parent Families Devote to Housework and Child Care, by Wives' Employment Status.

compared to 48 minutes and 43 minutes, respectively, among those whose wives have part-time or no jobs. Although these figures are in the direction that might be expected, the differences are emphatically small compared to the actual amount of housework women do, even if employed full-time.

Furthermore, the amount of time men devote to child care has no meaningful relationship to their wives' employment. Like women, men devote more time to child care when children are younger. However, this means that the men's mean contribution of about 40 minutes a day when the children are under four years of age falls to about 15 minutes as the children reach their teens.

Generally, even when both spouses have full-time jobs, men spend more time at the job (450 minutes vs. 392). However, when their wives are less fully employed, men work even longer, by an average of 35–40 minutes. The greater the extent of their wives' employment, the greater the devotion of time men make to travel (95, 77, and 75 minutes, respectively). While the woman with a full-time job spends as much time travelling as the average male, she still travels less than her own husband (95 minutes vs. 81 minutes). Housewives spend more time than their husbands in sleep and other personal activity, in passive leisure activities, and in socializing, but wives employed full-time have approximately 40 minutes a day less passive leisure than their husbands. Women generally shop somewhat more than men, regardless of their employment status, but spouses are relatively equal in time devoted to active leisure and education.

The more general time-use impressions about weekends, while confirming the inequalities shown on weekdays, are not so dramatic. Husbands are alone with some or all the children on weekends about 1½ to 2½ hours less than are their wives. See Table 4.6. Husband-wife differences remain clear-cut, but, in this particular instance, the ratio of wives' time to husbands' is not as great as in the aggregate of weekday child-care activities.

The comparison of husbands and wives from two-parent families reflects the means within subcategories according to wives' employment status. But it does not assess the complementarity of time-usage by specific pairs of spouses, pair by pair. It is possible that the means seen so far hide significant amounts of complementary effort of men in particular families when their wives are unable to keep up. Thus, correlation analysis may be insightful.

With respect to such activities as housework and child care, for example, such complementary efforts would lead to expectations of negative correlation coefficients, reflecting inverse relationships. That is, men would be expected to devote more time to an activity when their wives contributed less; when the wives could do more, the men would do less.

Table 5.1, however, indicates just the opposite. It shows a positive correlation between husbands and wives on every activity except minutes of paid employment. With respect to housework, for example, there is a direct relationship between the times men and women devote to the tasks, among all the couples in the sample; however, this relationship is low and not statistically significant. This suggests that, while there is certainly no support for the hypothesis of trade-offs between husbands and wives with respect to housework, there is little sign of any other pattern. What the husband does is relatively independent of what his wife does or doesn't do.

On the other hand, concerning respective times devoted to child care, the somewhat higher correlation of +.20 is statistically significant, given the large sample. This suggests that the amount of time men devote is directly related to their wives' efforts. In other words, when women put in more time on child care, so do men; when women devote less time to it, so do men. The aforementioned demands that come from a child's age, for example, are more critical determinants of men's child-care activity than are the constraints on their wives. Once again, this represents a form of response by men, but it is not evidence for a transformation in household sex roles.

The relationships shown for such activities as shopping and social life reflect that these are activities husbands and wives typically do together, making high positive correlations the expected pattern, in contrast to our hypotheses about obligatory household activities.

68 The Immediate Context: Household Division of Labor

TABLE 5.1

Correlations of Time Devoted by Husbands and Wives
to Activities on a Weekday by Employment Status of Wife

Activity	Employment status of Wife			All Married Couples Regardless of Employment Status
	Full-Time	Part-Time	Not Employed	
Employment	+.09	+.01	+.05	-.02
Housework	+.15*	+.44**	-.08	+.08
Child Care	+.22**	+.26**	+.18**	+.20**
Work, Housework and Child Care Combined	+.18*	+.18	+.14*	+.13**
Active Leisure	+.04	+.01	+.12	+.08*
Educational Activities	+.27**	+.09	-.02	+.19**
Passive Leisure	+.26**	-.03	+.22**	+.20**
Personal Care	+.15*	+.26**	+.13*	+.15**
Shopping	+.51**	+.22*	+.34**	+.36**
Civic Activities	+.12	-.04	+.43**	+.24**
Social Activities	+.52**	+.71**	+.45**	+.51**
Travel (total)	+.17	+.30**	+.10	+.19**
Public Transit	+.04	+.02	-.08	+.01
Travel by Auto	+.15*	+.17	+.21**	+.18**
n =	(141)	(80)	(173)	(394)

* $p < .05$

** $p < .01$

One might question whether the expected complementarity is not hidden when lumping all employment categories together. Breaking the data down, as in Table 5.1, to observe only women with full-time jobs and their husbands, strengthens most of the relationships. The positive correlation between husbands and wives with respect to housework increases to +.15, which represents a significant difference at less than the .05 level. The positive correlation on time devoted to child care increases marginally; those representing joint activities increase considerably.

In short, we have strong evidence that the husbands of employed women

The Immediate Context: Household Division of Labor 69

respond to some of the same demands and attractions as their wives but do not fill in for them at home in any systematic way.

The degree of responsibility for specific tasks is another way of looking at division of labor within the family. We asked about the differing degrees of responsibility among the various members of the family, including whether husband, wife, child(ren), or another was the main person responsible, helps regularly, or helps sometimes. Joint responsibility was possible, as was not doing the task at all. The female head of household was asked about sixteen different household tasks.

Women with full-time jobs are primarily responsible for an average 6.7 household jobs, compared to 7.7 for part-time workers and 8.3 for those not employed. As might be expected, these responsibilities are even more directly the mother's in single-parent households, averaging 10.1 among women with full-time jobs and 11.1 among those without employment.

Substantively, jobs break down according to traditional sex roles. For example, women remain heavily responsible for such activities as cooking, dishwashing, laundry, ironing, indoor cleaning, supervising school work, grocery shopping, and taking children for medical and dental care. In these kinds of activity, men are most commonly occasional helpers; responsibility seldom is fixed on them for these jobs. In contrast, such tasks as car maintenance, house repair, and garbage removal are traditional male preserves that are sustained in these analyses. In two-parent families, wives may do these some of the time, but not nearly so much as men.

Employment status introduces significant variations in the same general theme. The more complete women's devotion to outside work, the less likely they are to take sole responsibility for "women's tasks." For example, 53.2% of housewives take exclusive responsibility for the cooking, compared to 40.7% of part-time workers and 38.2% of full-time employees in the sample. Similarly, 79% of the housewives do the laundry exclusively, compared to 59% of those with part-time jobs and 55% of those with full-time jobs. The finding that fewer employed women take sole responsibility for such jobs does not mean that their husbands do so instead; respondents state that shared responsibility becomes more common.

In contrast, "men's jobs" are not likely to vary as greatly according to the wife's employment status.

Budgeting and bill paying are "unisex jobs." These are often shared, regardless of the wife's employment status, and husbands and wives are roughly equal in taking sole responsibility for such jobs. Nevertheless, there is a slight tendency in favor of either equality or exclusive wives' performance of these tasks when the wives have full-time jobs. For example, when the wife does not have outside employment, she has exclusive rights over bill paying in 32% of the cases, he does it 33% of the time, and they do it equally 16½% of the time.[2] When her job is full-time, however, she pays the bills 34% of the time compared to his 24%, with equality in 31%, clearly a difference.

Another tendency worth mention is that toward stated equality in caring for babies when the wife has outside employment, particularly full-time employment. Equal responsibility for child care by husbands and wives is claimed by 31.2% of the women with full-time jobs, compared to 26.7% of part-time employees and only 11.2% of housewives. Conversely, exclusive care by the mother declines from 31.9% among the housewives to 14.6% among women with full-time jobs, findings roughly comparable in their message to those of Kamerman (1980); no "control group" of housewives was included in Kamerman's study, however, and women with part-time jobs were few and not given explicit treatment.

Although this sign of a trend in the direction of equality is noteworthy, particularly but not exclusively with respect to child care, it is only fair to point out that the different times reported in the time-budgets for the average weekday by husbands and wives do not reflect such a commitment at all strongly. Although the wording of our responsibility questions, the areas covered, and the analysis differ marginally from those of Geerken and Gove (1983), the findings are quite similar, particularly in the comparison of stated responsibilities to time-use. (Note that their figures reflect respondent estimates rather than time-budgets and hence differ in some respects in their absolute values.)

Other questions we asked shed additional light on husband-wife division of labor. When children are sick and have to stay home from school and when teachers' professional-development days create a parallel need for nonroutine child care, the wife is much more likely than the husband to stay home to take care of the children. Those employed full-time are often allowed some flexibility in doing this without consistent loss of pay; part-time workers are much more likely to lose pay, because of the more tenuous and wage-oriented conditions typical of part-time work.

This general orientation toward the mother is reflected in a respondent's comment in the discussions:

> When your children are in elementary school, if there are any difficulties, the teacher phones you. "You come over. Can't we discuss this?" That's true when both are working, when they can't get the mother any more than the father. They just usually put through telephone calls to the mother. "We can disturb her, but don't look up the father." She's got two jobs.

What about children's place in the family division of labor? According to both the time-budget and responsibility data, children are much more of a subsidiary labor force than are husbands. About one of every five families primarily assigns dishwashing and garbage disposal to a child or children, who are also typical secondary and tertiary helpers if not the main doers. But children otherwise have relatively little to do with the sixteen tasks discussed in this section. Children four to six years of age typically devote about six minutes a day to housework; those seven to nine increase this to about ten minutes; and children ten to fourteen double that amount, to twenty minutes. These are all well below what their mothers and fathers devote to housework chores.

It is particularly ironic to note a high degree of gender differentiation in household work among the children in the sample, even those in two-earner families. For example, among the seven-to-nine-year-olds, girls average twelve minutes a day in such chores compared to seven for boys; among the ten-to-fourteen-year-olds, the differential increases to twenty-seven minutes vs. thirteen minutes.

As one might expect, children are most likely to help if their mother is employed. Here, though, the data on responsibilities and time-use conflict. According to the mothers, children whose mothers have part-time jobs take on the least in household responsibility. The children rally to their aid when they have full-time jobs, but mothers with part-time jobs appear not to divert responsibility to their children. Nevertheless, the time-budgets show that, within the relevant age categories, the children of women with part-time jobs contribute the most time in household work, about 30% above the means. Whichever is more pertinent to the situation, there appears to be some response to maternal employment by children, but still not one that takes away from the predominant devotion by women to household work.

Previous literature raised but did not settle the question of whether help from outside the household significantly substitutes for what the employed woman does not do in the home. In response to a direct question on the subject (question 31), so few persons reported housekeeping or other forms of help that no analysis was feasible. This may be a further reflection of many respondents' economic grounds for holding outside employment. They appear to prefer reducing the amount of time devoted to certain activities to transferring their earnings to substitute help. It was also evident that a certain number of the respondents were themselves employed as cleaning help. Hypotheses that originate with the upper socio-economic strata do not explain realistically whether cleaning women hire others to clean in their absence.

The point of this chapter was not to pass judgment on the division of labor within the various types of households. Nonetheless, for our forthcoming discussions of outcomes and implications of maternal employment, it is important to understand the underlying conditions of differential time-use and responsibility at home. The juxtaposition of responsibilities within the limitations of the twenty-four hour day is important as we turn in Chapter 6 to considerations of time pressure and tension.

Notes

1 This paper was originally published in 1978.
2 Other variations account for the rest of the percentages.

6
Outcomes of Maternal Employment

We have seen that the total daily workload of the employed mother is extremely high compared to that of others. Without significant help from either members of her family or outsiders, she has less time for virtually all nonemployment-related activities. On these grounds alone, it is no wonder that maternal employment has been viewed as problematic. As one respondent in our study remarked, "I can see it being an upsetting experience to have an outside job where you are proving you have talent and then coming home and not being able to get help from someone else who says he has talent."

Nonetheless, it is evident that women get something in return for such efforts. In some cases, this may be satisfaction intrinsic to a desired job. In many others, it is income women feel they need, which may permit a standard of living and a degree of upward mobility otherwise unlikely for their families. There is thus a rationale that supports maternal employment despite its logistical dysfunctions.

This chapter assesses the outcomes of maternal employment. Our particular foci in this regard are on how women feel about what they do during the typical weekday, as well as what contributes most to these feelings. Such information, however, must also be viewed in terms of more general feelings of happiness and factors that contribute to them. In other words, we want to measure the relative degree of daily hassle that accompanies maternal employment and to assess how important this is in women's lives more generally.

Outcomes Previously Pursued

Previous research indicates that outcomes arise from two major sources: the job itself (or its absence) and the context of the interaction of employment with other activities, people, and priorities.

Employment has been shown to contribute more than income. Self-esteem, self-confidence, competence, identity, and intellectual flexibility are said to result from maternal employment (e.g., Howell, 1973a; Mortimer and London, 1984). Contrary to some hypotheses, employment has been found unrelated among women to psycho-social disorders, but rather instead to personal satisfaction (e.g., Rutter, 1981). Indeed, the positive outcomes of employment have been shown to be passed down to the next generation, particularly to daughters (Hoffman, 1974a and 1979).[1]

Not all jobs are pleasant or uplifting, however. Fatigue and harassment are also direct outcomes of employment (Mortimer and London, 1984). There are the well-known problems women encounter in gaining equal pay for equal work and in being hired and promoted in recognition of their training and abilities. None of these negative aspects of work are exclusive to women, but outcomes along these lines are nevertheless potential entries into women's balance sheets.

Employment also interacts with a variety of other factors to produce additional outcomes (see Portner, 1983). We have already reviewed and documented the interaction of employment and other activities performed within a limited amount of time. This has been linked to feelings of overload and stress.

The interpersonal side of this interaction has led to decreased contact with spouses and children, for potential outcomes involving family life (Staines and Pleck, 1983), spousal affection and couple harmony (Geerken and Gove, 1983), and guilt (Mortimer and London, 1984).

Work can interact with other factors at the normative level as well. Women get it from all sides about what they should give priority to—or not do at all (Skinner, 1984).

The positive outcome of the interaction of women's employment with so many other considerations is less prominent in the literature. The ideal, of course, is to be able to combine all role requirements successfully, to enjoy the satisfactions both of the component parts and of successfully mastering the whole. The gist of the literature is that this takes a virtual superwoman/mom, in view of the number of demands this requires under current social and physical contexts (Lawe and Lawe, 1980; Holmstrom, 1972). Fine as it is when it works, this requirement is seen as an unrealistic prerequisite for positive outcomes from the everyday routine. Given the number and degree of role requirements currently placed on employed mothers, it seems more reasonable to require societal structures and institutions to adapt than to challenge the working mother to be a superwoman—a "seldom-win" situation (see Kamerman, 1980).

The various positive and negative outcomes of employment can be viewed one by one or together on paper, as on a balance sheet. The direction of the most general outcome reflects the interpretation of the person involved. Does she consider hassle or other negative outcomes worth bearing for the sake of positive outcomes? Research has turned to the conditions under which the balance of outcomes is determined. Rutter puts this issue rather simply: "Whether maternal employment is or is not a good thing for the family is likely to depend very much on whether the mother wants to work" (1981, p. 17). Ross, Mirowsky, and Huber (1983) found that whether women are in normative agreement with significant others about their occupational roles is an important factor in the avoidance of depression.

Given our view of the family as a system, the outcomes of maternal employment are not restricted to just the women involved. Their husbands, children, or both are potentially involved, as are others to whom they may be close (in some cases, for example, their mothers). We saw in the last chapter how small is the behavioral outcome of women's employment on their husbands. In this chapter, we can nonetheless examine men's more subjective feelings. Berk and Berk, for example, found: "Compared to husbands of unemployed wives, husbands of employed wives experience about 10% less of their household time as pleasant" (1979, p. 239). They suggest that women prefer to do household tasks alone, while men prefer their wives' company during this work.[2]

The literature has thus addressed direct benefits and detriments of employment, as well as others arising from the logistical and normative interrelationships of employment with other aspects of life.

What this chapter will address primarily and what has not been given extensive treatment in the literature is what outcomes emerge directly from the juxtaposition of the commitment to employment with the qualitative and quantitative systems of activity in the rest of weekday life. How great are the temporal conflicts of everyday role responsibilities? Which obligations tend to create the most negative feelings in this context? What is the relationship between these logistical considerations and more direct outcomes of employment? How do outcomes reflecting the logistics of the daily routine link maternal employment to such hypothesized but more remote outcomes as marital satisfaction?

Most of this chapter therefore deals with considerations seldom covered in the existing literature. Instead, these represent the next step toward understanding the outcomes of maternal employment in its complex context.

Outcomes of Daily Role Responsibilities

It is one thing to document the various patterns of time-use associated with women's outside employment, not to mention the intrafamilial division of labor. It is an additional step, however, to assess whether any pattern leaves an impact on those who exhibit it. Let us first look at data indicating what respondents saw as the types and degrees of outcome of their daily responsibilities and activities.

TIME PRESSURES

Chapter 2 discusses the rationale and structure of several questions about respondents' perceptions of time pressure. For example, "busy scales" solicited respondents' perceptions of whether they had too little, the right amount, or too much time for what they had or wanted to do in stated periods of time. One question asked, rather directly, whether respondents felt too busy all the time, most of the time, some of the time, or never.

Correlation analysis indicates that respondents' perceived "average-week" time pressures are most highly related to all the other busy scales. I shall refer to the busy scale for "yesterday" when discussing comparisons with time-budget data for that day, but otherwise I shall refer mainly to the average-week busy scale and to the direct question as to whether women feel too busy. It might have been possible to construct an index linking the various busy scales, but the average-week busy scale's high degree of representativeness did not indicate a need to do so.[3]

In any case, Figure 6.1 shows that there is considerable variation in the levels of perceived time pressures according to employment status. Married women with full-time jobs reported the most time pressures, and those with-

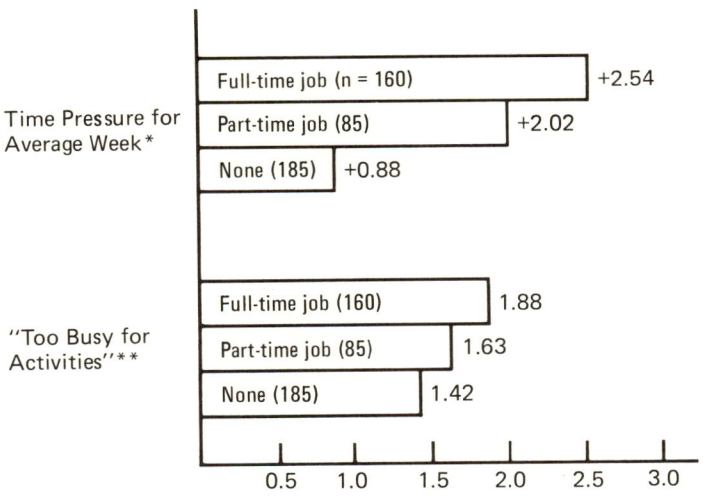

*Scale ranged from +10 (most time pressure) to −10 (least time pressure), with 0 an equilibrium between activity needs and time available

**Scale ranged from 4 (all the time) to 1 (never)

FIGURE 6.1.
Mean Time Pressures for Married Women by Employment Status.

out jobs the least; part-time workers were in between. Data on single mothers, to be reported in the next chapter, follow exactly the pattern of those on married women.

Some people say that women who become employed have a personal disposition to want to be busier than others: they have "bees in their bonnets." Women were therefore asked about their ideal busy-scale value. If the stereotyped image were true, employed women should be found to have higher ideal busy scales. In addition, we should then expect the difference between actual and ideal busy scales to be constant across employment groups. Neither hypothesis received support. Indeed, the contrary to the second hypothesis was found. There is a greater gap between actual and ideal time pressures among the married women with full-time jobs than among those working part-time and without jobs. For example, the gap between actual and ideal scores is +5 or more for 38.1% of full-time workers, 24.8% of part-time workers, and only 18.3% of those without jobs. That is, mothers, particularly those with full-time jobs, receive significantly more time pressure than they want, and this overload is greater among those with more rather than less or no employment. The mean ideal score was about +1, varying little by employment status. A very few respondents, mainly among the housewives, reflected scores in which actual time pressure was lower than their ideal. Once again, single mothers are exactly comparable.

A number of direct questions touched directly on the conditions under which people feel time pressure. For example, the single greatest perceived cause of daily time pressure among women is the attempt to fulfill multiple responsibilities; 35.4% of the sample mention this directly. The hypothesized interaction between employment and other activities becomes clear when employment status is controlled statistically. Among the married women with full-time jobs, 60.6% see multiple responsibilities as the main cause of time pressure, compared to 43.4% among those with part-time jobs but only 10.5% of those without jobs.

The most typical causes of daily pressures are getting other members of the family out in the morning and then preparing meals in the evening, while also fulfilling external obligations. Morning and early evening therefore become the most difficult periods, inasmuch as internal and external obligations become juxtaposed or overlap at these times. These are transitions from one kind and location of activity to another. Since travel is frequently involved, this puts an affective perspective on travel rarely pursued by transportation researchers and practitioners. This will be discussed in greater detail in Chapter 9.

The busy scales enable a deeper look at the conditions under which feelings of time pressure emerge. Women were asked if they had too little, just enough, or too much time for what they needed to do (on the same scale) with respect to such activities as employment, housework, child care, time for the husband, and time for oneself. It was then possible to analyze statistically the contribution of time pressures from these sectors of time-use to our central measure of perceived time pressure, the average week. Table 6.1 shows that, while there is a positive correlation between all the sectors and the busy scale for the average week, each highly significant statistically, two sectors are much more highly related than the others. Time pressures of housework and regarding time for oneself are correlated at +.64 and +.50, respectively, with the more general busy scale.

Breaking these down according to employment status does not lessen the significance of these relationships. But among women with full-time employment, having time for oneself is found to be more highly related to general time pressure than is having time for housework (+.56 to +.54). Among housewives, the opposite emphasis, on housework, is strengthened, with correlation coefficients of +.61 for housework and +.36 for personal time. Women with part-time jobs resemble more the pattern of the housewives, having the highest correlation concerning housework (+.65) but a stronger correlation between time for oneself and general time pressures (+.49), reflecting their characteristic combination of commitments to the home and employment-related pressures.

A regression analysis was also run on these variables. Putting time for housework first into the regression equation leads to a significant explana-

TABLE 6.1

Correlations of Women's Perceived Time Pressure for Average Week with Perceived Time Pressure for Particular Activities

Perceived Time Pressure for Particular Activities	Correlation With Perceived Time Pressure for Average Week	p =	n =
Employment	+.14	.009	(300)
Home	+.64	.001	(540)
With Children	+.32	.001	(540)
With Husband	+.17	.001	(440)
With Friends	+.19	.001	(535)
For Self	+.50	.001	(538)
Opportunities for Children Outside Home	+.26	.001	(507)
Children's Medical Care	+.14	.001	(539)
Self Medical Care	+.21	.001	(539)

tion for that factor, with a multiple correlation coefficient of .59 and an r^2 of .34, but relatively little residual explanation for the other sectors' busy scales. Once time pressures at home have been considered, time for oneself adds only .08 to the change in total explanation, with only .06 left for the remaining sectors of time-use. If the order of factors is changed, putting time for oneself before housework, the former is slightly more significant in its contribution to the change in the r^2, but housework still adds virtually as much — at .24 and .20, respectively.

These data suggest that women reserve time for their work responsibilities, for their husbands, their children, and their friends. That is, they set aside the requisite time for obligations to other people and for contractual requirements. The source of felt time pressures is the lack of sufficient time slots, on the other hand, for tasks uniquely required of women acting largely unaided around the house and, on the other hand, for time simply one's own — to relax, think, plan, clear one's head. Between time for housework and time for oneself, the former appears the stronger contributor to general feelings of time pressure, perhaps because even individual work in this regard involves fulfilling obligations to others.

Because these measures of time pressure are such an important part of the total picture, it is important to assess how much time pressure is related to other plausible explanatory variables. However, our results indicate that the above findings hold across various categories of socio-economic status, size of family, and age of children. Indeed, socio-economic status is unrelated in the present sample to feelings of time pressure. Family size is mildly related to feelings of time pressure, but not nearly as strongly or consistently as is employment status. In this regard, feelings of time pressure rise moderately as family size increases from one to four children, but then decline among families with five or more children. Contrary to expectations, time pressure increases slightly as children get older. In any case, none of these factors relates as significantly to reactions about the contents of the day as does employment status.

Employment status structures people's days in ways that result in differing amounts of time pressure, even if it is not necessarily work time itself that evokes the feeling of pressure. The feeling of pressure is brought by the activities squeezed by the allocation of time to other activities.

The sensitive situation of the time that women have available for housework is further indicated by data on the degree of worry underlying the feeling of time pressure. It is possible, for example, for people to experience severe time binds while maintaining a sense of humor about them, taking such pressures as part of the chosen territory. On the other hand, lack of time for some activities may be a genuine source of worry and concern. Therefore, whenever a respondent indicated a busy-scale response of +3 or greater on a sectoral time pressure, we asked her the degree of worry this feeling caused

Outcomes of Maternal Employment 79

her. As Table 6.2 shows, not only is housework a major contribution to general time pressure, it is far and away the greatest source of worry among the respondents, regardless of employment status. This contrasts strongly with the employment context, which is seen neither as a locus of time pressure per se nor as a source of worry. Having time for oneself, though contributing to general time pressures to some extent, is not seen as a major source of worry.

These data make somewhat clearer how women can potentially gain positive outcomes from what they do on the job, yet encounter potentially great difficulties from the logistics of holding employment under typical societal conditions. Furthermore, the sensitive picture of housework as a salient yet worrisome obligation for women, in that it reflects the expectations of others, helps bridge the gap in formulations that take maternal employment as an independent variable and marital harmony as a dependent variable.

Similarly, having time for husband and for children, while not explaining much about general time pressure, is shown in Table 6.2 as increasingly worrisome the greater the commitment women have to employment.

We analyzed the data to assess as well whether the amount of time devoted to specific activities during the previous day is related to perceived time pressure for that day. The findings, as outlined in Table 6.3, are mild but logical. There is a significant but not extreme positive relationship between minutes devoted to employment activities and feelings of time pressure for "yesterday." Time devoted to child care is even more mildly (and inversely) related to

TABLE 6.2

Percentage of Wives Reporting a Lot or a Great Deal of Worry About Being Too Busy for Particular Activities, by Employment Status

Employment Status						
Activity	Full-Time	n=	Part-Time	n=	Not Employed	n=
Job	25.0%	(72)	17.1%	(35)	—	—
At home	58.7	(104)	62.5	(48)	50.7%	(77)
With children	44.8	(87)	36.3	(33)	33.3	(60)
With husband	40.3	(82)	37.5	(32)	26.0	(77)
With friends	20.9	(72)	10.3	(39)	10.3	(68)
For self	24.2	(98)	14.3	(42)	17.8	(90)
Opportunities for children outside home	38.7	(49)	23.1	(13)	32.2	(28)
Children's medical care	33.3	(21)	0	(3)	33.3	(9)
Self medical care	37.5	(32)	0	(12)	28.0	(25)

TABLE 6.3

Correlations Between Minutes Devoted to Specific Activities
and Women's Perceived Time Pressure "Yesterday"

	Correlation With Time Pressure "Yesterday"	$p \leq$
Professional work, outside home	$r = +.19$	.001
Professional work, brought/at home	+.13	.001
Food preparation, cooking	−.08	.05
Home repairs, operations	+.09	.05
Repair and other services outside home (e.g., laundry, car wash)	−.07	.05
Travel by bus	+.12	.01
Meals and snacks at home	−.09	.05
Meals outside home	+.10	.01
Night sleep	−.09	.05
Nap or rest	−.12	.01
Visiting friends	−.10	.01
Hobbies	−.09	.05
Unspecified leisure	−.09	.05
Watching television	−.21	.001
Reading mail, writing letters	−.10	.01
Relaxing	−.07	.05

time pressure. Travel by bus and streetcar is positively related to time pressure, as is eating nonsocial restaurant meals—functions of employment. In contrast, again, having time for personal activities, particularly sleep, is related to ease, as is visiting with friends. The single highest correlation coefficient is inverse, linking greater amounts of television viewing to lesser feelings of time pressure ($r = -.21, p < .001$). As we have learned, television viewing is more common among housewives, who tend to report less time pressure.

Turning to the question of division of household responsibilities, it is worth noting that the number of these for which women are primarily responsible is ever so mildly but inversely related to feelings of time pressure ($r = -.08, p = .03$). This counterintuitive result turns out, however, to reflect only the housewives in the sample. It is they who feel more at ease with the greater number of tasks they accomplish at home ($r = -.17, p = .012$). Data for women working full-time and part-time, while not revealing positive relationships between household responsibilities and time pressure, simply show no relationships at all between the number of household jobs and feelings of pressure or ease.

TENSION

A second measure of the outcome of the daily routine is degree of tension. As noted in Chapter 2, this was an integral part of the time-budget and hence directly reflects the content of the day. Information was provided on the degree of ease or tension associated with each activity, as well as a general measure of tension constructed by aggregating the individual activity ratings across the day, weighted according to the amount of time devoted to them.

The picture that emerges from analyzing daily weighted tension scores is similar to conclusions drawn from time-pressure data. Tension varies directly and significantly with both minutes of employment ($r = +.16$, $p = .000$) and minutes of obligatory activity ($r = +.15, p = .000$). Married women with full-time jobs have the highest tension scores (5.09); housewives show the greatest ease (5.37); married women working part-time are in between (5.2). Single mothers show the same differences according to employment.[4]

Although still in the expected direction, differences by employment status in the degree of tension women feel when doing housework are minuscule—considerably less than in the daily weighted scores. Clearly, the difference employment makes is primarily in whether one gets the time to do these chores.

Turning to the degree of tension associated with individual activities, Table 6.4 shows that some of the tensest activities at home for women are, first, waking children, getting them ready, and "leaving and arriving," and, then, household jobs. Thus, women's feelings about activities on the day in question support their more general comments about what gives them the most time pressures and when these occur. Transitions are indeed tense. Men are shown as generally more relaxed when doing these activities. Employment, on the other hand, is generally equally tense for men and women.

Thus, although men and women share one tension-producing activity, one which generally accounts for a lot of time among men and considerable time among a growing number of women, women are more likely to have a range of other responsibilities that also produce tension during the day, if only because they are primarily responsible in most families for getting them done. A number of women in the respondent discussion groups said, for example, that men are more likely to feel relaxed when doing household chores because they are not regular, ongoing responsibilities for men.

TABLE 6.4

Mean Tension in Selected Daily Activities (Men and Women)

	Women	Men
Getting children ready	4.3	5.7
Arriving, leaving	4.5	5.0
Employment	4.5	4.4
Waking children	4.6	5.0
Care to older children	4.8	4.4
Care to babies	4.9	5.5
Food preparation	4.9	5.4
Indoor cleaning	4.9	5.9
Dishes	5.1	5.6
Shopping for everyday things	5.1	5.7
Laundry	5.2	5.8
Meals at home	5.3	5.6
Putting to bed	5.3	5.8
Sleep	5.3	5.8
Personal hygiene	5.4	5.5
Conversations	5.5	5.7
Gardening, animals	5.5	6.0
Talk with children	5.5	5.5
Correspondence	5.6	5.4
Naps and rest	5.6	6.2
Visits	5.7	6.1
Joke, play with children	5.8	6.2
Relaxing, thinking	5.9	6.2
TV	6.0	6.2
Reading	6.1	6.1

1 = highest tension
7 = lowest tension

There is no noteworthy relationship between household division of labor and the aggregate measure of daily tension; household activities, as a function of their duration during the twenty-four hour day, are not weighted heavily in the construction of the latter measure. On the other hand, if we look at tension during employment, which is a major contributor to average daily tension because its high tension-producing potential and its duration, we see that, the greater the tension women experience at work, the greater is the number of household tasks for which the husband takes primary responsibility ($r = +.22, p = .013$).[5]

The only other specific activity related to household responsibilities in terms of tension is daily travel. The more jobs at home children do, the less tense women employed full-time are in their daily travel (especially coming home, one presumes).

Such specific findings are certainly logical, but they stop short of associating household division of labor with generalized feelings of tension or relaxation. Indeed, our overview of findings about both time pressures and tensions indicates that it is the need to collate and condense daily nonemployment activities, demanded by employment, rather than the degree of performance of any single activity, that enhances or diminishes women's feelings of pressure and/or tension.

Furthermore, we note that part-time work establishes the conditions for outcomes that, like behavioral phenomenon, are clearly between those of women working full-time and those of women without jobs. In many instances, the data for part-time employees lie closer to figures reflecting the housewives than to those for full-time employees. Even though women working part-time appear to take pride in carrying out nearly the full platter of household jobs while still keeping one foot in the employment market, such a combination of daily activities appears significantly easier to carry out than does the combination of a full-time job and the load of household activities still accepted by the female head of household.

CONFLICTS AND SATISFACTIONS

The importance of degree of employment is underlined when viewing women's degree of contentment with their decision to seek employment. Among married women who have full-time jobs, this satisfaction is inversely related to their perceptions of time pressure "yesterday" ($r = -.21, p = .005$). Among women who work part-time, however, the correlation is exactly zero, confirming the feeling that part-time work is not seen as an impediment to what women wish to do in the course of the average week.

A correlation of zero is also found between the average-week busy scale and housewives' satisfaction with their choice not to undertake outside employment. Again, women with part-time jobs react very similarly to housewives and significantly different from women with full-time employment.

It is therefore not surprising that there are major normative differences between women who have full-time and those with part-time jobs. Two questions from a Harvard Graduate School of Education study (Belle, 1982), about typical "conflicts" between

1. "being a mother and having a job" and
2. "family and work," were asked of all the employed women.

Table 6.5 shows, once again, major differences between full-time and part-time employees. In this case, we are going beyond the feelings of pressure and tension to a more general normative conflict, which is more pronounced among those with full-time jobs.

TABLE 6.5

Typical "Conflicts" Among Employed Mothers by Employment Status

Reported Frequency of Conflict Between Being a Mother and Having a Job	Employment Status	
	Full-Time	Part-Time
Very and Quite Often	37.4%	18.3%
Some of the Time	35.5	39.0
Seldom or Never	25.8	36.6
Other	1.3	6.1
n =	(216)	(99)

Reported Satisfaction with Balance Between Work and Family	Full-Time	Part-Time
Very Satisfied	24.7%	53.0%
Somewhat Satisfied	44.8	28.9
Dissatisfied	29.2	10.8
Other	1.3	1.2
n =	(216)	(99)

The literature has shown that maternal employment can provide direct and often beneficial outcomes that serve as a basis for undertaking and then continuing a daily round which, in turn can prove trying. Therefore, we sought to assess the extent that maternal employment affects women's feelings of well-being and happiness at an even more general level. For this purpose, we utilized measures employed in the Canada Health Survey (questions 2 and 3). The first listed a series of ten items, in response to which respondents stated the extent that they were "on top of the world," "very lonely," "depressed," "pleased about accomplishments," "bored," "proud," and more. A second item asked whether respondents were, "all in all," "very happy," "pretty happy," or "not too happy."

Employment among married women makes little difference with respect to these very general measures of well-being. Such measures are not as specifically related to the logistics of daily life as are time pressures and tension measures, which are keyed to the annoyances found in the daily round. These latter considerations, however central to this inquiry, are nonetheless not the only things in life that contribute to happiness or its absence. People can be extremely hassled on a day-to-day basis, yet be working for some higher goal toward which they aspire. Indeed, working toward what appears to be a realistic aspiration has been found to help sustain in the short run what would otherwise be considered an untenable situation (Biderman, 1963; Michelson, 1977).

Moreover, there is no intent here to disparage the importance of time pressure, tension, and normative conflict in everyday life. These can prove debilitating in and of themselves and can defeat the achievement of cherished goals in the long run.

In contrast, the so-called happiness scales are pertinent to single parenthood and will be examined again in this regard in the next chapter.

Although married women do not differ in their general personal well-being according to their employment status, there are some signs that their husbands do. Husbands of women with full-time jobs are somewhat less positive on many of the individual traits, and they are marginally less happy. For example, 14% of the husbands of women with full-time jobs often felt "on top of the world," compared to 24% of men married to part-time workers and 20% of those whose wives do not have jobs. Similar percentages of men who are never "very lonely" are 49%, 57%, and 62%. Moreover, only 41% of men whose wives have full-time jobs are never "depressed," compared to 48% and 47% of those whose wives are part-time workers or housewives, respectively. Men whose wives work full-time are often "pleased about accomplishments" only 28% of the time, compared to 46% and 43%, respectively, of the other two categories of husbands. Such findings from husbands reflect more than the employment status of the wife, however. One must keep in mind that many of the men whose wives work full-time are themselves earning lower than average incomes, which was indeed a stimulus to the decision of the wife to work full-time. In this respect, low male income and a wife who is absent from home somewhat more may be negatively reinforcing for the husband's view of his own well-being and happiness.

OTHER LIFE CONCERNS

We asked also about other problems respondents might have been experiencing, to ascertain the linkage of time pressures and tension to other sources of concern. Such concerns included ill health, employment, education, marriage, being a parent, and money.

Given the chain of reasoning linking employment and the various forms of pressure, it is illuminating to examine employment status with respect to specific types of concern. For example, with respect to concern about money, a great deal is reported by 25.7% of those with full-time jobs, compared to 17.5% and 17.7% of the others, reinforcing the more objective data about financial conditions cited earlier.

Employed women, whether with full- or part-time jobs, are more likely than housewives to express concern about their marriages (40% vs. 20%). Mothers employed full-time express somewhat more concern about being a parent; 16% mention quite a bit or a great deal of concern, compared to 9.3% and 10.1% of those with part-time and no jobs.

The converse, however, is shown with respect to concern over ill health. Women with full-time jobs are less likely to mention health concerns. Only 57.8% of them mention any sort of concern about ill health, compared to 71.9% of women with part-time jobs and 66.5% of housewives. This relationship can work both ways, of course; it is hard to work full-time with severe health problems.

Operationalizing employment a second way, in terms of minutes a day doing paid work, shows these relationships to be strong and significant. As before, minutes of employment are *positively* correlated with worries about marriage, parenting, and money, but *inversely* related to concern about ill health.

Time pressures are definitely related to feelings of concern about these other problems. A correlation coefficient of $+.31$ was established between the average-week busy scale and the number of other problems pertinent to respondents.

A logical but modest link joining employment to a specific concern through time pressure is confirmed in the case of worries about marriage. The correlation coefficient between the average-week busy scale and the degree of concern about marriage is a positive and significant though not dramatic $+.16$. In contrast, the correlation coefficient linking this kind of time pressure to worries about parenting is only $+.07$, well below significance. Thus, the fact of employment, not the associated time pressure, is involved in parenting concerns, although the attentent time pressures do enter into potential marital difficulties. (We would not assess worry about money the same way, as this would be logically prior to employment and feelings of time pressure.)

One would not expect a relationship between such a collection of potentially troublesome concerns with time pressures or tension alone. It is not surprising that socio-economic status is independently (and inversely) related to the number of concerns people have ($r = -.25$). Family size and age of children, though, are unrelated to the number of such concerns.

CHOICE, PRESSURE, AND TENSION

In this chapter, we have examined time pressures, tensions, normative conflicts, and more specific concerns with respect to women's employment status, noting many specific though not global relationships between degree of employment and personal outcomes. Such findings have been seen in the light of data on why women take various degrees of employment and how much help they get with domestic tasks. The connection between independent and dependent variables is clarified by looking at the relationship between choice and tension among the various activities people perform each day. The correlation for women's average degree of choice and their tension is $-.44$, with a significance level of .0000. As might be imagined, most individual activities show significant correlations in the same direction, with employment ($-.69$) and various household tasks among the areas in which choice and tension are more strongly related. Thus, if full-time work is involuntary for many and if logistical problems are not solved, it is no wonder greater degrees of tension are encountered.

The same relationship between choice and tension holds equally well for men ($r = -.46, p = .0000$). However, the absolute levels of tension and choice are not as difficult on many activities (apart from employment) for most men, compared to women.

In short, nothing in these data says that employment for women is inherently difficult, any more or less than for men. But when employment is undertaken for extrinsic reasons, takes time and effort, and it not accompanied by people or mechanisms to lessen preexisting responsibilities, then logistical difficulties with personal outcomes may arise. It is noteworthy that, while general personal outlook does not vary significantly by employment status per se, it is related very significantly to the degree of choice involved with their work among those with jobs ($r = +.25, p = .0000$), joining with other findings to reinforce Rutter's previously cited conclusions (1981) about satisfaction with work.

I shall turn later to the impact of women's employment on children and to the effects of external conditions on both. First, however, more attention should be paid to the single mother. When I focused on the effects of employment for women in contrast to those of men in the same families, the emphasis was naturally on the married women, so as not to compound explanatory factors. At this point, we examine the differences between married and single mothers, assessing the contributions to daily life and to personal outcomes of both employment and marital status.

Notes

1 In a personal communication, a staff member of a Swedish commission that had completed a wide-ranging assessment of factors affecting youth stated that one of the greatest influences on young people's development is the image of the work world that parents bring home with them every day.

2 We shall also examine certain differences among children by maternal employment in Chapter 8.

3 Indices were created from other questions when that approach seemed more appropriate.

4 The absolute level of this scale, toward the ease side of the continuum, continues respondent traditions toward expressions of relative optimism in answer to social-science surveys. As in so many other studies and in some instances in this one, I focus here on the direction and consistency of differences between categories. The plusses and minuses given on correlating coefficients are reversed to reflect the logical view of the variation of tension and other factors.

5 One hopes that he is responding to her employment tensions, not that she is tense because she knows he is doing things around the house!

7
Single Parenthood: How Special?

There is no question that single mothers are special. They do not fit the societal norm of the nuclear family (indeed, they exist in such numbers as to challenge the norm!). Their children have primary reference to only one sex of adult. The single parent has gone through the trauma of widowhood, separation, divorce, or birth out of wedlock. The economic status of most female-headed households is markedly low. One fewer person is available to take up the obligations and responsibilities of daily life. The multifaceted situation of the single parent is said to promote isolation and loneliness.

The major objective of this chapter is to look at the everyday life of the single mother, to ask how special it is. Taking employment status into consideration, what concerns do single parents encounter that "normal" parents do not? In what ways do their actions differ? Their outcomes?

The Context of Single Motherhood

The literature on single parenthood takes as a given that men, women, and children involved have experienced a major personal shock and are living in an unconventional social situation. There is recognition of and concern for the psychology of these individuals (e.g., Vincent, 1961) and for strategies and structures by and in aid of single parents (e.g., Schlessinger, 1978).

First, one ominous aspect of single parenthood for most women is economic marginality. Many, though clearly not all, single mothers come from the lower socio-economic levels. Hence, they have little personal wealth or occupational solidity. In any case, the full-time housewife who is single does not have a spouse to bring home a full pay check. The single mother with an outside job reports more income, but even then there are relative deficiencies. "Women's jobs" still pay less than most men's and there is no husband's salary to soften this discrepancy. At the least, child-care and transportation costs are usually incurred to earn this income and are absorbed by it: income-tax deductability for such expenses is not of much assistance when taxable incomes are low at the outset. Hence, the single parent is usually in a far more difficult economic situation than the reduction from two adult heads of household to one would suggest. Some of the most serious studies of single parenthood have focused on the socio-economic milieu and subcultures common to many — but, again, not all — single mothers (e.g., Belle, 1982; Kriesberg, 1970; Marsden, 1969).

Among women who did not come from poor families or whose marriages had been economically satisfactory, downward mobility, with accompanying belt-tightening and personal stress, is noted as common (Hogan et al., 1983).

Pragmatically, having few personal resources means that single mothers are in less of a position to possess human or material means to fulfill wants and responsibilities. For example, where public transportation is expensive and inefficient, it takes money to purchase more acceptable personal means of travel and to get baby sitting or help for housework.

Second, the time for and responsibilities of housework and child care are placed absolutely on one person rather than, at least potentially, two. There is some dispute and ambiguity about the exact time requirements, but there is substantial agreement in the literature that both authority and responsibility fall into the hands of the single parent and that this is frequently found to be a source of stress. Parents want to do the best for their children and often find decisions and the need for subsequent action overwhelming when not shared with or supported by others. In a small sample of single women in Toronto, for example, Schlessinger found that two-thirds reported that the difficulty of child rearing increased when they became single, largely because of the assumption of total parental responsibility (1978). Marsden (1969) had found identical outcomes in an English sample.

There is less unanimity about everyday activity and hassle. Theoretically, throwing all potential domestic activities onto one person adds up to more for that person to do. In her study of only employed women (90% of them with full-time jobs), Kamerman spots a trend toward significant sharing of domestic tasks by husbands. Though noting that "single parenthood may be never having to explain 'why' to a spouse," it still means that the everyday "costs outweigh the benefits" (1980, p. 79).

Weiss (1979), however, in his in-depth study of single parents, feels that single women escape having to be attentive to a husband's many needs. These include cooking requirements and standards, as well as expectations about housework and entertaining. He concludes:

> Indeed, insofar as she has a husband to care for as well as children, the working married mother, just like the nonworking married mother, has somewhat more to do around the house than does her single counterpart. [p. 57]

Weiss observes that, when faced with the logistics of an overload of things to do, in the absence of pressure from a husband, the single mother will simply skimp in certain areas.

Nonetheless, as a result of child-care responsibilities, tasks that *are* done, the need for income, and the economic inability to pay for substitutes or for mechanical means of increasing efficiency, single mothers are said typically to lack the time and energy for an external social life. They have been observed to be isolated, lonely, and anxious. Regular external obligations, such as employment, are thought necessary for contact with other adults (e.g., Weiss, 1979).

While the literature describes and illustrates the compelling general situation of the single mother, it is relatively short on detail about the content and consequences of the daily routine. Time-budget studies have apparently not addressed the behavioral substance of single parenthood, perhaps because, while it is not uncommon, it does not fit the mode expected, or because time-budget studies typically have focused on either individuals within households or else have selected only two-parent households.

In this chapter, we shall examine many of the findings, ambiguities, and disputes about single mothers in considerable depth, by drawing on time-budget, responsibility, outcome, and socio-economic/pragmatic data from the Toronto study, to see how "special" single parenthood is. Not only can mothers who are single and married be compared, but the effects of everyday life and outcomes of marital status can be compared with those of employment status.

Effects of Marital and Employment Status

The data in Chapter 3 (Table 3.1) confirm the expected economic position of single mothers. Their incomes are extremely low, compared to the other types of household, markedly more so among single mothers without jobs. Indeed, low income should be kept in mind as perhaps the most prominent feature of the situation of the single mother. Let us, however, examine a number of less cut-and-dried aspects of her everyday life.

RESPONSIBILITIES AND NON-SPOUSAL AID

It would seem that, by definition, the single parent would have a greater number of household responsibilities. There is no spouse with whom to share them. While the data from our study surely support this premise, the differences between single and married women are not as great as might be expected. Married women take on more household tasks than do their husbands, leaving room for only marginal rather than profound differences from single mothers. Moreover, employment-status differences found among the married women are to be found as well among the single women. Among those with full-time jobs, 10.1 household tasks are primarily done by single women, compared to 6.7 married women. Among those without employment, the comparable means are 11.1 and 8.3, respectively.

One part of the lack of an overwhelming difference, between the married and single parents with respect to household responsibilities in fact stems from their economic differences. Some of the responsibilities men typically fulfill in two-parent families come with better financial circumstances; outdoor jobs, car maintenance, and house repairs are seldom part of the routine of the single parent who does not have a house or car.

Furthermore, children take up some of the slack in single-parent families when the mother has a full-time job. For example, among these families, children had primary responsibility (sometimes shared with the mother) for cooking 11% of the time, dishwashing (28%), laundry (14%), indoor cleaning (17%), and garbage (42%) — all well above the figures for all other family categories. The single mother without employment does not get such compensating help from her children.

In addition, single parents benefit from nonspousal mutual aid somewhat more than do mothers in two-parent families, if we hold employment level constant. Table 7.1 details data on seven forms of nonspousal assistance respondents have received during the month before the interview.

The hypothesis that children and outsiders help provide some of what spouses customarily contribute is confirmed by a direct question on what busy mothers do to save time (question 14). Looking at those with full-time jobs, 20% of the married women say they get help from their husbands, which has of course no comparison among the single; the latter, however, call on children a third more (25%) and on outsiders twice as frequently (15%).

TABLE 7.1

Forms of Nonspousal Assistance Received During Past Month, by Employment and Marital Status

	Percent Receiving Specific Forms of Nonspousal Assistance			
	Full-Time Job		No Employment	
Form of Personal Assistance	Married	Single	Married	Single
Babysit For an Hour	34.4	44.0	40.0	33.3
Babysit For a Weekend	8.3	14.3	12.0	11.8
Run an Errand	21.7	37.4	21.7	51.5
Advice on Children	40.6	38.5	30.7	45.7
Borrowing	17.2	32.6	13.5	24.2
Talk about Personal Problems	41.8	60.8	35.4	57.1
Information on Children's Opportunities	39.8	31.2	38.1	56.2

Furthermore, consistent with the literature, single mothers in our study are more likely to eliminate certain jobs (36% vs. 26%), and women in two-parent families are more likely to do tasks in advance (32% vs. 13%).

Thus, our data suggest that, while women in single-parent families are in a different structural position from those in two-parent families, the former have mobilized personal resources to compensate at least partially for the lack of a spouse.

TIME-USE AND TRAVEL

A major question our data enables us to pursue is the difference that single motherhood makes in everyday life. In what ways do the daily activities of single mothers differ from those of women in two-parent families? A relatively objective apprpach is to examine daily time usage. Table 7.2 compares

TABLE 7.2

Mean Minutes Devoted by Women to Major Activities on a Weekday, by Employment and Marital Status

Activity	Full-Time Job		No Employment	
	Married	Single	Married	Single
Employment	392	360	–	–
Housework	128	98	302	253
Child Care	64	57	134	127
Total Obligatory Time	584	515	436	380
Active Leisure	13	12	28	55
Education	9	15	4	0
Passive Leisure	93	152	171	178
Personal Care, Sleep	570	582	611	614
Shopping	33	29	48	49
Civic, Organizational Activity	8	1	12	10
Social Activity	34	27	45	84
Travel	81	92	44	38
(Public Transit)	(25)	(35)	(3)	(5)
n =	(160)	(55)	(155)	(35)

single and married women, controlling for employment status. As in similar tables, data on women employed part-time are not presented, because of the paucity of such cases among single-parent families ($n = 13$).

The chief message of Table 7.2 is the importance of employment status in how time is divided among daily activities, regardless of marital status. Though, on the day in question, the average devotion of time to outside employment is about half an hour more for married women with full-time jobs, the fact that both married and single women allocated between six and seven hours to outside work sets limits on what else can be done. Hence, married and single women with similar employment status resemble each other in time usage more than all marrieds and all singles do each other. The difference between married and single women, once controlled for employment status, are minor for such activities as personal care and sleep, shopping, and travel.

Nonetheless, there are also some marital-status differences in activity worth noting. At any given level of employment, the single mothers spend less time on housework, perhaps reflecting dwelling units that are in fact smaller (which in turn reflects financial status). As the literature suggests, this difference may also represent, to some degree, the absence of pressure from husbands in this regard. Single women also spend somewhat less time in child care, probably reflecting the average of half a child less in their families. The combination of differences in time devoted to employment, housework, and child care ads up to a difference between married and single women in obligatory activity of 69 and 56 minutes for employed and nonemployed mothers, respectively.

In contrast, single mothers log in much more time across the various leisure activities. Single mothers differ by employment status, though, in the kind of leisure to which they devote more time than the married women. For example, although housewives as a group devote more time to leisure than do women with outside employment, single housewives spend disproportionate time in active leisure and social activity, while single mothers with full-time jobs spend more time in passive leisure, probably reflecting limited opportunity and energy at the end of the workday.

Single mothers spend more time traveling than married women, if they have a job, but less, if they don't.

One might surmise that lack of travel reflects poverty. An analysis of trip making only partially supports this hypothesis. Twice the percentage of women with incomes under $5000 (29%) made no trips during the day studied as among the most affluent group (15%), with others almost exactly in between. Nonetheless, staying home is as characteristic of married housewives, who are typically not poor, as it is of the poorer single housewives. Among both married and single mothers, those without external employment are three times more likely to stay home on the weekday studied. Among the married women, only 10% of those with full-time jobs did not report a trip on the day surveyed, compared to 31.9% of housewives. Among the single women, figures were 9.1% and 28.6% respectively. Such data are additional evidence of the influence of work in structuring daily activity.

One might speculate further about the influence of geography on daily trip making. However, exactly 21% of women do not report a trip on the day studied, whether they live downtown, in the inner boroughs, or in the outer boroughs, of Metropolitan Toronto.

Direct questions on the interview schedule dealt with excursions children might take, potentially with parents. The relationship of these to employment status was described in Chapter 4. In this regard, single parents accompany children to activities at least as often as do married parents, and children do not lack excursions because their single parents are too busy. Differences accounted for by marital status are even less consistent and less substantial than by employment status.

Other direct questions dealt with eating out and getting take-out food, which employed people were shown more likely to do. Figure 7.1 suggests that, holding employment status constant, single mothers are also somewhat more likely to use these external sources of prepared food—much more so

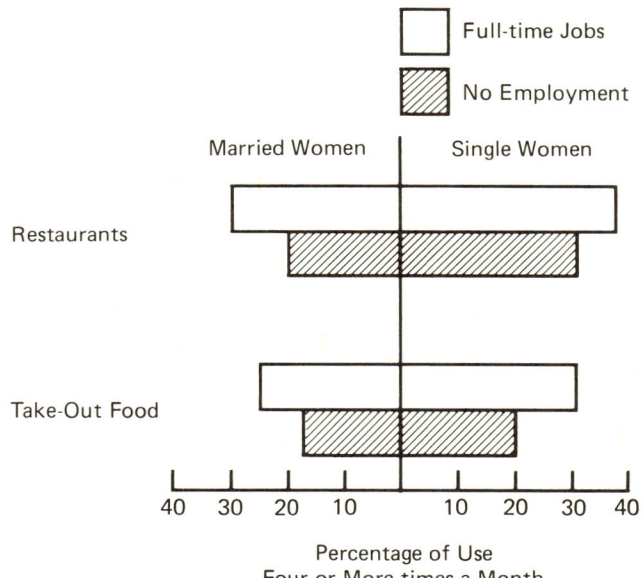

FIGURE 7.1.
Frequency of Use of Restaurants and Take-Out Food for Dinner, by Women's Marital and Employment Status.

96 Single Parenthood: How Special?

than their financial situation would suggest. Single mothers with full-time jobs are 28% more likely than fully employed married women to have dinner in restaurants and 25% more likely to buy take-out food for dinner four or more times a month. Among housewives, these differentials are 55% and 18% for restaurants and take-out, respectively—again in favor of the single parents.

PRESSURE, WORRY, TENSION, AND HAPPINESS

A third approach to everyday life is to look at the pressures, worries, tensions, and accompanying self-characterizations people in different life situations report. We have seen, for example, that increased external employment of mothers is accompanied by greater feelings of time pressure and stress but not necessarily by a different general outlook on life. Do single mothers exhibit more severe outcomes because they lack spouses, or do various mechanisms compensate?

We did not find differences we would have hypothesized in reported time pressures according to degrees of personal responsibility at home by marital status. Indeed, if anything, the single mothers report somewhat less time pressure than married women in both employment-status categories. Figure 7.2 illustrates this. It is clear that, regarding perceived time pressure, level of employment is a more potent explanatory factor than is marital status. Their joint influence is considerable. Thus, without question, the married woman

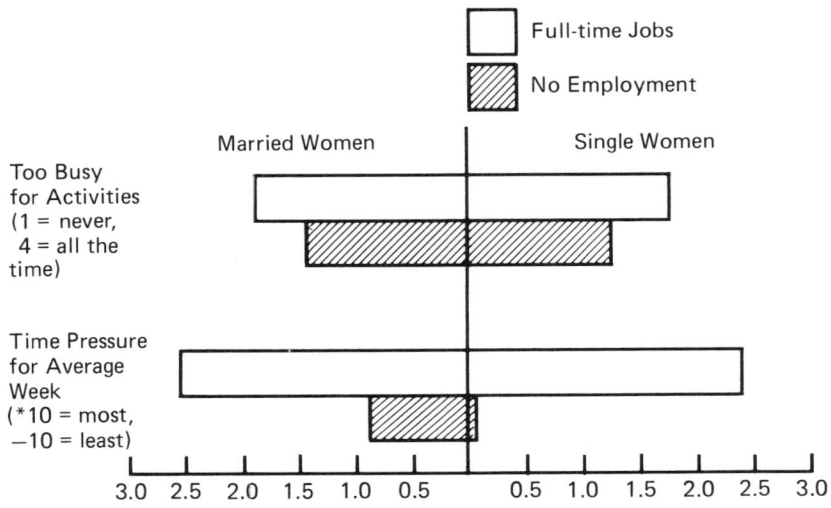

FIGURE 7.2.
Perceived Time Pressures for Women, by Employment and Marital Status.

with a full-time job feels the most pressure, and the single housewife, the least, indeed virtually to the point of equilibrium between time and activity on the busy scales.

Furthermore, the sectors of life that were shown in Chapter 6 to statistically explain time pressure, most notably time for housework and for oneself, apply as well to the single mothers as to those who are married. Even the variation in salience concerning these two major factors between married women with and without jobs holds for single mothers.

The degree of worry behind various sectoral causes of time pressure is illuminating, however. Single mothers with full-time jobs worry much more about having sufficient time for their children than do married women, if they feel this as a source of time pressure. "Quite a lot" or "a great deal" of worry is expressed by 66% of single women with relatively high time pressures regarding child care, compared to only 45% of similar married women. The former, however, worry less about housework pressures (44% vs. 59%), again reflecting the likely place of the husband in worries about housework but without discounting the general importance of housework to women.

Aggregated daily tension also is no more severe for single parents. Among women with full-time jobs, tension is slightly lower for the single mother (5.16 vs. 5.09, on a scale of 1–7 with higher values representing less tension). Among nonemployed women, it is an identical 5.37 for the two marital-status groups, representing somewhat greater ease than for both categories of employed mothers.

Thus, these findings are contrary to the several grounds for hypothesizing greater pressures and tensions among single parents, but they confirm Weiss's observations (1979).

This was a major point of discussion during the feedback phase of the study, and the respondents who attended these discussion sessions, whether married or single, were unanimous that the findings are accurate. The husband, they said, requires additional concern and work — he is still another person around the house to take care of. Thus, husbands add to, rather than diminish, time pressures and tensions. This did not mean that men were thought to be without redeeming features, but their contribution to the daily round was not in the main seen as positive.

> ... the single mother with a child can set up whatever kind of schedule she wants, and she does not have to confer with a husband to see what, well, what is your schedule and how can we fit this so that there's no conflict? It's just herself. And so, I can see, perhaps, less tension.
>
> When I get a little behind, if someone would just go away and leave me alone. My husband and my son have been away this week. . . . I've just had a fantastic time. I've pulled everything apart and washed everything in sight, and I feel like the squirrels and the birds; winter is coming, and I am going to be ready when it gets here. It's a great feeling. Really, because I love work. I love to be able to just get at it.

I have a routine that I like to follow, and everything gets done. So once my routine gets out of order, it doesn't all get done; so then I get upset.

These comments complement the data in suggesting that there are practical advantages in fixing responsibility on one person. There may be more to do, but the one person responsible can organize the work, if she chooses, without the need to consult another adult. In psychological terms, this represents more of a feeling of control.[1] And, as the data indicate, many single mothers do get assistance from others, as well as finding time for recreational and social activities.[2]

Daily time pressures and tensions do not represent the entire fabric of satisfaction or happiness for single parents any more than for the married mothers. Indeed, while there were few employment status differences among the married women in their more general outlook, there are significant differences between the married and the single. Despite somewhat "easier" daily routines, single mothers are somewhat less positive about themselves.

Table 7.3 summarizes answers to the question about general happiness: "Taking things all together, how would say things are these days — would you say you're: very happy, pretty happy, not too happy?" Holding employment status constant, the majority of both married and single women are "pretty happy"; but a higher percentage of the married women are "very happy," while a similarly higher percentage of single mothers are "not too happy" (by about 250% in each case).

More insight can be gained from looking at specific self-characterizations on the part of the single parents, particularly at the extreme values. No single pattern is revealed in Table 7.4. However, single parents without outside employment more frequently than others describe themselves as very lonely, not interested in something, bored, and not having things go their way. The common aspects of these items suggests that, under the right conditions, employ-

TABLE 7.3

General Happiness Among Women by Employment and Marital Status
(in percent)

	Full-Time Job		No Employment	
	Married	Single	Married	Single
Very Happy	23.4%	7.7%	26.6%	14.7%
Pretty Happy	58.9	67.3	60.3	62.9
Not Too Happy	12.0	23.1	9.8	26.5
Other	5.7	1.9	3.3	5.9
n =	(158)	(52)	(184)	(34)

TABLE 7.4

Self-Characterizations Among Women by Employment and Marital Status
(in percent)

	Full-Time Job		No Employment	
Self-Characterizations	Married	Single	Married	Single
On Top of the World (Never)	8.2%	17.0%	12.0%	17.6%
Very Lonely (Often)	10.1	11.3	10.9	23.5
Interested in Something (Often)	32.9	37.7	32.8	20.6
Depressed (Never)	32.3	17.0	27.5	26.5
Pleased About Accomplishments (Often)	39.9	37.3	29.3	29.4
Bored (Often)	13.3	17.3	11.4	26.5
Proud (Often)	22.8	9.6	15.4	32.4
Restless (Often)	21.5	21.2	7.7	11.8
Things Are Going Your Way (Often)	26.9	21.2	26.2	17.6
Upset About Criticism (Often)	6.3	5.8	4.9	2.9
n =	(150)	(53)	(182)	(34)

ment can add something to how single parents feel about themselves, as hypotheses from other studies had suggested. Daily feedback from other adults, which is usually part of the work situation, can mean more to the single parent than to someone with a spouse at home. One also must not underestimate the value to the psyche of a paycheck. In the words of one respondent: "That's a lovely sign—it's the sign that gives you value."

Nonetheless, single parents with jobs report more depression, which urges some caution in the interpretation of these data.

I should note also that women with jobs, whether single or married, are more likely to describe themselves as "restless." This suggests that some types of self-conceptions may predispose women to employment, although our attempt to assess this through the ideal busy scales did not support this hypothesis. Other self-conceptions, of course, appear to be logical outcomes of employment.

In any case, it is clear that lower time pressure among single mothers does not necessarily mean positive feelings in general. Some of their specific concerns are indicated in Table 7.5. On every item of concern except one (ill health, among employed women), single parents are more concerned than those in two-parent families. Single parents are logically much more con-

TABLE 7.5

Women's Specific Concerns, by Employment and Marital Status
(in percent)

	Full-Time Job		Housewives	
Concerns (Percent Reporting "Quite a Bit" or "A Great Deal" of Concern)	Married	Single	Married	Single
Ill Health	26.6	23.6	25.0	37.1
Employment	12.8	33.1	15.1	25.7
Education	23.9	27.2	17.9	18.6
Marriage or Relationship	7.6	18.9	3.7	19.1
Being a parent	16.0	29.0	10.1	11.7
Money	25.7	49.1	17.1	42.0

cerned about money, employment, and relationships with the opposite sex. That is, these major human concerns are not solved by a marginally easier daily routine.

How special is single parenthood? Despite challenges, the daily routines of single parents are not impossible for most, but manageable routines do not define or serve as the basis for evaluation of their situations. The contacts and activities that go with outside employment are helpful, not to speak of the income, but the single mother still does not consider her life a panacea.

I do not argue that these data detract from policies designed to support the daily obligations of single parents, particularly when special or local conditions demand them. They suggest, though, that major attention should also be paid to basic aspects of the human condition that are frequently problematic for the single parent, such as money, employment, and relationships. Moreover, these comparisons of the behavioral and logistical aspects of the daily lives of single and married mothers underscore the influence of employment on the daily routine and its implications. Specific attention to employment can clearly assist women, regardless of marital status.

Findings about children of single parents and supportive institutions and practices are covered in the following chapters.

Notes

1 Unfortunately, in the need to select a manageable number of measures for a survey of limited duration, we did not include any measuress of control. As Principal Investigator, I am responsible for this omission.

2 Single mothers who are unable to escape overload still have potential problems, however, which should be recognized and dealt with.

8
Implications for Children of Maternal Employment

If employment of mothers of young children is a marked new trend in North American society, this becomes even more immediate when viewed in terms of children, roughly half of whose mothers now have jobs. The degree and pace of this nontraditional tendency has put great numbers of children into a relatively unchartered context. As I noted in the Preface, it was our interest in learning more of what was happening to children under this rapidly emerging societal trend that prompted this study. It was also our perspective that, in that the family is an interactive system, one cannot understand what is happening to children without exploring first what is happening in the lives of parents and with what personal outcomes. Now that these latter concerns have been examined, let us turn to children.

Previous Views: Outcomes versus Process

Psychologists have long since devoted their efforts to predicting personal outcomes among children. Their focus has been on a variety of plausible influences coming from family structure (e.g., birth order), schools, (e.g., size of class, pedagogy), and even greater institutional and societal structures (e.g., poverty, racial discrimination). In recent years, subjects of psychological interest have included the effects of having an employed mother.

The impact of maternal employment has been viewed directly and indirectly. In the former perspective, the direct impact of the mother's altered role and her differential daily schedule (i.e., availability) draws attention. In the latter, the focus turns to an institution to which so many preschool children are exposed as a consequence of maternal employment—the child-care arrangement, not the least of which is the day-care center.

The early preschool years are an object of inquiry common to both approaches. According to Hoffman (1979, p. 860), "In considering the effects of maternal employment on the child, perhaps the period about which it is most difficult to be sanguine is infancy." Yet, studies are equivocal about any kind of regular effect of maternal employment. Discussions rage about such possible outcomes as young children's feeling less comfort and security, suffering lowered abilities to interact with other people, and possessing greater anxiety, aggression, or both. But sophisticated reviews consistently point to the importance of viewing these possible outcomes in terms of the de facto situations children face: How extensive is the mother's employment? How does the mother feel about her work? What is the nature and quality of substitute child care, including but not restricted to such considerations as caretaker/child ratios, training of caretakers, constancy of caretaker(s), program, and facilities (e.g., Rutter, 1981; Kagan, 1979; Hodgson, 1979; Gold and Andres, 1978a)?

Even with respect to some of these conditions, the evidence is not consistent. For example, Woods (1972) states that full-time work by mothers is better for children than part-time work; Hoffman (1974b) claims the opposite; and, according to Howell (1973b), there are "almost no constant differences" between children of employed and nonemployed mothers.

As children go to school and develop toward and through adolescence, certain outcomes are considered. Hoffman, for example, has noted a series of positive outcomes thought to accompany maternal employment. Girls in particular are felt to develop a greater sense of independence. They are less likely to accept traditional sex roles and to be fearful and inhibited; they are more likely to be motivated, outgoing, and have higher self-esteem (1974a, 1974b, 1979). Yet other research has not agreed on all these points. Van Vliet, for example, found less-traditional roles and attitudes among the daughters of employed mothers, as expected, but also found them to be less independent and to have lower feelings of self-esteem and control (1980). Howell's earlier review (1973b) had not found differences in the degree of independence or in teacher ratings of student maladjustment and emotional problems.

Hoffman raises the question of whether older children run more of a risk of delinquency if less supervised at home after school (1974b); the evidence does not permit her any definite position. In contrast, Hansson et al. (1981), while noting opportunities for greater promiscuity under such circumstances, conclude that children who are home alone more gain self-discipline and responsibility from it.

Looking at somewhat more specific causes of such potential outcomes, Gold and Andres (1978a) feel that employed mothers are less restrictive in their child-rearing practices. These researchers also feel that children in these families have more contact with their fathers and that this is a helpful influence, not least for the development of nontraditional roles among both boys and girls.

In short, while there are many concerns and claims about how children may encounter negative outcomes as a consequence of maternal employment, the literature as a whole does not support these or very many of the hypothesized positive outcomes. As Skinner put it (1983, p. 268), "There is no evidence to suggest that the dual-career lifestyle, in and of itself, is stressful for children. What may be more significant for the children is the degree of stress experienced by the parents which may indirectly affect the children."

In the concentration on outcomes, this largely psychological literature has said little about what children actually do. Knowledge of their round of activity (behaviors, contacts, locations) has perhaps suffered from time-use researchers' aforementioned lack of attention to children. Yet, regardless of outcomes, one would expect that the situations in which parents are increasingly finding themselves would greatly alter children's daily life styles. The process of children's daily lives is clearly of importance to those coping with it at various levels and to the prevention of future problems.

The one reasonably common aspect of this process that has emerged in the literature is the relatively specific set of housework activities. The consensus is that the children of employed mothers, particularly the girls, help out more around the house (Howell, 1973; Van Vliet, 1980). We saw some support for this hypothesis in Chapters 5 and 7, especially among the children of single mothers.

Van Vliet (1980) studied some aspects of daily time-use and concluded that children have less contact with their mothers when the latter are employed; not surprisingly, the mothers chauffeur children less. Furthermore, the ninth-grade students he studied whose mothers are employed are 20% less likely than students whose mothers stay home to think that their mothers have enough time for them.

A major exception to the prevailing emphasis is a work by Medrich et al. (1982), which reports their study of the nonschool activities of a large number of eleven- and twelve-year-olds in Oakland, California. They found, for example, that the percentage of children who are unsupervised after school varied from about 10% among two-parent families with one wage-earner to nearly 50% among families with an employed, single parent (p. 106). On the other hand, there were no significant differences by employment in the time children spent with their parents watching television (considerable) and doing homework. In the main, however, while this book provides a wealth of information about what children of a particular grade level do after school, it does not provide a wide range of answers to questions of how children's daily lives vary by the employment status of their mothers or of how the lives of children of other ages may differ.

The current study data, however, enable some assessments of activity, contact, and location, including gender differences within these areas. I shall look into the utilization of different child-care alternatives, including the so-called latch-key practice, and their implications for children. Some evidence is available as well about certain outcomes for children of both parental employment and the type of child care. Finally, some results focus on women's child-raising techniques under particular circumstances.

Children's Activities, Contacts, and Locations

Table 8.1 covers many aspects of daily activity, even though it is selective. Its complexity reflects one obvious consideration: children of different ages, because of that fact alone, do different things during the day. We have therefore broken down children's data, somewhat more finely than elsewhere in the book, into age groups of 0-3, 4-6, 7-9, and 10-14 years of age, each analyzed according to mother's employment, but restricted at this point to those in two-parent families.[1]

The most crucial general conclusion from Table 8.1 is that differences that reflect maternal employment are greatest for the youngest children. As children grow older, they experience society's formal institutions, such as mandatory schooling, alongside such informal but widespread practices as neighborhood play. The timetables of older children are hence much more standardized than are those of younger ones. Indeed, the degree of choice noted in daily activities of children ten years and over is markedly lower than that of their mothers and fathers; children in this age range average about 2.7 on the scale between 1 (least choice) and 7 (most). Very young children, on the other hand, have neither as many of the universal institutions available to older children in North America nor equal compulsion to use those that are there. Therefore, variations according to their mothers' needs are high for these younger children.

Most differences are predictable. Children aged three or younger whose mothers have full-time jobs spend about nine times as much time on the average day in a school, day-care center, or other child-care arrangement than do similar-aged children whose mothers do not work outside the home. They spend less time at home and more time in institutional buildings and the homes of other persons. They spend much less time with their mothers, but more time with persons who are neither neighbors nor kin (e.g., teachers, child-care workers) and with peers.

When psychologists such as Hoffman speak with urgency about the effects of maternal employment during infancy, it is usually because they consider this a crucial stage in a child's development. Such concern grows as we see that this is also the period of the greatest employment-related differences among children's activities, contacts, and locations. While nothing in the literature suggests that any life style is inherently better or worse than another in terms of its outcomes, it is important to recognize the behavioral side of a trend that emerged without explicit planning or prediction, as an indirect consequence of widespread maternal employment.

TABLE 8.1

Selected Aspects of Time Usage (in minutes) by Children, by Employment Status of Mother (2-Parent Families Only) and Age of Child

	Age of Child and Employment Status of Mother											
	0 - 3			4 - 6			7 - 9			10 - 14		
	Full Time Job	Part Time Job	No Job	Full Time Job	Part Time Job	No Job	Full Time Job	Part Time Job	No Job	Full Time Job	Part Time Job	No Job
Selected Activities												
School/child caretaking	221	28	25	245	137	164	358	320	319	342	339	364
Night-time sleep	562	606	597	626	642	649	580	628	603	555	530	571
Television	13	40	60	81	59	91	106	73	75	113	113	112
Reading	8	4	3	8	3	5	7	6	3	9	15	7
Housework	—	—	—	6	11	6	7	13	10	21	26	15
Shopping	11	30	25	15	21	26	11	4	13	13	4	10
Social Activity	10	17	18	16	31	18	7	6	14	28	27	29
Time with Persons												
Mother	346	458	611	310	417	413	190	211	217	150	158	155
Father	182	154	202	173	126	140	112	96	109	116	93	101
Immediate Family	558	788	755	538	602	618	517	484	490	364	328	366
Other kin	12	53	7	24	25	4	1	3	1	5	10	7
Neighbors	20	8	3	24	1	1	0	1	1	3	1	2
Peers	96	7	32	188	118	147	327	274	301	298	313	300
Others	112	16	7	57	6	2	9	4	15	9	14	5
Time in Place												
At home	956	1,162	1,223	891	1,038	1,024	855	891	873	840	839	837
Outside home	34	69	46	53	65	70	32	47	40	38	22	20
At school	141	24	32	196	152	150	357	297	325	316	282	321
Home of another	103	60	24	99	42	25	29	16	24	44	30	39
Travel	39	28	29	38	58	33	53	57	58	71	74	54
n =	(69)	(43)	(103)	(52)	(23)	(79)	(50)	(38)	(68)	(101)	(46)	(97)

A number of more specific observations are in order. First, while many of these findings are clearly part of the conditions that accompany maternal employment, others are not. For example, it is not a foregone conclusion that children whose mothers are home will have significantly less peer contact than those whose mothers work full-time (32 vs. 96 minutes a day), while children whose mothers have part-time jobs report significantly less yet (7 minutes). The part-time situation, moreover, does not result in significant time away from home in formal child-care institutions but involves much more contact with kin, notably grandmothers.

Categories of children's time-use are not directly comparable with respect to all activities, nor are the data always complete, because the interviews did not pursue what children actually did during their child-care time. Even time in peer contact is understated when reflecting time in child-care settings.

Nonetheless, some comparisons are worth discussion. Children whose mothers have full-time employment sleep less at night. Respondents noted in discussion that this reflects desires by parents for "quality time" with their child(ren) during the only period in the day where this is practical—after dinner and before a sometimes-delayed bedtime. Children under four whose mothers have part-time jobs sleep the most—44 minutes a night more than those whose mothers work full-time.

As would be expected, because of the need to get to child-care settings, the youngest children whose mothers have full-time jobs spend more time during the day traveling, but the differences—39 minutes vs. 28 (part-time) vs. 29 (housewives)—are not startling. The latter categories of young children spend two or three times more time shopping with their parents, another need for travel. It is ironic that children spend the most time shopping at an age where this simply reflects the need that they be taken along, if not placed in somebody else's care. As they get older, there is less need to take them along, and they also have alternative demands on their time.

Children's general development in the direction of self-generated activity is illustrated well by their travel. Time devoted to travel not only increases as children grow older, but it changes its character. Figure 8.1 shows these trends. The youngest children are obviously taken where they go, and most of such travel is by automobile. On the average, only 2 of the 30 minutes a day the youngest children spend traveling are by public transportation, and far more time is spent driving (16 minutes) than walking or cycling (a total of 9 minutes). The 4–9-year-olds add to their travel by walking and cycling much more but still do not go on public transportation very much. Only among the 10–14-year-olds does public transportation surpass travel by car; but even in this cohort of children who travel more widely than the younger ones, public transportation accounts for a relatively minor portion of travel time (18%).

In the youngest age group, there is also a considerable difference in re-

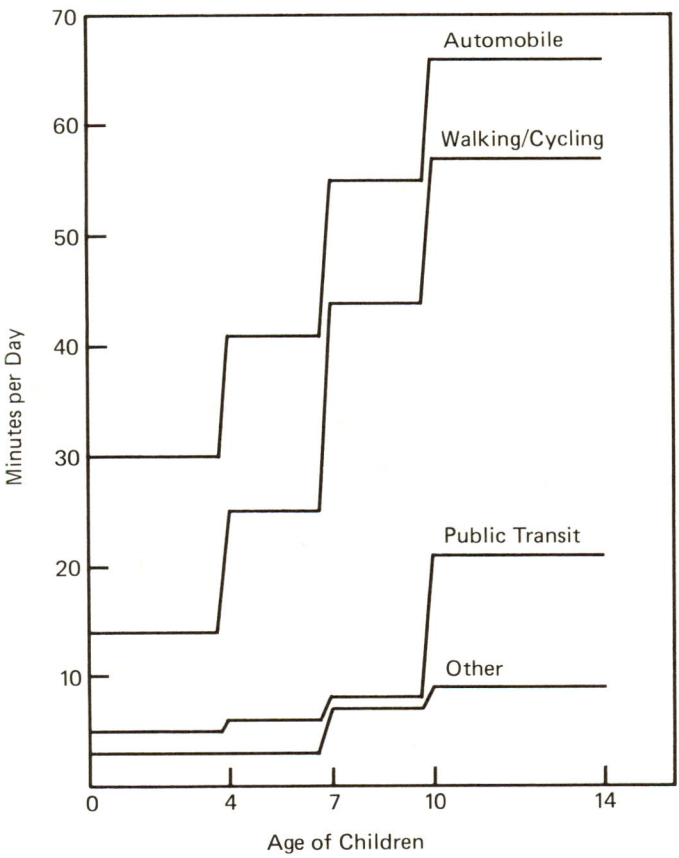

FIGURE 8.1.
Cumulative Chart of Mean Minutes in Specific Modes of Travel per Day, by Age Category of Child.

ported television viewing. Those whose mothers have full-time jobs watch far less at home, like their parents. We cannot tell, however, how much they watch elsewhere. Yet, even with time elsewhere unaccounted for in detail, children whose mothers have full-time jobs spend more time reading.

Table 8.1 indicates that older children spend their time differently from younger ones—they get less active play and more passive activity (particularly television), more school time and homework, less sleep, and more social activity, much less time at home and more traveling, much less family contact, and much more peer contact. Moreover, the reflection of maternal employment in time-use virtually disappears among the older children. Our concern, then, about the children of employed mothers should be particularly focused on the very young, for whom universal education, recreation, child and health care, and the like have yet to be developed in North America and for whom these years are highly formative.

The amount of time children spend with their fathers is not seen to vary in any great or systematic way according to the mother's employment status, as had been hypothesized by optimistic observers. Inasmuch as fathers' times with children usually come before and after work and mothers' jobs are usually within the time periods of the fathers' work (obviously excepting shift and night work), the times fathers spend with their children do not typically touch periods when the mother is unavailable. In other words, there is typically an asymmetry between the amounts of time mothers and fathers spend with their children alone and together. At present, it is the mother who is typically alone with a child, and it is this type of parent-child contact that gets taken away in larger or smaller amounts when external employment enters the daily timetable.

The employed mothers themselves indicated awareness of many of these differences when asked directly how they thought their children's day was affected by their job. More answered "less time with mother" (47%) than in any other way. About 30% cited an objectively different daily routine for the children, and 23% mentioned that children had more responsibility. More contact with other adults and children were noted by 13% and 10%, respectively. Only 18% of the mothers felt their child(ren)'s day is not affected by maternal employment.

Results parallel to but not included in Table 8.1, concerning children of single mothers, show no significant or interesting differences in children's behavior according to their mothers' status. The differences accountable to external employment are exactly similar to those of the two-parent families.

Boys versus Girls

Certain differences in activity by sex are nonetheless noteworthy because they indicate that sex roles still account for major differences in behavior, even among the children of presumably emancipated parents.

Table 8.2 shows that girls in every age group spend more time in household jobs, for example, while boys spend more time in both active play and, as they get older, in outside employment. Indeed, the differences between boys and girls in the age group that contributes the most household labor, those ten to fourteen, are greatest among the families in which the mother works full-time; boys devote 6 minutes a day to these chores, compared to 23 minutes for girls. Boys and girls spend 14 and 31 minutes, respectively, in the context of part-time maternal employment, and 9 and 11 minutes, with none. Such data certainly do not provide evidence that equality is near.

Moreover, just like their mothers and fathers, girls are more tense than boys when doing these chores.

TABLE 8.2

Mean Number of Minutes Children Devote to Selected Activities on a Weekday, by Age and Sex

Selected Daily Activities	Age and Sex of Children			
	0 – 3 Female/Male	4 – 6 Female/Male	7 – 9 Female/male	10-14 Female/Male
School/child care	69/136	184/221	340/324	356/342
Housework	17/4	7/8	12/7	27/13
Outside job	0/0	0/0	0/0	2/12
Active play	240/254	203/207	117/144	81/108
Special educational activity	0/0	0/0	4/2	3/2
Shopping	24/21	22/19	10/10	12/10
Passive activity	74/54	115/109	111/109	139/152
Nighttime sleep	581/600	649/640	594/594	553/547
Social activity	17/16	21/13	7/13	27/26
All travel	27/33	36/45	52/58	61/71
Auto travel	13/18	11/21	7/15	10/8
Public trans.	2/2	3/2	1/2	9/14
Walking/Cycling	8/9	21/18	38/34	33/40
n =	(101/103)	(84/70)	(76/80)	(118/124)

I did not anticipate or indeed even think to consider that there would be sex differences in child-care activities. Yet there are clear differences in the preschool years between the times boys and girls in our sample spend in schools and other child-care situations. On the averge, boys spend much more time in such situations in the earliest years, and this is not restricted to two-paycheck families, where boys average 245 minutes in child care vs. 195 for girls; in traditional households, boys average 37 minutes in child care, compared to 15 among girls. It is possible that such differences are an aberration, which further study of the breakdown according to sex of larger numbers of various child-care settings would support or refute. Are parents possibly more protective of girls and hence reluctant to make external arrangements for them? Are parents more anxious to dispatch rambunctious boys, as some of my colleagues suggested in rebuttal? In any case, there is no special feature of the current sample, which is well balanced by sex in every subcategory, that would introduce such large differences as functions of the methodology. Only once children advance into the years of full-time compulsory schooling do girls approach (and then surpass) boys in how much time they spend there.

Boys spend more time traveling than do girls, at every age level. In the earlier years, this could be accounted for by the greater exposure to outside institutions, but this would not be the case among older children.

Child Care Settings and Children's Life Styles

The families in the sample draw upon a variety of child-care alternatives, formal and informal. A number of arrangements specified in question 4 were used by anywhere from 33 to 98 children each. The distribution of providers does not, however, represent the real distribution in the population; an oversampling of less frequently used providers took place, to assure comparisons. As an additional effect of the sampling, the more frequently used arrangements are probably underrepresented in the sample, having made room for the oversampling of nonmodal arrangements.

There is also a major omission in our discussion of child-care arrangements made to support outside employment by mothers. The wording of question 4 did not allow the analysis to differentiate between baby sitting conducted on a full-time, all-day basis and that which fills in on occasion for specific purposes. Hence, one form of child care often preferred by career women, child care in the family's own home by a regular sitter, housekeeper, or au pair, goes unanalyzed. Somewhat the same difficulty occurs in the analysis of data on use of grandparents, but the probable confounding of two different situations appears less in this case, and results about use of grandparents are included.

Use of different types of child care within the samples varies by mothers' employment status. Among families with children under four, day-care centers are used almost exclusively by mothers with full-time jobs, married and single; 83.3% of users are from this employment category. Home day care (that is, in somebody else's home), on the other hand, is used about as equally by all categories except housewives, who do not use it at all. Preschools are used most by married women who have part-time jobs. Finally, grandparents are called upon in a wide range of situations, but once again excepting the housewives.

It is logically difficult to compare the daily lives of children who are taken care of in such different ways, in that different child-care alternatives cope with different ages of children. Taking the three that most commonly cover preschool children (center day care, home day care, and grandparents), there are few major differences in daily time-use, apart from the obvious expectation that center day-care users will spend more time in formal institutional locations. However, users of center day care do more traveling by car (25 minutes, compared to 19 and 11 for the latter two categories);[2] in contrast, center day-care users spend the least amount of time walking (8 minutes, vs. 21 and 24, respectively).

Children in day-care centers average 3 minutes a day shopping—well below the average for their age cohort. Children in home day care average 10 minutes, still well below average, and children taken care of by grandparents are out shopping more than twice as long, 21 minutes. Thus, the more formal types of child care take away the need to bring younger children along during shopping, provided the parent can find time to do it on the weekday, among other obligations.

One question often raised in the context of child care and children's subsequent behavior has to do with the prevalence and consequences of the so-called "latch-key" situation, in which parents who are (usually) out working leave children under about twelve without supervision some hours of the day. We searched through the data to identify for analysis children between the ages of six to twelve whose mothers had jobs and who were not said to be cared for by any of the forms of child care we asked about. This search identified 48.4% of these children as fitting the formal qualifications for latch-key status.

How is daily life for latch-key children different from life for children of employed mothers who have child-care arrangements? These two categories do not differ significantly in contact with parents and kin, but the latch-key group spends nearly 50% more time with neighborhood children (i.e., not schoolmates or day-care associates per se)—114 vs. 81 minutes a day. Sex differences, however, are crucial. Latch-key boys spend 144 minutes with friends, compared to 87 minutes among the others. Latch-key girls, however, see a bit less of their friends—74 vs. 77 minutes; in any event, they spend less time with friends than do boys.

These sex-role differences are reinforced by examining where children spend their time. Boys spends no more or less time at home if they are latch-key or in a child-care arrangement (840 minutes a day in both situations). Girls, on the other hand, are at home more than three-quarters of an hour longer, on average, if latch-key (913 minutes vs. 867 minutes)—in both situations longer than are boys, consistent with the findings of Medrich et al. about sixth-grade students (1982). The data show that the locational differences are made up by latch-key boys' spending more time than latch-key girls at other people's homes (42 vs. 11 minutes) and in public places (42 vs. 21 minutes).

Personal Outcomes among Children

While it is a relatively straightforward matter to assess daily behavior, it is another question to discover what outcomes emerge among children under the conditions studied. As we have seen, a large and sometimes sophisticated literature provided many issues but few conclusions. All things considered, including the heavy demands placed on respondents by the sections of our survey dealing with the basic conditions of responding families, we took a relatively simple and direct approach to characterizing children. We asked the mothers whether they thought their children were high, medium, or low on each of eight traits, seven of which represent considerations in the literature on maternal employment—achievement, adventure, happiness, independence, getting along, patience, and ambition. Table 8.3 shows considerable variation among the categories of children, according to their mothers' marital and employment status and according to their own ages. As with behavior, differences tended to smooth out by the time children reached the highest age range.

Humor was listed as a characteristic only to help respondents get used to answering the question. There was no expectation of differences between categories, and there was in fact only minimal variation.

Achievement and ambition are hypothesized as greater when the mother

TABLE 8.3

Mother's Characterization of Children by Their Age and Her Marital and Employment Status (in percent)

	Married			Single	
	Full time Job	Part time Job	No job	Full time Job	No job
Children, Age 0 - 3					
Humor (high)	76	80	75	85	70
Achievement (high)	Not applicable				
Adventure (high)	79	79	59	71	78
Happiness (high)	89	77	85	80	78
Independence (high)	58	61	39	71	38
Getting along (high)	64	55	59	43	33
Patience (low)	35	34	37	50	60
Ambition (high)	69	72	55	35	50
Children, Age 4 - 6					
Humor (high)	60	48	61	60	57
Achievement (high)	72	73	64	78	71
Adventure (high)	60	57	48	60	71
Happiness (high)	76	71	73	60	71
Independence (high)	53	52	51	70	43
Getting along (high)	69	32	58	30	43
Patience (low)	27	38	31	70	29
Ambition (high)	66	56	44	33	43
Children Age 7 - 14					
Humor (high)	61	53	75	54	59
Achievement (high)	54	60	62	51	59
Adventure (high)	66	59	54	60	65
Happiness (high)	66	61	60	33	65
Independence (high)	55	55	55	63	71
Getting along (high)	61	48	70	60	48
Patience (low)	21	24	25	35	53
Ambition (high)	53	45	47	66	38

sets an example in the outside world. The married, employed mothers do characterize their children as greater in these two respects in the younger age cohorts. The single-housewife mothers of seven-to-fourteen-year-olds are farthest from the norm, in characterizing relatively few of their children as high in ambition.

Independence is thought engendered by both employment and single status among parents. In this respect, the children of single mothers with full-time jobs are most consistently said to be independent. Among the children under four, those whose mothers do not have outside jobs are said to be markedly less independent than those whose mothers are employed.

Proponents of day care claim that children learn to cooperate with peers at an earlier age; others have sometimes found children in day-care centers with poorer social skills than other children. Doubtless, much depends on the specific institution involved. There is similar (i.e., little) consistency in our data across age groups with respect to "getting along." Among the youngest children, those with single parents are ranked much lower, but this does not remain consistently true among older children. Among the children in two-parent families, those whose mothers have part-time jobs are described as considerably lower than the others.

Less patience was hypothesized as more characteristic of children in external child-care situations, who are thought to yearn for their parents' attention at the hectic end of the day. The data, however, show lower patience as more characteristic of the children of single parents than of employed parents per se.

Finally, as the literature suggests, happiness varies relatively little among the categories of children. The only emerging exception is that of children of single mothers with full-time jobs, as the children get older. These children are perhaps thrust into adult responsibilities at an earlier age, with less active choice.

It is important to remember that there is no external validation for these characterizations. It is entirely possible that mothers describe their children in wishful, projective ways—or that many of them read the same literature. Still, there is no perfect measure for such phenomena, and the variations appear logical in many respects.

This study is unusual in that, under a uniform analytic framework, the same measures are applied to children in a variety of age groups. Contrary to the outcome documented in previous literature, our empirical findings of differences by maternal employment and parental-marital status are greatest among the age cohort that psychologists regard so seriously. What our data can not answer is whether this is in fact a cohort phenomenon, reflecting the recent increase in maternal employment when children are very young, or is instead a pattern that, like everyday activity, is homogenized as children grow older.

Analyzing mothers' characterizations of children by the form of child care utilized gives some variations worth noting. Patience among the youngest group is considerably lower for children having center and home day care (56% and 48%, respectively), many of whom are children of single parents. Among the four-to-six-year-olds, children who attend day-care centers are still lowest in patience, but the differences are more narrow. In addition, however, day-care children are said to be the greatest by far in achievement (83% "high") and, marginally, in ambition (57% "high"). Thus, several of the hypotheses are sustained by these data, though their validity must, once again, be viewed with caution.

Child-Raising Practices during Periods of Overload

To this point, then, we have seen that children—particularly younger children—have differences in daily lives and some variation in reported traits according to their mothers' situations. A final question on outcomes for children has to do with how mothers treat them during periods of parental overload, which, as we have seen, usually involves mothers more than fathers.

About two-thirds of parents feel their children's behavior changes during certain time periods to an atypical pattern—mostly for the worse. The most prevalent reactions by children are various combinations of overt negative behavior (e.g., screaming, fighting), passive negative behavior (e.g, whining, delaying), and demanding attention (interrupting, being silly).

These changes are said to occur most frequently during the morning and evening "rush" hours (52%) and when the parent is otherwise busy (44%). Only to a much lesser extent do parents see these occurring when children are tired (28%) or burdened (10%), or when parents are tired (7%).

On their part, virtually all mothers admit to times of impatience with their children. About two-thirds of mothers feel that such impatience is precipitated by what the children themselves do (i.e., disruptive or demanding behavior), while 40% feel that such impatience is an outgrowth of the mothers' being already upset from other causes.[3] The prevalence of such situations does not vary by employment or marital status. The mothers see themselves as far less positive when impatient. Their responses are said to be largely verbal, but about 20% threaten or employ corporal punishment.

More specifically, about 80% of the mothers say that they are less patient when busy, and 60% are less affectionate under the same circumstances—both without significant variation by employment or marital status. Presumably frequency and duration of overload do vary, though, weighting parental responses accordingly.

Just under a quarter of the mothers say they are less strict when busy, but 42% claim to be more strict. Indeed, 57% of single mothers with full-time jobs say they are stricter when busy. These mothers are also significantly less comforting when busy than other mothers (51% less so, compared to 37% among the others). That single mothers with full-time jobs say they are more strict and less comforting than their married counterparts probably reflects more need by the single parent to exercise control during critical periods.

Women also say they are less consistent (40%) and helpful (48%) to their children under these conditions, without significant variation by employment or marital status.

In short, the various implications for children of their mothers' overlapping responsibilities, particularly relating to outside employment, are considerable in number and impact most fully on the youngest children.

There are, nevertheless, a number of institutions, practices, and other tangible aspects of our communities that are intended to help people in general and employed mothers in particular with their daily needs and routines. Let us now examine a selection of these external supports to see how they relate to the everyday logistics of the employed and/or single mother.

Notes

1 We shall return to an examination of differences between boys and girls, but for the moment the figures represent both sexes, which are found in even measures within subcategories.

2 More detailed logistical considerations of location and travel will be examined in the next chapter.

3 More than one response was permitted in answer to the question, and the percentage of responses totals more than 100.

9
The External Context: How Supportive?

I stressed in Chapter 1 the need to go beyond blaming the victim for dysfunctions attached to maternal employment. To this point, I have traced:

1. Some broad forces that lend urgency to the pursuit of maternal employment,
2. behavioral implications for women and how men's behavior differs,
3. how little internal (familial) contexts have adapted to these implications of maternal employment,
4. pressures and tensions women feel as a consequence, and
5. effects on children's daily lives and upbringing.

Now it is time to ask how such phenomena relate to the external context — factors outside the immediate control of both the employed mother and her family members but yet highly relevant to the opportunities and constraints of her daily life.

Institutions, facilities, and more general arrangements at the community or urban level presumably serve supportive, collective functions. Those paid for at least in part by taxes are legally bound to attempt to enhance the health, welfare, or safety of the population, and, in theory at least, the limitations of the public purse make for natural selection among collective responses to support citizen needs, according to their effectiveness. Private-sector activities are based on the premise that they fill needs, gaining profits in return; it is another question whether profit-making enterprises meet all needs and whether everyone is in a position to pay for satisfying the needs. And the nonprofit sector presumably supplements government in addressing needs that fall through the cracks of the private sector.

Certain aspects of the extremely complex and varied everyday world beyond the family are highly relevant to the daily routine of the employed mother. Some institutions address themselves directly to the needs of such women. Child-care settings are obvious examples. Others address needs that are not exclusive to women but appear to pertain more to them than to any other single segment of the population. Workplace practices that provide flexibility within employment, including various forms of part-time employment and flexible hours, fall within this category. Still other aspects of the context people live in make certain daily patterns easier or more difficult. In this case, the question is how the particular situation of employed women interacts with the availability, organization, and structure of this community infrastructure. Land-use, timetabling (i.e., setting the many opening, closing, and office hours of the various organizations, enterprises, and services in a local community), and transportation are among these considerations.

All of these aspects of the external context themselves face multiple, sometimes conflicting demands. The interests created by limited budgets, management concerns, and profit necessities need not be harmonious with the special interests of employed mothers. In transportation, for example, of which women are but one sector of users, the interests of some users are perhaps better recognized and served than those of others. In the case of child care, which presumably focuses on employed women and their children, some of women's interests in child care may be served better than others, not to speak of whether any given interest is optimally satisfied. With respect to some of the more general characteristics of the community structure—land-use and timetabling—there is the question of how explicitly any logistical interest that reflects the everyday life of the average citizen has been considered, in comparison to land economics, blue laws, professional and managerial prerogatives, etc.

Therefore, in this chapter, I shall direct attention to how well selected major aspects of the external context support the everyday lives of employed women, keeping also the situation of nonemployed and single mothers in the picture. I shall first focus on child care, then on transportation, on workplace flexibility, and on land-use and timetabling—each of which is highly relevant to the logistics of daily life among employed mothers.

Child Care Arrangements and Everyday Pressures

Child care is typically analyzed with respect to such considerations as availability, cost, instrumental value for labor-force participation, facilities, and the quality of the experience for children. Here, the focus is on the effect of selected child-care arrangements on mothers' abilities to fulfill daily responsibilities.

A significant effort to relate day-care centers as institutions to the other institutions upon which women rely in their daily routine was conducted by

Mårtensson (1977, 1979). She discusses the degree of overlap in time schedules of such functions as day-care, typical jobs, shopping, and medical care. The study indicates that, while the typical day-care center fulfills its mandate to care for children while mothers are employed, its hours provide little margin for variability in employment time, distances to be covered between job and day-care center, or the fulfillment of other needs within overlapping time parameters.

In the present case, our focus shifts from the relationship of the timing of institutions to the person who may need to utilize more than one of them within the confines of daily timetables. These are, of course, two sides of the same coin, and Mårtensson provides an extremely helpful basis for understanding what the employed mother encounters and experiences.

An immediate expectation is that more comprehensive child-care services should help relieve feelings of time pressure among mothers. A facility such as a day-care center has more continuity and resources than does an individual provider, and the growing professionalism of the day-care worker is generally considered a comfort to concerned parents. Noting the absolute degrees of time pressure among women using each of the selected child-care arrangements, as in Table 9.1, provides quite an opposite picture. This suggests instead that users of child-care services are generally above average in time pressure; the day-care center, the most comprehensive arrangement, is associated with the greatest degree of pressure. Fortunately, this is a misleading picture of the support provided by such arrangements, because it does not compare the varying external responsibilities of users of these respective arrangements to others. It is necessary to control for the employment-status composition of users.

For example, center day care is accompanied by a mean busy-scale of +2.2

TABLE 9.1

Mean Time Pressure Scores for Women by Type of Child Care Services Used

			Time Pressure Scales		
	Too busy to do what want (4=most 1=least)	Average week (+10=most −10=least)	Time for housework (+10=most −10=least)	Time for children (+10=most −10=least)	Time for self (+10=most −10=least)
Centre daycare	1.9	+2.2	+2.6	+2.1	+3.3
Home daycare	0.8	+2.0	+1.9	+1.8	+2.4
Preschool	0.5	+1.4	+1.1	+2.1	+2.3
Grandparents	0.6	+2.1	+1.4	+1.3	+2.3

on the average week—the most representative busy scale. This score is tied for highest among users of typical child-care alternatives for young children, indicating the greatest feelings of pressure. If, however, we select our scores for the most typical user groups, i.e., married and single mothers with full-time jobs, we see that those who utilize day-care centers report less pressures than the groups as a whole. For all women with full-time jobs in two-parent families, the average busy-scale score is +2.5; for those using day-care centers, it is +2.1. For single mothers with full-time jobs, the mean overall score of +2.4 improves to +1.9 for users of day-care centers.

The same kind of logistical support appears to be given by home day care, with improvements to +2.4 and +0.7, respectively, again indicating a greater positive effect for the single mothers than for the married.

In contrast, the married women with part-time jobs report greater time pressure with use of home day care (+3.3, compared to their average of +2.0)—and indeed also with preschools (+2.9) and grandparents (+2.6), their other common external sources of child-care services. Preschools better serve the purposes of their other major user group in the sample—married women without employment, whose scores are marginally more relaxed than their average (+0.6 vs. +0.9).

Use of grandparents appears the least successful in alleviating time pressures, despite the potential flexibility of grandparents. Four of the five categories of employment and marital status show more pressure when relying on grandparents than the category averages, in some cases much more. For example, married women with full-time jobs who receive child care from one or more of the child's grandparents report a mean average-week busy-scale score of +3.5, well above the +2.5 average for the category and the highest score for any category of child-care users. One possibile explanation is that grandparents require a personal investment by the mother not associated with more institutional forms of child care.

The other measures of time pressure follow the same explanatory pattern. Formal child care appears successful in marginally reducing the time pressure of particular employment and marital-status categories, but not to the point that the disparate levels of time pressure in these categories are substantially altered. In other words, these data provide evidence that the more formal child-care settings provide some degree of support but do not in and of themselves greatly change the pressures mothers face.

Additional qualified evidence for the support offered by day-care centers in particular comes from an analysis of answers to the question on how content women are with their decision to undertake outside employment. Among the employed mothers of children six or younger using these main child-care alternatives, there is roughly equal contentment with this decision to undertake outside employment. Between 63% and 70% of those using any of these categories of child care express medium satisfaction. In all categories except those using home day care, most of the remaining respondents report high rather than low contentment, led by day-care centers, with 31.3% high and only 6.3% low. Preschool users are a close second, at 28.6% high, with grandparents third, at 22.2%. Users of home day care, in contrast, report only 11.6% high contentment with the decision to work, with 19.2% low.

Thus, even with the more favored arrangements, daily life does not thereby become easy — only less difficult. Some explanation for this lies in the interaction of considerations about child care with those in other aspects of community infrastructure, as Mårtensson would have us suspect. Transportation is highly relevant in this regard. Let us examine at this point how transportation contributes to the everyday logistics of employed mothers.

Women and Transportation: Convergence or Divergence?

When we consider how the external context affects the ease or difficulty of everyday life, the geographic locations and temporal availability of the various nonresidential activities become meaningful to the individual routine largely in terms of how much time and effort it takes to get around to these activities within a twenty-four-hour day. Transportation is a crucial dynamic factor linking a host of other considerations. Another writer put it aptly in a recent review:

> Transportation centrally affects the relationship between physical space and society.... [It is] part of the environment and a key mediator between that environment and the individual.... [Yago, 1983, pp. 171, 185]

He goes on to note that transportation resources are not divided equally within the population, leading to different levels of opportunity and resulting in different situations among subgroups.

This is the essential starting point for the discussion in this chapter, insofar as the qualitative experience of daily travel provides or does not provide support for employed women. Hence, we have to ask how different women's transportation situation is from men's. This requires some insight beyond the sheer amount of travel, focusing on the demands for and nature of travel, available resources and eventual mode of travel, and the outcomes of the interaction of all these factors.

I should note as well at the outset that transportation represents an intersection of internal (intrafamilial) and external contexts, in that some transportation resources are privately owned and controlled by the family, though subject to unequal distribution, but other, qualitatively different resources and a range of broader considerations come from the external context.

We have seen in previous chapters that the time women devote to travel varies directly with the extent of employment and, to a lesser extent, with the age of their children. Neither of these is true for men. Even though women with full-time jobs approach the mean daily-travel time of the average employed male, they remain below that of their own husbands. Similarly, children's travel varies in nature and amount by the ages and sex of the children and by the responsibilities of their mothers. While these figures help indicate the content of daily activity, they say little or nothing about the qualitative nature of transportation, how it is experienced, and the degree it supports the demands placed upon it.

These findings are consistent with many previous studies, cited earlier, that centered on time-use aspects of women's travel, as well as with literature on the lack of change in men's travel in response to maternal employment (Hanson and Hanson, 1981) and on the effects of children on women's travel (Zimmerman, 1980). However, there are additional signals from previous work that the interrelationship of women with transportation is qualitatively unique.

1. Functions served: Women have been found to make trips in order to satisfy a wider range of activities and tasks than do men (Madden, 1981; Koppelman et al., 1978; Pickup, 1981). Shopping in particular is in women's purview, as are a variety of trips with children associated with child care and children's activities (Vanek, 1974; Skinner and Borlaug, 1978; Hanson and Hanson, 1981). These trips are shorter in distance than are those men typically take, which revolve more around employment and recreation (Giuliano, 1979; Madden, 1981). Thus, it is only logical that women are said to be more likely to combine multiple functions into single trips. That is, they link potentially independent trips into one (Madden, 1981; Pickup, 1981; Koppelman et al., 1978). This is done more successfully in most instances with an automobile than with public transit (Damm, 1978).

2. Transportation resources and mode of travel: Most persons of both sexes prefer automobile travel over the alternatives (Studenmund et al., 1978); indeed, women prefer it for transporting children, because of its relative flexibility, reliability, and capacity (Koppelman et al., 1978; Pickup, 1981). Yet, women have less access to cars, for several reasons. In many places they are about half as likely as men to have driver's licenses (Pickup, 1981; Sen, 1978). Married women are said to choose work location as a function of residential location, placing logistical ease higher in priority than career development (Palm and Pred, 1974). They most typically cede usage of a single family car to their husbands, as the latter are most typically considered the chief wage-earner (Koppelman et al., 1978; Levine, 1980). Single women are, on the average, poorer and hence less able to afford automobiles (Giuliano, 1979). Hence, women use public transit disproportionately to their numbers and to the number of trips they make; even when traveling by automobile, they are more typically passengers than drivers (Giuliano, 1979).

The general picture emerging from this literature, that women are increasingly traveling as much as men but over shorter stretches, on less-favored means of transportation, but for more functions, shows that women are "transportation deprived and transit dependent" (Carp, 1974, p. 6).

To date, there has been a virtual vacuum in the literature of studies that relate personal or structural characteristics and travel data to personal outcomes. Indeed, even the studies showing greater travel demands on employed women have failed to distinguish between full-time and part-time employment and therefore between the differences in how travel fits within the confines of different routines.

However, Renwick, Lawler, and the *Psychology Today* staff (1978) presaged the finding reported in Chapter 6 that the typical daily transitions to and from household and other activities are the most difficult to manage for employed mothers. Since transportation is a vital component of most such transitions, this suggests that employed women will find considerable affective significance in certain major components of daily transportation, not least in the means by which such trips are taken.

Data from our Toronto study provides insights into a number of aspects of how employed women experience transportation and what this means for them.

TRAVEL DEMANDS AND CONDITIONS

First, women's daily travel occurs in the context of such pressures as child care and housework, beyond "just" employment, as is the case with men. A regression analysis indicates that the employment-generated set of role responsibilities is not the only one affecting degree of women's travel. A second set involving most women, housework, is independently significant in explaining women's travel time—in this case inversely ($r = -.35$). The more time women spend on housework, the less time they spend traveling; this relationship is stronger for driving than for public transportation, though roughly similar. Men's daily travel is almost totally unrelated to how much housework they do ($r = +.02$).

Hours of employment and hours of housework explain relatively independently time spent traveling. Time spent on housework increases the multiple correlation coefficient of employment hours on travel time from .26 to .36. Even just among those with full-time jobs, those who do more housework travel less. As we have seen, housewives generally do lots of housework and only a moderate amount of travel; hence, the housewives who invest relatively more time in housework undertake extremely little travel.

Previously reported results underline the finding that, not only is housework a constraining trade-off with women's travel, but the need for time for housework is the basis for the pressure that colors the experience of many daily activities. There is no reason to believe travel is an exception to these activities.

Second, women's weekday travel is less often solitary than men's. For example, comparing just work trips between women with full-time jobs and their husbands, the men are about 30% more likely to travel without other family members and twice as likely to travel completely alone. Table 9.2 shows that, in aggregate, women take children along on 44% of their trips, of which about a quarter (or 11% in all) include the husband as well. Moreover, children accompany women on more than half of all trips except those to work.

Housewives are most likely to take trips with children; almost two-thirds of all their trips include them. They take relatively few trips alone. Even employed women, nevertheless, have children as company on over 30% of their trips.

Third, the purposes behind trips are consistent with employment status and associated levels of accompaniment by children. For example, Table 9.3 shows that work trips are replaced in part among the housewives by trips to other persons' houses and to shopping—more hospitable destinations for children.

The interrelationships of employment status, accompaniment by children, and mode of travel are brought out in Table 9.4, which indicates that women seldom travel with children by public transportation. Given the findings of the literature that mothers prefer travel with children by car for logistical reasons, it is not surprising that housewives take so few trips by public transportation; in the absence of employment, most of their trips are with children. Nonetheless, Table 9.3 shows that employed mothers, especially if working part-time, take a reasonable number of noncommuting trips each day, dur-

TABLE 9.2

Company on Trips From Home by Married Women

	Alone or with non-family	With children only	With husband and children	With husband only	# of trips
Full-time job	59.0%	22.5	8.7	9.8	(205)
Part-time job	54.9%	29.1	8.6	7.5	(93)
No outside employment	27.8%	46.6	16.5	9.1	(176)
All married women	46.6%	32.7	11.6	9.1	(474)

TABLE 9.3

Destination of Married Women's Trips From Home by Employment Status

Employment Status	Destination					
	Residential	Work	Shopping	Recreation	Other	n=
Full-time job	31.7%	45.4	8.8	8.3	5.9	(205)
Part-time job	36.0%	25.8	20.4	10.8	6.5	(93)
No outside employment	54.5%	–	25.0	11.4	9.1	(176)

ing which time their children are typically with them. This helps make clear the cleavage between trips by auto or on foot, which include other family members, and those by public transportation, which are solitary. It appears that a mother will consider going by public transportation only if she is taking the kind of trip where she travels alone. These figures provide stark confirmation of the preferences noted in the literature reflecting women's particular child-care functions.

Nonetheless, the reverse is not valid: because women may travel alone does not mean that they will go by public transportation. The mode of travel women use is determined by a complex of considerations, which again differ from those for men.

TABLE 9.4

Company and Mode of Travel in Trips by Married Women, by Employment Status

Employment Status and Mode of Travel	Company on Trip				
	Alone or with Non-Family Members	With Children only	With Husband and Children	With Husband only	# of trips
Full-time job					
Car	46.7%	26.7	13.4	13.3	(105)
Public Transit	97.0%	0.0	0.0	2.9	(34)
Walking	42.9%	47.6	0.0	9.5	(21)
Part-time job					
Car	50.0%	27.5	10.3	12.1	(58)
Public Transit	70.0%	25.0	5.0	0.0	(20)
Walking	64.7%	29.5	5.9	0.0	(17)
No outside employment					
Car	23.1%	38.5	26.4	12.1	(91)
Public Transit	100.0%	0.0	0.0	0.0	(4)
Walking	19.1%	72.3	6.4	2.1	(47)

MODE OF TRAVEL

Consistent with the percentage of trips they take with children and the feelings they have about how best to travel with children, the majority of women go by automobile to and from the majority of their destinations. Table 9.5 provides data on trips leading home, in terms of where they originated and the mode of transportation used. It shows that public transportation is prominent only among those taking work trips; about a quarter of the trips home from work were on public transit, compared to less than 6% of trips from other origins. Viewed another way, about 70% of trips home on public transit were from work.

Table 9.5 also shows how mode of transportation varies by the degree women are employed. The full-time employee is most likely to take public transportation, obviously to and from work, but also for trips with other purposes. Women with part-time jobs and housewives take only 3.3% and 2.4%, respectively, of their daily trips on public transportation. The housewives, however, are not more likely to drive by virtue of this; a greater percentage of their trips are on foot.

Let us turn from the analysis of mode of transportation on the basis of trips to the time spent traveling during the day. This reinforces the previous picture of variations by degree of employment. Table 9.6 shows that women with full-time jobs spend a much greater mean time during the weekday on public transportation—more than seven times the amount of the housewives and almost three times as much as those with part-time jobs. Single mothers

TABLE 9.5

Mode of Travel Used for Married Women's Trips Home,
by Selected Trip Origins and Employment Status

Origin Trip Home	Auto	Public Transit	Foot	Other or Unspecified
Residential	56.0%	4.0	26.4	13.6
Work	55.0%	25.5	8.1	11.4
Shopping	63.4%	5.9	22.8	7.9
Recreational	69.4%	3.2	21.0	6.4
Employment Status				
Full-time job	59.2%	17.7	11.0	11.9
Part-time job	67.3%	3.3	18.5	10.9
No outside employment	58.4%	2.4	28.3	10.8

TABLE 9.6

Mean Minutes a Weekday in Travel by Mode of Transportation
and Employment Status of Married Women, for Husbands and Wives

	Employment Status of Wife					
	Full-time job		Part-time job		No employment	
Mode of Travel	Wife	Husband	Wife	Husband	Wife	Husband
Automobile	43	74	43	54	25	56
Public Transit	25	9	9	6	3	9
Walking, Cycling, and Other	15	12	19	17	16	11
Total Minutes	83	95	71	77	44	76
n =	(160)	(141)	(86)	(80)	(188)	(173)

with jobs spend much more time traveling (100 daily minutes, of which 38.4 are by public transit and 37.6 by car); single housewives spend the least (32 minutes, of which 6.2 are by public transit and 19.6 by car).

The men in the sample nearly all have full-time jobs, so no analysis was made of the effects on their mode of travel by this consideration. Nonetheless, as can be seen in Table 9.6, men spend very much more of their time driving and relatively little in public transit (about 10% of daily travel time, compared to 30% for wives with full-time jobs). Futhermore, how men get to and from their destinations is totally unaffected by whether and to what extent their wives are employed. Going back to trips, 50% more men drive to work than women.

Answers to a direct question on how respondents and their husbands travel to work give an impression of more public-transportation usage than the time-budgets document for the weekday in question. Women with full-time jobs say they take public transit to work in 46% of cases, while 37% of women working part-time claim to do so. Among their husbands, 16.3% and 8.9%, respectively, say the same. This discrepancy is puzzling, but the gender differences remain constant.

We have now seen that women's travel is more constrained by manifest or latent domestic pressures and involves children to a greater extent, which effectively militates against use of public transit, and hence this travel depends on automobile use except among a strong minority of women with full-time jobs who use public transit largely to get to work. Yet their husbands, who do not operate under the same conditions, are more likely to drive a car to almost everything, including work. It becomes obvious that women's interrelationship with transportation differs greatly from men's. Women's choice of how to get to work is of particular curiosity.

The matter boils down to the conditions under which women take public transit to work.

If a woman has a job and exclusive access to an automobile, then she drives to work. Only one married woman out of forty-five who are employed full-time and have exclusive access to a car takes public transportation. Of twenty-five women with part-time jobs and auto access, none takes public transportation.

Women are less likely than men to have access to an automobile for their exclusive use. The literature shows this as related to both income and the intrafamilial distribution of transportation resources.

Our data show that, contrary to what would be expected from family-income figures, married women in the three employment-status categories show nearly no differences in the percentage of women who have exclusive access to a car (just under 40%). Over 90% of these families in all categories have at least one car, and between 30% and 40% have two. Thus, the husband-first dynamic applies to the distribution of family cars: the husband usually gets to use the first one in the family; if there is one, it does not sit idly during the workday. If there is a second one, it falls under the jurisdiction of the wife, who uses it if she takes a work trip. The housewife is less likely actually to use hers on a given weekday, because her trips lack the obligatory regularity of work trips.

Thus, among the married women, both the mode and the amount of travel vary by employment status, while access to a car remains stable. Among single mothers, there is a major difference in access. The majority (56%) of employed single mothers have a family car, compared to only 30% of nonemployed single mothers — surely a function of both income and need. Nonetheless, this is difficult for the single housewife, who is less likely to have the mode of transport mothers customarily use for the kind of trip she makes (i.e., shopping and other child-accompanied trips). Even without exclusive access to a car, married housewives have the services of a husband and/or his car for such trips.

Our central questions remain. Why do not more married women with full-time jobs have the second cars their family incomes might enable? Why do more full-time than part-time workers take public transportation? Why do so many women with part-time jobs have cars and not take public transportation?

The answers lie in a variety of interacting factors. Income does have a limited effect. Within women's employment-status categories, the woman's access to a car is a function of income. The more affluent families in every category are significantly more likely to own cars. The categories themselves represent different income strata, though. This means that the lower-income segment of two-parent families where the wife has a full-time job may not have two cars, but probably could. The upper-income segments of two-parent families where the wife has a part-time job or of single-parent families do have a car for the woman's exclusive use, even though probably less likely to be able to afford it. The lower-income segments of these categories do not have one but almost certainly want and would use it, given their typical transportation uses and preferences. So income helps determine who does not get to use a car, but not necessarily who does.

Many women's failure to have a driver's license is probably part of the same sex-role syndrome that underlies family division of labor and transportation resources. At any given moment, a number of women can not drive for that very reason. In the current sample, 38% of all the women interviewed lack a driver's license, and this is as high as 62% of nonemployed single mothers. Contrary to expectations, the average woman without a driver's license is a shade younger than the average woman who has one (32.8 years vs. 34.4).

Locational and transport-system considerations are helpful in going beyond the limitations of income to explain the purchase of a car and use by female heads of household.

Women with full-time jobs are more likely to commute to the central city than are those with part-time jobs. The latter are more likely to have their workplaces in the same concentric ring of the metropolitan area where they live, minimizing their distance to work.

Among both men and women, it is work trips to or (less likely) from the center that create larger than average commuting trips. Men are even more likely than women to work in the central business district and to have a longer mean commute, regardless of the concentric zone in which they live.[1]

Like the time devoted to many other activities, husbands' and wives' work trips do not complement each other; if one is long, the other will be, too. Correlation coefficients concerning wives' and husbands' distances from home to work are $+.27$ $(p < .003)$ and $+.40$ $(p < .001)$ for families in which the wives have full-time and part-time jobs, respectively. Therefore, the husband's preempting of the family car reflects primarily his desire to use available resources himself, rather than significant differences in commuting distance.

Most families desire and own a car. The question is how many more are both desired and affordable,[2] and to some extent this is a function of the particular urban area and the types and locations of the trips which would be made. Downtown Toronto is relatively congested and places disincentives on all-day parking, and women working full-time are more likely to need to retain their incomes. So women working full-time downtown have both positive and negative reasons to use the excellent public-transportation system, which focuses on downtown destinations via subway and commuter train lines, rather than to purchase a second car.

As one respondent observes the dilemmas of driving to downtown Toronto: ". . . Parking is very expensive and scarce. . . . Subways go downtown. Who wants to drive downtown? No one wants to, I am sure!"

The greatest percentage claiming use of the Toronto Transit Commission (TTC) for the work trip is that of suburban women working full-time downtown (68.9%), indicating that, whether for good or bad reasons, suburbanites will use public transportation, if it is available. Public transit is used far less by part-time workers (about 40%) and by women who both live and work in an outer borough of Metropolitan Toronto (25%).

Moreover, the subways and commuter trains that primarily take people to and from the central city have a female ridership in our sample of whom 50% lack driver's licenses. Among women traveling to work by bus or streetcar alone, which are slower and less centrally focused means of transport, 73% lack licenses.

Work trips that do not follow the lines of relatively fast, efficient connections to and from the center, but primarily involve intrasuburban commuting, are much more efficiently taken by car. Virtually any trip is possible by public transportation in Metropolitan Toronto, but the timing and connections among suburban bus lines are not close (which is felt directly in terms of travel time and flexibility and in winter chills). These data suggest that such travel by public transit is more commonly taken by those who have no alternative, in contrast to use of the subway and commuter trains.

The prevalent choice of mass transportation for full-time work trips from the suburbs to the central city, when joined with the use of cars for suburban work trips within the same zone and closer part-time work when feasible, leads to a possibly surprising relationship. In Toronto, with its well-organized public transit system and a focused center for full-time employment downtown, women associate public transportation with more distant work trips and driving with shorter ones (with a mean difference of 1.1 kilometers). The competitiveness of public transportation is shown in a zero correlation between access to a car (and hence its use for commuting) and daily travel time for both married and single mothers with full-time jobs.

Is there another reason besides job location, in view of the relative efficiencies of public transportation, that women with part-time jobs are more likely to drive to work? Various data suggest that those working part-time are more likely to take care of shopping and social visits during the daytime on weekdays, leaving themselves available for their families in the late afternoons and evenings. Having a car would facilitate this, which is something those with full-time jobs haven't the time to do in between jobs and home and which they make up for on weekends. Among just the married women working part-time, 71% of drivers make stops (i.e., link other functions to their work trips), as compared to only 28% of transit riders. To take another example, women with full-time jobs are as likely as their husbands to take a shopping trip on a weekday (.226 vs. .213 mean shopping trips). Those with part-time jobs are much more likely to do so (.413) than either the women with full-time jobs or than their own husbands (.147), but still a bit less likely than the housewives (.496). The same tendencies are present, but somewhat less pronounced, for recreation and similar trips.

It is often said that women drive to work if they can so as to be able to get home sooner, in response to housekeeping pressures. However, our data show that women who drive to work spend no more (or less) time at home than those who don't drive. This is not to discount these pressures, but the locational data suggest that women drive to work in part to help keep their time away from home from escalating to a higher level, rather than to reduce it to lower levels.

Women's access to automobiles appears to support the participation in certain activities by children. We analyzed how many of the six types of excursions mentioned in question 36 children had gone on during the previous six months. Children whose mothers have exclusive access to a car had gone on 4.4 of them; whose whose mothers have licenses but not exclusive access, 3.7, compared to 3.3 for those whose mothers do not have licenses.

Furthermore, the question arises as to what full-time housewives do if about 60% do not have exclusive access to a car but are almost entirely restricted to walking or driving, in view of an apparent reluctance to take public transportation.[3] About 10% more of the married housewives go places with their husbands than do the employed women. And, as we saw earlier, women without employment are simply more likely to stay home on the average day.

In sum, then, when outside employment requires that women take commuting trips, their mode of travel is a complex function of income, possession or lack of a driver's license, job location and direction, intrafamilial division of transportation resources, traffic and parking disincentives and the merits and focus of the public transit system, and such activities as shopping and chauffeuring that auto travel permits, relative to the length and timing of daily employment. Those who take public transit may be exercising an option not to buy a second car for pragmatic reasons. At any time, however, many women feel they have little option to travel to work in any other way.

Those who have opted not to get a second car or who are unable to do so are thereby dependent on public transportation. It is therefore no surprise that women view travel by public transit as having the least degree of choice of any major activity they perform (2.66 between 1 and 7, i.e., less than work: 2.75, housework: 3.34, and child care: 3.67). Men have more choice when taking public transit (3.42), because most who do so could preempt the family car.

Women without outside employment who lack access to automobiles are similarly constrained, but their travel is more likely to be optional. The travel they do is hence more likely to reflect some degree of choice, but this is reflected largely in reactions to travel by automobile.

In any case, the factors explaining women's mode of transportation and how they experience this mode, lie in both their intrafamilial and external contexts, a blend of subjective sex-role practices and highly objective characteristics of the community and its infrastructure.

PERSONAL OUTCOMES OF THE TRAVEL EXPERIENCE

We have seen that women's travel serves more purposes and involves more other people than men's, yet it involves less choice in the mode by which it is taken. All of these occur under pressures that do not typically enter men's lives to the same degree. Indeed, this situation pushes women with full-time jobs toward one mode of transportation for work trips and toward another for most others, in neither case with the feeling of an actual choice. On such a basis, one would expect greater feelings of time pressure and tension associated with women's travel than with men's, particularly in those situations where choice is low.

Various results support these expectations.

We saw in Chapter 6 that women's busy scale for "yesterday" is mildly but significantly related ($r = +.18$) to the total time spent traveling. Analysis of the average-week busy scale not only shows a similar relationship with travel time for women ($r = +.15, p < .00$) but suggests that public transit contributes more to time pressure than does travel by car.

One could ask if these findings don't just reflect the greater time pressures among employed women. However, these outcomes are noted when just the women with jobs are analyzed. Travel mode to work is observed in relationship to previous-day time pressures, for example, in Table 9.7, which shows that over 35% of women using public transportation for commuting are in the highest time-pressure bracket, compared to about 19% of drivers and those who switch mode en route. In contrast, only 22% of transit riders felt they had the time they needed, compared to over 42% of drivers. Among men, the relationship is reversed: riding the TTC is more of a choice for them.[4]

Women's "yesterday" time pressure is unrelated to the number of trips they made ($r = +.04$) or to trips by car ($r = -.01$), but it is significantly related (given the size of the sample) to the number of trips they took by public transit ($r = +.12, p < .01$).

TABLE 9.7

Time Pressure Yesterday by Mode of Travel to Work, by Sex

Mode of Travel to Work	Time Pressure Yesterday				
	High (+6 to -10)	Medium (+1 to +5)	Equilibrium Between Time and Activity (0)	Ease (Too Much Time) (-1 to -10)	n=
Women:					
Car	19.3%	38.5	37.3	4.8	(83)
Car and Public Transit	18.2%	36.3	45.5	0.0	(11)
Public Transit	35.1%	43.2	19.0	2.7	(37)
Men:					
Car	20.8%	31.9	41.5	5.8	(207)
Car and Public Transit	33.3%	40.0	20.0	6.7	(15)
Public Transit	8.0%	44.0	48.0	12.0	(25)

We can narrow in on outcomes directly attributable to travel by assessing tension as measured in the time-budgets. Travel tension in particular is somewhat greater among women who take public transportation to work (4.7 vs. 5.0 on the 7-point scale); this is not a function of trip length.

Average daily tension is also mildly but significantly related to travel time for women ($r = +.10$, $p < .012$), highlighting time on public transit ($r = +.13$, $p < .001$), but again not time spent driving ($r -.01$, $p = .403$).

In contrast, no relationships between tension and travel time or mode are significant for men. The gender diffferences are easily understood in view of the kind of difficult transitions to and from pressing household responsibilities facing women but not men, transitions that are part of the experience of daily transportation.

Moreover, I noted in the previous section that more women, particularly those with full-time jobs, take public transportation than men and that the women regard it as a very low-choice situation, whatever its absolute merits. The general relationships between degree of choice and amount of tension are upheld specifically with respect to travel for men, women, and children. Women, however, not only have the greatest exposure to public transit under current conditions, but show the highest correlation between choice and tension ($r = +.43$); men are second ($r = +.37$), followed by children ($r = +.30$).

In short, public transit, the mode of travel many women take as a consequence of a number of factors in the intrafamilial and external contexts which lead to less choice in travel than men have, is associated with feelings of greater time pressure and tension. These are just not generalized feelings of hassle associated with employment, they are feelings of tension associated directly with transportation and its specific modes, which in turn contribute to the implications of maternal employment.

CHILD-CARE TRAVEL: AN ILLUSTRATION

In the first part of this chapter, we examined several forms of child care, noting that more institutionalized forms appear to alleviate but not substantially alter the levels of time pressure associated with different degrees of maternal employment. The travel logistics of child care in the daily routine make this situation somewhat clearer.

External child-care services require that the child(ren) get to them. We have seen that children whose mothers have full-time jobs spend more time traveling and that the children who go to external child care travel different amounts of time by varying modes of transportation.

Obviously, most children are accompanied to the child-care arrangements, creating a situation whereby at least two people commute to and from a particular location each workday, which neither would be likely to do without maternal employment in the family.

Mothers are involved in most trips for child care, consistent with the data on who accompanies whom on trips. They are the lone adult family chaperone in 55.6% of such trips, and they and their husbands go together another 14.8% of the time, totaling over 70% of child care trips. Husbands make child-care trips without their wives in only 13% of the trips; children go alone or by a collective service in 11.1% of child-care trips.

Let us look at the distances of women's child-care and work trips. If child care were immediately adjacent to home or workplace, it still might take longer to get from door to desk or bench, but the child-care drop-off would not represent extra distance. Our calculation of distances was very conservative—as the hypotenuse joining the center of the square kilometer of one location to that of another. This is conservative because activities in the same grid are considered to involve no distance and because people are seldom able to travel from one location to another in a straight line.

As shown in Figure 9.1, women's mean distance from home to work is 6.46 kilometers. The mean distance from home to child care is 1.71 kilometers (taking a mean of 19 minutes), and from child care to work, 5.23 kilometers. The mean "perimeter" distance, i.e., from home to child care to work, is therefore 6.94 kilometers.

Thus, not all child-care travel is out of the way. Nonetheless, according to

134 *The External Context: How Supportive?*

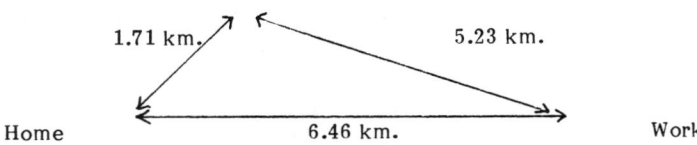

Figure 9.1

Distances Between Women's Homes, Child Care Locations, and Places of Employment

these distances, no less than 28% of travel with children to a child-care setting is beyond the requirements of home-to-work commuting, not counting extra time for starting and stopping, which are additional daily transitions. Going to a child-care setting adds at least a half kilometer each way to the daily commute. The greatest increments in work trips caused by child-care drop-offs are among those who either live or work in the central city (.65 km and .89 km). Actual distances are probably higher, if only because few are able to take straight-line routes and because these figures include a variety of ages of children and types of child care, some of which situations make minimal demands on the parents.

Indeed, as might be expected, extra travel is particularly pronounced among mothers of younger children. The one-way perimeter distance for employed mothers of children under four years of age is 8.9 kilometers, a conservative 4-kilometer difference in the round-trip commute, compared to the general mean of 6.9 kilometers.

It is not surprising to see in Figure 9.2 that child care in the most institutionalized form is farthest on average from home. The day-care centers families in the current sample use are, on average, 3.58 kilometers away. In

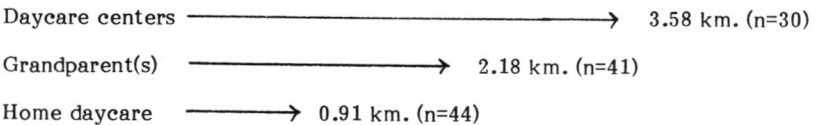

Figure 9.2

Distance From Home to Three Child Care Alternatives

contrast, home day care, sometimes preferred for its flexibility, averages within a kilometer of home (0.91 km). Grandparents, a third common source of support for employed women with small children, are found in between (2.18 km), not because they are more institutional, but because they are chosen on neither institutional nor logistical grounds.

Users of day-care centers show the longest one-way perimeter distances (11.26 km). This reflects in part the longer investment in travel that accompanies full-time work (10.11 km home to work for users of day-care centers), but the relatively large-scale character of day-care centers and their typical locations near neither home nor work leads to a greater mean additional distance to be covered during the day than for other forms of child care.

The upshot of all these locational considerations is seen in Table 9.8, which shows personal outcomes in terms of tension in daily travel. This tension does not vary significantly by either the distance from home to work or by the perimeter distance of home to child care to work. Rather, the amount of extra distance added by the child-care drop-off is significantly related to travel tension over the day. Furthermore, the tension corresponding to marginal increases in distance is greater for those driving ($r = +.21$) than for those taking public transportation ($r = +.10$), consistent with customary ways of transporting children.

One mother expressed the situation very clearly: "When you're halfway across the city and caught in a snowstorm, and you know the day-care center has to close, that produces tension!"

Fathers do not show the same pattern of tension ($r = -.03$), reinforcing the view that the child-care drop-off is significant primarily in the mother's routine.

TABLE 9.8

Tension in Employed Women's Travel by Selected Types of Distance (Correlation Coefficients)

		Correlations with tension in daily travel
A.	Straight-line distance home to work	$r = +.10$ (NS)
B.	Straight-line distance, home to childcare to work	$r = -.04$ (NS)
C.	Marginal distance added to work trip by childcare dropoff (i.e. B - A)	$r = +.16$ ($p = .004$)

(N = 263)

Flexibility in Employment

When dealing with how full-time work affects a person's day and the other activities potentially in it, I have so far appeared to assume that this work obligation takes up a fixed, unchangeable period of time, whatever the individual's preferences and needs. Large and external it is, and the kinds of conflicts it creates for individuals have become increasingly recognized as married women have entered the labor force more and more. Other community problems, such as traffic jams and transit-system overloads, when everybody leaves work at once, have also been acknowledged as a function of inflexible scheduling of employment. Therefore, a number of practices have been tried in efforts to introduce more flexibility into employment timetables.

Part-time work is obviously one form of response. It provides the worker some of the desired benefits of employment, without the degree of pressure on other activities in the daily routine that comes from a seven- or eight-hour workday. Some employers are able to attract workers for some of their overload periods through part-time positions, and others have been able to get needed workers back into the work force by making work available part-time (e.g., nurses). Yet most employers, who are worried about extra costs, obligations, and administrative work, differentiate part-time from full-time work by paying wages rather than salaries and by failing to provide fringe benefits and job continuity to part-time workers (Commission of Inquiry into Part-time Work, 1983).

The traditional alternative of fixed employment hours is shift work, a very old concept. A recent and highly sophisticated study of the effects of shift work on family life, including the interaction of two spouses' shifts, was conducted by Staines and Pleck (1983). While generally findings that nontraditional working hours have negative consequences within families, Staines and Pleck show that a crucial factor that plays a part in the explanation of how employment hours affect families is the degree of individuals' flexibility within a given system. The more they have, the more positive the consequence. Parent-child contact, particularly, is fostered when workers have a sense of control in the timing of their employment activities — or in occassional exceptions to established routines.

Various efforts have been made in recent years to introduce more flexibility into full-time employment. One type of flexibility has come in the form of alternatives to the approximate nine-to-five, five-day workweek. Planners largely concerned with eliminating effects of lock-step practices on community infrastructure find merits in such innovations as staggered hours, in which different employers require different hours of their employees, so as to spread out the morning and evening rush hours, and the four-day week, in which workers put in more hours on their workdays but work one fewer day, thereby reducing the number of commuters on any given day by as much as a fifth. Practices like this have fewer documented benefits for individual workers, who still do not have sufficient flexibility to fit working hours to idiosyncratic family needs (Jovanis, 1983).

Another attempt to introduce flexibility, which makes the individual the center of attention, is *flextime* or *flexitime* (Ronen, 1981). Under this approach, employees are free to select their own hours, within a certain daily range, usually with a core of hours in the middle of the day when nearly everyone is expected to be available. In some variations, workers are free to decrease their number of hours on some days, provided that they compensate by putting in more time on others. The number of hours have to balance with an agreed-upon standard within a period, such as a month. In some cases, surpluses or deficits may be carried over; in others, payroll implications ensue. An advanced punch-clock system, called the Flextimer, which can record and account for employee arrivals and departures over a long period of time, has been placed on the market to support such arrangements (*The Financial Post,* 1984). Sullivan (1984) writes, "Currently 17% of the U.S. companies and 23% of government agencies offer flexitime options to employees" (p. 315).

A few studies of flextime indicate some minor benefits for some employees, but not the drastic improvement that might have been hypothesized, particularly on those with multiple responsibilities, such as employed mothers (e.g., Bohen and Viveros-Long, 1981). Nonetheless, work performance is said to improve with flextime (Nollen, 1982). It was, however, open to question whether the cases studied were broad enough in their operationalization of flextime.

Regardless of specific employment schedules, some individual places of employment and kinds of jobs permit more flexibility than others. Salaried and independent professionals, for example, often have a high degree of freedom as to when they perform their duties. The responsibility for performance is on their own shoulders, and the timing is their own business. This generally gives them freedom to respond not only to the ebbs and flows of the work itself but to family and other personal demands. The results recorded by Staines and Pleck probably reflect more of this side of flexibility than enter a well-designed evaluation of a particular flextime arrangement, such as that by Bohen and Viveros-Long.

In any case, in this section, I would like to explore the evidence in the Toronto data dealing with whether one or more of the different conceptions of flexibility in employment help support the daily round of the employed mother. As Staines and Pleck put it (p. 85), "The notion here is simply that micro-adjustments can diminish the impact of macro-arrangements." This is precisely the point of this section.

One form of flexibility is the ability to work part-time. In the present sample, which did not involve stratification for employment status in any deliberate way, less than half as many of the mothers had part-time as full-time work. We have seen up to this point that part-time work gives women sufficient flexibility to engage in remunerative extra familial activity, while still performing social, commercial, and domestic chores during the daytime and acting as the traditional mater familiae during the evening (except, of course, when the part-time work is in the evening).

There are now other aspects of flexibility to explore, not losing sight of how they might apply differentially to full-time and part-time employment.[5]

First, does the work situation itself allow flexibility? Female respondents were asked whether they had much, some, or no flexibility on their job. Part-time workers are much more likely to have jobs that are structured flexibly; 36% say they have a lot of flexibility. Even in full-time situations, about a quarter of the women feel they have a lot of flexibility, and three-quarters have at least some.

For most of the respondents, it was possible to assess whether their degree of flexibility is a function of office rules and procedures or of the nature of the work itself. Among full-time workers, flexibility comes from the former in 57% of individual situations; part-time employees owe their flexibility to the nature of the work in the same 57% of cases, an exact reversal. Flexibility has more of a price, though, for the part-time employees; as they are more likely to be paid wages than salary, more of them lose pay when, for example, they take a child to the doctor than do women working full-time.

A second question has to do with variations to traditional hours of employment. There were many variations to the standard working week, which 56.8% of the employed women still followed. These variations include weekday evenings (3.5%), one or more weekend days (1.3%), shift work (4.8%), staggered days (29.8%). Due to the variety of alternatives and the small n of each, comparisons were made between those working on standard weekday nine-to-five schedules and those not (a very rough kind of comparison). As might be expected, part-time workers are much more likely to be situated in jobs without the standard schedules. More than three-quarters of them are on nontraditional hours, with the reverse true for full-time employees.

The underlying question, however, is the impact of the two kinds of flexibility on full- and part-time employees.

First, with respect to the amount of time spent traveling during the day, flexible work schedules, regardless of how defined, are associated with less travel time. Those working the standard weekday average 87.6 minutes a day traveling, compared to 69.2 minutes for those with nonstandard schedules. Such a difference is not simply a function of the full-time vs. part-time difference. Full-time workers travel 18 minutes a day less if on a nonstandard schedule (88–70 minutes), while part-time workers save 15 minutes (82–67 minutes).

Similarly, those whose work situations permit flexibility, regardless of the hours, spend somewhat less time traveling, particularly if it is the nature of the work that allows this flexibility. Those with no flexibility travel 83.6 minutes a day; those with some flexibility, 82.9 minutes; and with much flexibility, 75.6 minutes. Full-time workers whose flexibility lies in the work spend 75 minutes en route, while similar part-time workers average 4 minutes less.

What do women do with travel time saved as a function of work flexibility? Flexibility on the job enables women to carry out more household responsibilities. This is not a self-evidently positive value or one necessarily endorsed in this text, but many women, particularly those with part-time employment, find pride in the number of household responsibilities they can manage to carry out. Therefore it is consistent with findings in previous sections that the data show that the degree of flexibility among part-time workers permits an increase in the number of household chores for which the mother takes responsibility, over full-time workers. While both types of flexibility account for differences, flexibility in the job situation appears somewhat more important than whether hours are standardized, not least because the differences are found in both full-time and part-time employment. Table 9.9 shows these data.

Table 9.10 gives an idea of which household responsibilities the wife is more likely to do if her job situation is flexible, as well as the differences between full-time and part-time employment status. The biggest and most consistent differences in activity "allowed" by flexibility and its accompanying reduction in travel time are in times the mother supervises children's homework, deals with their medical and dental care, and copes with household repairs (inside and out). Part-time workers are more likely to use their flex-

TABLE 9.9

Mean Number of Household Responsibilities by Employed Mothers, by Type of Employment Hours and Flexibility of Job Structure

	Average Number of Household Responsibilities	
	Full-time Employment	Part-time Employment
Standardized hours	7.5	6.8
Non-standardized hours	7.6	8.1
Flexibility of job structure		
None	7.3	5.9
Some	7.3	7.7
Much	8.3	8.7

TABLE 9.10

Differences in the Percentage of Female Respondents Responsible for Specific Household Chores by Degree of Workplace Flexibility

Household Chores	Difference between Much and No Flexibility in Percentage Responsible for Stated Chore		Difference between Non-standard and Standard Working Hours in Percentage Responsible for Stated Chore	
	Full-time Job	Part-Time Job	Full-time Job	Part-Time Job
Cooking	6	0	(2)	6
Dishes	3	2	(15)	9
Laundry	(5)	0	(9)	0
Ironing	(3)	0	(1)	(3)
Indoor cleaning	6	(3)	(4)	(5)
Outdoor jobs	15	22	0	26
Car maintenance	2	(1)	12	6
Repairs to home	20	8	11	2
Family budget	18	15	(3)	27
Paying bills	8	15	(8)	24
Caring for baby	3	8	4	6
Supervising schoolwork	22	18	4	15
Children's medical care	9	1	4	16
Children's dental care	15	11	12	16
Grocery shopping	6	7	6	(5)
Take out garbage	8	5	(15)	(13)

ibility to assume family budgeting and bill-paying, compared to a mixed picture in this regard among full-time workers.

There are, then, some significant differences in daily activity related to flexibility at work. Does varying flexibility also affect feelings of time-pressure and tension? Again the answer is positive.

If we examine, as in Table 9.11, the busy scale for "yesterday," always a weekday, we see that it is related to both types of flexibility. Those who work standard schedules report greater feelings of time pressure than do those on other schedules (+2.3 to +1.5). These differences in working hours also carry over to the two major aspects of perceived pressure in the daily routine, time for housework and for oneself, with differences of 0.7 and 0.2, respectively, in the direction expected.

Flexibility in the job structure has the same positive effects. These are greater between the categories of no and some flexibility than between some and much. Table 9.11 shows these data as well. The effect of flexibility in the job situation is relatively large with respect to time pressures for housework and for oneself.

Data on tension show the same outcomes from work schedules, though on the more narrow (1-7) scale. The average tension for those on a standard schedule is 5.0, compared to 5.3 (greater ease) for those on nonstandard schedules. Tension at work and in travel, whether by car or public transit, vary similarly. These differences, once again, are not functions of employment status, as they hold equally within categories of full-time and part-time employment.

Data on the influence of different work situations on tension are less consistent. Average daily tension and tension at work vary as hypothesized (i.e., flexibility associated with ease). On the other hand, despite lesser travel times through flexibility, travel tension is slightly higher with more flexibility in work. This last difference, while not supportive, is extremely small.

Despite the ambiguity just noted, the overall picture emerging is that job flexibility, particularly in work scheduling, does help ease daily time pressures and tensions. Flexibility in working hours is associated with quantitative and qualitative differences in everyday life. With increased flexibility, daily life still is not a bed of roses, but pressures seem to be fewer the greater women's freedom to arrange for fulfillment of their multiple responsibilities.

TABLE 9.11

Mean Time Pressure Scores by Kinds and Degree of Flexibility in Employment

	Time Pressure Scales		
	Yesterday (+10 = most −10 = least)	Time for Housework (+10 = most −10 = least)	Time for Self (+10 = most −10 = least)
Standard hours	+2.3	+2.7	+2.7
Non-standard hours	+1.5	+2.0	+2.5
Flexibility in job structure			
None	+2.5	+3.3	+3.6
Some	+1.9	+2.5	+2.5
Much	+1.9	+1.4	+2.0

Land-Use and Timetabling

Mårtensson's work, cited in the first section of this chapter in conjunction with child care, is a prime example of a larger interest Swedish researchers have had for some years in the interrelationships of the locations and timetables of the many workplaces, stores, services, institutions, and transportation networks that help comprise a local infrastructure (Carlstein et al., 1978, vol. 2). Their work shows both logically and empirically how the extent of an individual's activity can be limited when nonemployment activities overlap too closely in time with working hours. Similarly, even with extensive timetable flexibility, dispersed land-use distributions and poor transportation can hinder the fulfillment of needs or desires for multiple activities.

Stores have increasingly recognized that fewer and fewer female shoppers are available during traditional weekday daytime hours and that being open more in the evening and on Sundays serves their customers better. Deliveries are made in the evenings and weekends, too. This, of course, raises questions in the minds of some store personnel, who may be asked to work hours that are not traditional or that clash with typical family, religious, or recreational timetables. Not all employees, however, oppose nontraditional hours; some welcome timetables (full- or part-time) that complement those of their spouse, to minimize the need for external child care or to mesh with other activities (e.g., school or second jobs). It is interesting to note that stores began to be open longer hours first in the western U.S.A., where lower population densities and dispersed land-uses make for long travel by automobile for most purposes, making a near coincidence of store hours with standard working hours frustrating to consumer and merchant alike.

Various institutions have been slower to respond. Those selling necessary services, such as banks, physicians, and bureaucracies, are likely to feel that consumers will get to them during traditional hours because they have to. Even here, though, there have been innovations in recent years, such as automatic twenty-four hour tellers, night clinics, and more. Yet, such phenomena as hospital emergency rooms' being filled with (often juvenile) flu victims in the evenings and children's failing to get expected innoculations because their parents now both work during "business hours" are signs of a disjunction between consumer need and the extent of reaction by these institutions. Even as I write this, I pick up a community newspaper with a full-page advertisement on behalf of local physicians by an area hospital. Five physicians list their hours. Two are 9:00–5:00, and one is 9:00–5:30. A fourth lists "9:00 a.m. to 5:00 p.m. with extended hours" but does not specify the latter. Only the last goes explicitly into the evening, closing at 7:00 p.m. on Mondays through Thursdays and at 6:00 p.m. on Fridays.

This study was not designed to examine in depth a number of other important aspects of urban communities. Yet the location and opening and closing hours of a number of other services and facilities clearly affect how efficiently a day can be lived.

For example, about 20% of the sample specified more flexible working hours in answer to a question (#16) about the desirability of changes in opening and closing hours. Virtually the same percentage prefers longer hours for stores in general and banks in particular, which is related to the problem addressed by flexible working hours. Just over 5% mention the need for expanded medical hours, about 1% more than want longer hours for child-care services and public facilities, respectively.

These preferences are grounded to some extent in the conditions facing the respondents. With the exception of public-facilities hours, a greater percentage of respondents that desire changes in opening and closing hours are "too busy to do all you want to do" than of those not desiring such changes; in some cases there are great differences. The exceptional case of desired change in public-facilities hours is made primarily by women without jobs, whose time pressures are lower; support for change in job, bank, child-care, and medical hours comes, as expected, from those with jobs. Support for longer, later store hours comes equally from all categories of respondent.

Regarding distance to facilities (question 17), those desiring change want them closer. What they want closer reflects somewhat different considerations than those underlying opening and closing hours. Almost a quarter of the sample wants recreation facilities closer, virtually regardless of employment status. Another 10% each want child-care and public facilities closer; desire for the former reflects employment, while the latter does not.

There is also confirming evidence for this set of preferences. Respondents currently living closer to such facilities as food stores, variety stores, drug stores, banks, public-transit stops, and the like report consistently lower busy-scale scores — on both the periods and sectors of time pressure.

In short, the various sections of this chapter suggest that a number of external aspects of the community mediate in part, for better and worse, the relationships between obligations and responsibilities, on the one hand, and activities and subjective outcomes, on the other.[6]

Notes

1 Nonetheless, men tend also to work in the zone in which they live. About as many men who live in the outer suburbs also work in one of them as work in the central city and inner suburbs combined. Men whose home and work are both in the outer suburbs have lower than average distances to work, 6.7 kilometers.

2 Canadian income-tax regulations do not permit deductions for interest paid on loans for personal goods.

3 The word *reluctance* is chosen because almost all respondents live within a few blocks of at least a bus stop and hence accessibility to the TTC's dense, interconnecting network.

4 "The better way" according to TTC advertising — but only if you have a choice.

5 Sherry Ahrentzen took considerable initiative in organizing this analysis.

6 In addition to the several external supports mentioned up to this point, social support from other persons could be mentioned. This lies somewhere between the microworld of the family and more formal world of the community. Chapter 7, for example, showed that single mothers receive somewhat more extrafamilial support than do women in two-parent families. There is, however, no evidence from the data that the nature of support the respondents receive at present makes major positive contributions to their daily round. The various forms of mutual aid we explored do not vary systematically with the time-pressure measures.

10
Summer Vacation: How Free (and for Whom)?

In the previous chapter, we went beyond the undifferentiated picture of the full-time work schedule as a monolithic constant. The same must now be done for the weeks and months of the year. To this point, it has appeared that the whole year is made up of working weeks, schools, child care, and weekends. This is no different from the view one gets from other research on the subject, with few exceptions (cf. Harper and Richards, 1979; Michelson, 1971). For many, however, there are great changes in one or more of the factors of the daily routine when school is not in session — particularly during the long summer vacation.

What do mothers do during the summer to compensate for the hours when their children would be cared for in school? Do women alter their work situations? What are the differences in activity and time pressure?

To address such questions, a subsample of the original respondents was taken at random. Seventy-eight families were interviewed again during July and August 1980. They completed time-budgets just as before, and the mothers also answered a short list of relatively straightforward questions about changes in domestic conditions that might have occurred as a function of the season.

Differences for Children

Summer conditions are certainly different for children of school age. A glance at Table 10.1 confirms the obvious, that older children (i.e., seven to fourteen in the sample) shed tremendous amounts of school time, when comparing summer to school-term weekdays. "Obligatory activities" show the same change, since school makes up an overwhelming percentage of that kind of time-use among children. The question is what they gain instead. The greatest gain is as expected — active, usually outdoor, play (up to 126 minutes

TABLE 10.1

Average Minutes on a Summer Weekday a Subsample of Children
Spend on Selected Activities (and Differences from School Term
Time Distributions for the Same Children), by Age

	Age			
	0 - 6		7 - 14	
	Minutes	(Change in Minutes)	Minutes	(Change in minutes)
School/Child care	64	(-89)	25	(-300)
House work	12	(+2)	34	(+23)
Child care	—	—	0	(-4)
Shopping	57	(+29)	26	(+19)
Personal care/sleep	808	(-98)	785	(+45)
Lessons	17	(+17)	44	(+44)
Social activity	51	(+34)	49	(+29)
Active pastimes	286	(+95)	250	(+126)
Passive pastimes	68	(-19)	157	(+24)
Travel	52	(+13)	74	(+23)
by foot or bicycle	(12)	(-3)	(26)	(-5)
by public transportation	(2)	(+1)	(2)	(-1)
by car	(38)	(+15)	(46)	(+28)
All obligatory activities	80	(-87)	59	(-281)
Number of respondents	48		38	

a day). One would not necessarily expect to see passive leisure increase, in view of improvements in the weather, but the overall loss of obligatory activities leaves a sizable vacuum that passive activities help to fill. School-age children also do more housework during the summer (+ 19 minutes, or 271%). They spend more time taking care of themselves (+ 45 minutes), taking lessons (+ 44 minutes), and in social activity (+ 29 minutes). They travel more by car but less by foot, bicycle, and public transportation.

The younger cohort of children (those aged six or younger) also decrease their obligatory activities, which in this case include school and child care. The mean decrease of 89 minutes is not so great as for the older children, because the younger group is not so uniformly engaged in a regular program. The activities gained are thus not so great as for the older children, but many follow the same pattern — leading to much greater similarity between younger and older children in their summer use of time than during the winter. There appear to be two exceptions, however. The younger children substantially decrease their time in personal-care activities (by 90 mintes) and in passive pastimes (by 19 minutes).

Differences in younger children's time-use according to mothers' employment status remain, though these are not so great as during the school year. Children whose mothers have full-time jobs are in school or child care 148 minutes, compared to 97 minutes if the mothers work part-time and 7 if they have no job. The only other activity with almost exactly complementary figures is personal care, including sleep, with 753, 802, and 886 minutes, respectively. As before, such differences among the older children are minimal.

Mothers' Adaptations

What does this pattern of children's time-use mean for the parents? Few mothers formally altered their positions in the work world. Five women decreased from full-time to part-time work; two went the opposite way, and one housewife took on a full-time job—of seventy-seven reporting this information.

For the summer season, however, women with part-time jobs were more likely both to take holidays and to lower the number of hours worked. Half the part-time workers took time off during the summer, compared to 30% of those working full-time. These percentages are somewhat greater than those found in a study by Harper and Richards (1979, p. 292), but the differences by employment status are consistent. Similarly, 61% of part-time workers lowered the number of hours worked per week (most commonly by from one to nine hours, but some for greater amounts); only 19% of full-time workers did so.

The mothers do not see that taking care of children is affected, on balance, by an increase or decrease in the amount of external help available for this purpose during the summer. In fact, 70% do not feel any services are less available during the summer; 54% don't feel any are more available. Respondents noting changes in external support identified no single form as disappearing, but just under 30% say relatives are more available in summer.

The single biggest change in their children's activity that mothers themselves observe in the summer is more outdoor play. Housewives, who spend many cold months of the year "cooped up" with younger children, are much more likely to cite this difference (80% of them) than married women working part-time (50%) or full-time (47%). Nearly as many parents (57%) say that children make more excursions and visits during the summer, and another quarter send one or more away to camp or cottage. While in town, children are said to spend more time with friends (26.4%), take more lessons and courses (29.2%), have summer jobs (11.1%), stay home more (13.9%), and, in general, have fewer routines (38.9%). Not least, 23.6% report an increase in parent-child activities. Taking lessons or courses and staying at home are more prevalent among children whose mothers have full-time jobs, and excursions and visits are much more common when the mothers work part-time; otherwise the summer changes are the same, regardless of the mothers' employment status.

On their part, the parents report more time in the summer with their children (50%), planning for them (22.9%), supervising them (18.8%), and driving them (10.4%). Much more planning and supervision is characteristic of the mothers with jobs (full- and part-time) than of those without jobs. About a third of the parents report their personal time more restricted during the summer, but virtually the same percentage say it is freer then—both without variation by employment status.

Mothers' general outlook in view of what they and their children change or do not change during summer school holidays is, on balance, that summers are easier for parents than winters. Just over half (52.6%) find them easier, 26.8% see no change, and only 20.4% deem them harder. Women who take time off from work are significantly more likely to feel summers are easier than those not taking time off (62.5% vs. 37.5%). Half the working mothers who do not take time off see no change in child-care difficulty in summers, compared to only 19% of those taking holiday time.

Summer Time-Use by Parents

So far, this chapter has dealt with how children's lives change during the summer, what mothers do to take care of these changes, and how they view summer child care in light of their own adjustments. Because so much of this book has been on women's use of time and on its outcomes, let us also examine women's time-use and pressures during the summer holidays. One should keep in mind that time-budget data do not reflect time taken off from work and devoted to other activities as an all-or-nothing phenomenon. These data average what is observed on the day in question among the many persons in a category. For example, if 20% of a cohort are on vacation on a given day, the time change may be dramatic for them, but it reduces the minutes-worked figure in the category by only 20%.

In any case, regardless of absolute time-use statistics, it is important to note that there is great individual consistency from school term to summer. While people's own routines may change during summer conditions, what they do relative to what others do stays reasonably constant.[1] Table 10.2 shows the correlation coefficients of time devoted to selected activities by individuals during the school term and summer interviews. Most correlations for women are positive, high, and statistically significant. The exceptions are minutes devoted to active pastimes ($r = +.02$), clearly a function of time and weather; organizational activities ($r = +.03$), a minor time-use which

TABLE 10.2

Correlation Coefficients Describing Relationship of the Amount of Time
Individual Respondents Spent on Specific Categories of Activity
During the Weekdays Sampled in the School Term and Summer Surveys

	Women (n=75)		Men (n=50)	
	r =	p =	r =	p =
Paid Work	+.55	.000	+.32	.009
Household jobs	+.35	.001	+.55	.000
Child Care/Contact	+.44	.000	+.09	.253
Shopping	+.22	−.023	+.58	.000
Personal care/sleep	+.19	.046	+.27	.024
Education	+.40	.000	—	—
Organizational Activity	−.03	.395	−.02	.456
Social Activity	+.23	.019	+.15	.134
Active Pastimes	+.02	.404	+.36	.004
Passive Pastimes	+.25	.015	+.40	.002
Travel	+.18	.060	+.03	.408
All Obligatory Activities	+.34	.001	+.26	.029

virtually ceases during the summer; and travel ($r = +.18$),[2] whose changes vary according to employment status.

Men are nearly as consistent, with two notable exceptions. Their time devoted to child care and contact does not reflect consistency from school term to summer ($r = +.09$). In contrast, active leisure does ($r = +.36$); men are not so dependent on the season as women in the relative time they devote to sports and similar activities.

Turning to absolute amounts of time (and changes from winter to summer), let us look at them activity by activity, as in Table 10.3. Since this is a small subsample of the original respondents, the number in each employment-status category is much smaller than before, undoubtedly leading to considerably more random variation in the time-use means. One must, therefore, treat the figures with a degree of tolerance. Nonetheless, there are logical and relevant results. Wives are more likely to reduce their working hours, take time off, or both during the summer than are their husbands. In-

TABLE 10.3

Mean Minutes on a Summer Weekday a Subsample of Husbands and Wives Spend on Selected Activities
(Differences from Winter Time Distributions for the Same Respondents),
by Wives' Employment Status

	Wives			Husbands		
Activity	Full-time Job (n = 21)	Part-time Job (n = 12)	No Job (n = 23)	Full-time Job (n = 19)	Part-time Job (n = 10)	No Job (n = 21)
Work	305 (−118)	52 (−70)	—	374 (−51)	505 (−33)	462 (−85)
Household jobs	158 (+40)	194 (−56)	233 (−41)	47 (−26)	45 (+26)	53 (−17)
Child Care/Contact	49 (−5)	63 (−33)	123 (−42)	17 (−12)	21 (−15)	21 (+8)
Shopping	24 (−1)	62 (−10)	54 (+25)	12 (+1)	35 (−10)	16 (−25)
Personal Care/Sleep	603 (−2)	651 (+63)	633 (+18)	627 (+44)	582 (+37)	561 (+9)
Organizational Activity	0 (−9)	0 (−30)	0 (0)	0 (−21)	0 (0)	14 (+14)
Social Activity	62 (+9)	93 (+60)	60 (+34)	38 (+21)	25 (+13)	44 (+37)
Active Pastimes	10 (+1)	61 (+16)	63 (+32)	28 (+16)	42 (+40)	24 (+6)
Passive Pastimes	154 (+55)	188 (+86)	183 (−8)	176 (+44)	122 (−17)	141 (+30)
Travel	58 (−26)	79 (+4)	46 (+4)	91 (−4)	75 (−22)	113 (+44)
Walking/Bicycle	4 (0)	6 (−16)	13 (+6)	1 (−4)	0 (−48)	7 (−1)
Public Transit	18 (−3)	7 (−13)	3 (−1)	6 (−1)	0 (−6)	8 (+3)
Automobile	36 (−23)	66 (+33)	30 (−1)	84 (+1)	75 (+32)	98 (−2)
Obligatory Activity	512 (−82)	308 (−160)	372 (−81)	437 (−89)	571 (−21)	537 (−94)

deed, the men reducing their work-time the most are those whose wives do not have jobs themselves. While we have already seen that women working part-time are more likely than those with full-time jobs to reduce their workloads during the summer, the average amount of change is greater among the full-time workers.

Women continue to do the bulk of household work. Indeed, a major part (40 minutes) of the time full-time workers gain from work during the summer is rechanneled into housework; their husbands lower their domestic commitments by 26 minutes. Part-time workers lessen their housework, while their husbands increase their share. Housewives decrease housework, as do their husbands. The net result is a narrowing of the differences in housework time by women's employment status during the summer, though the remaining differences are still in the same direction; the husbands even out almost entirely.

Despite children's freedom from school, all categories of women spend less time during the summer on child care. Housewives save the most time (42 minutes), those with part-time jobs next (33 minutes), and full-time workers, the least (5 minutes). Differences in child-care time remain large, despite the narrowing. Husbands of employed women decrease their child-care time, in contrast to those of nonemployed women.

Total time children spend with their parents (not necessarily the parents' primary activities) is fascinating to view. Table 10.4 shows these data. Children under seven spend close to 500 minutes a day during the summer with their mothers and 200 with their fathers, whatever the mother's employment status. As expected, children seven to fourteen average less time with both. However, during the summer, these older children spend time with both parents in direct relationship to their usual degree of employment. In other

TABLE 10.4

Mean Weekday Time in Minutes Children Spend with Their Mother and Father During the Summer, by Age of Child and Mother's Employment Status

Mother's Employment Status	Ages 0 - 6 With: Mother	Father	n =	Ages 7 - 14 With: Mother	Father	n =
Full-time job	485	250	(14)	345	279	(16)
Part-time job	509	188	(10)	279	78	(7)
No employment	480	199	(24)	126	71	(15)

words, older children of full-time employed mothers spend the most time during summer weekdays with both mother and father (345 and 279 minutes). Older children whose mothers work part-time are next (278 and 78 minutes), and older children whose mothers are not employed spend the least time in their mothers' and fathers' company (126 and 71 minutes).

Summers give most people more time to care for themselves. Sleep, not specified as a line item in Table 10.3, is not found to be relatively low among full-time workers (471 minutes); those working part-time, with 445 minutes recorded, lag behind them and the housewives (481 minutes).

Social activities increase for all, though least for full-time employed women. Relative equality in increases between men and women probably reflect joint activities.

Time for active pastimes also increases across the board, but again those with full-time jobs do the least. Devotion of time by the employed women to passive activities, though, gains greatly—virtually to the point of equality with housewives, who lose a little of this time-use in the summer.

Women with full-time jobs, who traveled most during the winter but lost the most worktime during the summer, also lose nearly half their daily travel time. The other women gain slightly; men by and large still travel more.

The net result of the various changes is that most men and women devote less time to obligatory activity during the summer than during the school term. Men and women lose about the same amount, though the category with the greatest time saving and the least obligatory activity time during the summer is that of women with part-time jobs. In any event, these data provide some factual support of women's views that summer holidays tend not to provoke child-care crises.

Personal Outcomes

Are these views supported by feelings of time pressure during the summer? The measures of time pressure confirm again that summers are somewhat easier to manage. Busy scales that deal with the immediate time period, "yesterday" and "last week," indicate considerably less pressure than those relating to periods which are more typical (e.g., "average week"), which the respondents have not been lulled into forgetting.

Table 10.5 compares, for example, the last-week and the average-week busy scales for the married respondents in the summer survey (the single are too few, but do not distort previous patterns). This table shows somewhat less perceived pressure for the previous week (a summer week) than for the average week among employed mothers, but somewhat more among the housewives.

Thus, the fact of greater free time school-age children have in summer is not translated into additional hassles for the employed mother. More plan-

TABLE 10.5

Married Women's Perceived Time-Pressures for Last Week
(During Summer) and the Average Week, by Employment Status

Time Pressure

1. Last Week (During Summer)

Employment Status	High (+6 to +10)	Medium (+1 to +5)	Equilibrium between Time and Activity (0)	Ease (Too much Time, -1 to -10)	n =
Full-Time Job	18.2	60.0	18.2	4.5	(22)
Part-Time Job	7.1	50.0	28.6	14.3	(14)
No employment	19.0	38.1	42.9	0.0	(21)

2. Average Week

Full-Time Job	18.2	77.2	4.5	0.0	(22)
Part-Time Job	7.1	57.0	21.4	14.3	(14)
No Employment	14.3	33.3	52.4	0.0	(21)

ning may be necessary to arrange for this period of the year, but these data indicate that steps parents take (particularly mothers with part-time jobs) are relatively successful in making summers logistically viable.

Notes

1 This is parallel to the results showing that external supports mitigate but do not substantially change employment-related levels of time pressure and tension.

2 Reflecting the lesser size of the subsample, $p = .06$.

11
Emergent Implications for Policy and Practice

Many of the findings in previous chapters cry out for remedial action. They show that maternal employment may be a rational activity, according to some societal demands, but that society has not sufficiently recognized and dealt with the situations that accompany maternal employment—a cultural lag. One of our respondents expressed this notion clearly:

> To me, the coldest thing of all is taking a woman into the employment field, then ignoring the fact that she has other pressures from society to be a mother and a homemaker and a cleaning lady. Equality at work is one thing, but the total demands haven't changed.

With so many mothers employed, the world is aware of many aspects of the problematique around it. Great numbers of solutions have been proposed, many implemented in a preliminary way. Given, however, a society that has largely organized its traditional terms of employment and public infrastructure on the assumption that the public and work worlds are composed of physically and economically healthy males, able to work full-time (or more), with wives to care for their needs and those of their children, it would be premature to say that this society has sufficiently reorganized its practices to give appropriate support to the needs of such other emergent subsectors of the population as employed mothers.

Therefore, in this chapter I would like to take one inferential step away from the literal interpretation of our results, turning to what they mean for policy and practice. At present, this hardly requires great originality, considering the number of innovative responses to maternal employment already discussed. Nonetheless, believing society can benefit from evidence of the directions of its eventual adaptation, I must direct the weight of the current evidence to those areas of policy and practice in which, I believe, it is most commanding and potentially fruitful.

Both the initial perspective of this study and the variety of its implications at the intrafamilial and external levels of context, within differing categories of employment and marital status, suggest that no single solution can be advanced for every situation. Different situations call for different solutions. Furthermore, a number of the results, particularly in Chapter 9, show that individual ameliorative practices do not by themselves significantly change a complex, interactive situation. Each may help, if appropriately thought out and implemented, but a complex problematique requires the simultaneous, joint application of adaptive measures to improve the underlying situation more than marginally.

My focus here is on aspects of the external context. This hardly means that I consider intrafamilial dynamics unimportant. As long sections of this book have documented, lack of adaptation by other family members contributes directly to behavioral obligations and pressures, which are then either addressed or compounded by external factors. But pragmatic suggestions for changes in policies and practices find their way into families only indirectly. Arrangements husbands and wives work out in the privacy of their own homes and lives may change, but not by external fiat. Adaptation occurs when the parties involved understand its desirability. Huge changes in birth-control practice, for example, occurred within a relatively short period of history, once technology allowed, despite culture-based traditions. At present, results from other studies have suggested a trend of ideological changes concerning maternal employment and its ramifications within the family. Behavioral changes are obviously slower, but they are not inconceivable.

Pragmatic steps apply more feasibly outside the family, even though the territory is more clouded. The community context involves very many disparate interests. The fact that they join in creating a living environment does not mean that they originated or are managed with that in mind. Sometimes a public authority can step in to attempt to avoid practices that are considered to produce excessively negative results. For example, labor laws regulate the length of working hours. Planning processes and zoning laws prevent—or are supposed to prevent—juxtapositions of land use thought to be dangers to health, welfare, and safety. Blue laws are sometimes established, partly to protect the sabbath of some constituents, but also to prevent some businesses from undercutting others through longer or different hours. Nonetheless, there has been very little comprehensive coordination of attempts to fine-tune the timing and spacing of enterprises in the various sectors throughout the community in the interest of optimizing opportunity, ease, and efficiency in the everyday lives and routines of rank-and-file citizens.

Although this manuscript is being completed in 1984, I do not have Big Brother (or Sister) in mind. The challenge facing democratic societies is how to mobilize the organization and activities of many people and interests *voluntarily,* in ways that benefit the majority, without jeopardizing the rights of

156 *Emergent Implications for Policy and Practice*

minorities. Recognizing objectives, observing empirical evidence, and voluntary cooperation on behalf of an explicit set of mutual interests are not totalitarian processes. Indeed, regularly budgeted governmental programs are not, in and of themselves, solutions to a problematique like maternal employment. Adjustments to hours, more flexible use of personnel, and a more judicious selection of locations, for example, require little or none of the downward dispensation of money, services, or controls people customarily associate with assistance to given sectors of the population. Making a community function more efficiently for its citizens in large part depends on their interactions and their economic activities.

Today, however, employed women are a large and growing minority, for whom relevant measures have been downplayed by those forming the basic assumptions about how community and its many activities are organized and orchestrated. A number of suggestions derived from the previously discussed results follow. These address different concerns and apply differentially to employed mothers and other people, but they remain part of an overall community context, deserving comprehensive coordination.[1]

Job Sharing

Our results find many advantages for women in part-time employment. It enables them to arrange various responsibilities more easily within the confines of the working day, with less time pressure and tension in the process, and with better opportunity to take care of children, particularly young ones. Part-time jobs enable more flexibility on the job and make summer adjustments easier.

Moreover, there is no reason to ascribe part-time work as beneficial just for women. Presumably, the same underlying dynamics hold equally well for men who are faced with a similar set of obligations. Husbands and wives themselves have to settle household division of labor. The current discussion of part-time employment for women reflects how respondents report things are, not necessarily what they could be.

A final table, Table 11.1, shows how very content women with part-time jobs are with their decision to undertake employment, even granting the lower level of economic need behind their decision. Workaholics show the same level of contentment. Both levels are markedly higher than those for people with relative normal full-time loads.

This does not mean that part-time employment is optimal as it now stands. I noted in Chapter 9 a number of disadvantages typically faced by those with part-time jobs. Job sharing is a way to achieve the benefits of part-time work without losing the perquisites of full-time work. It is the chance for two or more persons to divide a regular, continuing full-time job, at regular salary levels and benefits (prorated by proportion of the time worked). The initia-

TABLE 11.1

Women's Hours of Employment a Week and Contentment With Decision to Work

Job Hours Per Week	Contentment With Decision to Work			
	Discontent	Neutral	Content	n =
50 and over	0.0%	18.2	81.8	(11)
40 - 49	11.5%	32.2	56.3	(87)
30 - 39	12.9%	27.7	59.4	(101)
20 - 29	3.6%	21.4	75.0	(28)
Less than 20	0.0%	16.7	83.3	(48)

tive for job sharing can be taken by either the employees or by employers, provided it is acceptable to both. The workers obviously have to agree on their respective hours and days. Employers are often leery of this kind of arrangement, as they may be of some other flextime arrangements, because of its unfamiliarity and because of concerns about the potential administrative difficulties and costs (cf. Meltz et al., 1981; Olmstead, 1979). But there is ample evidence not only that employers can manage this alternative, but that it more than pays them back in terms of the productivity of highly motivated, relatively unhassled employees (Commission of Inquiry into Part-time Work, 1983; Meier, 1979; Meltz et al., 1981; Nollen et al., 1978).

Advocates of job sharing in the interests of women with children, among others, are not advocating work sharing in the larger sense, which is an across-the-board tool to shrink the working time of those who want full-time employment. The latter kind of sharing is often a temporary response to market conditions and to potential unemployment. Rather, as an ameliorative, long-run practice, job sharing should be a regular option for those to whom it represents the best compromise among competing pressures — wthout exploitative aspects.

More General Flexibility

However helpful job sharing (and the minimum notion of part-time employment) might be for some persons, many if not most people — men and women alike — will probably still want or need to maintain full-time jobs. Our data show that a certain amount of flexibility is already present in many such jobs, and it is clear that innovative practices are increasingly directed to that objective.

The results here indicate that effective forms of flexibility in employment not only make daily activities more efficient but also result in measurable improvements in personal outcomes for the women involved. Therefore, we urge support for flexibility in employment that allows the individual worker to key adjustments to personal family needs. The types of flexibility most likely to redound to the benefit of the employer in terms of productivity are those creating an impact on the problematic nature of the individual employee's daily routine or ability to deal with unexpected domestic crises, rather than those that "merely" attempt to smooth out the load on the public infrastructure. While women are in a situation which flexibility can often tangibly assist, the same beneficial effects should accrue to men as well. The intensity of a problematic situation within one group hardly implies that it is not shared, though perhaps to a lesser degree, by others.

Research should accompany various attempts and experiments at flexibility, to help assess

a. who benefits and who does not from each, and
b. which sources of flexibility are compatible within organizations that allow variability in the types of flexibility.

Comprehensive Response to the Needs of Families with Young Children

One of the most striking series of results deals with how much impact a mother's employment has on the daily lives of very young children. Maternal employment alters young children's activities, contacts, and loci. Employed mothers of young children have far more time-consuming obligatory activities at home, and their commutes to work are stretched out by extra travel to child-care services with less than optimal locations.

In general, public services and practices are oriented much more toward school-aged children. The relatively standard daily timetables of older children are a function of services provided by both the public and private sectors. Even within the younger cohort, day care for preschoolers is much more readily available than is infant care. The vestigal public attitude that mothers of young children should stay home to care for babies runs up against the reality of the number who do not, not least in response to economic conditions.

CHILD CARE LOCATION

A first point is simple and unoriginal, indeed without basis in the results reported here. But it needs to be said in any such discussion. There are not sufficient places in child-care facilities for the number of young children whose mothers have outside jobs.

Our emphasis spotlights the less than optimal location of such institutions as do exist. If travel tension is positively related to the extra distance the child-care drop-off adds to the work trip, then the question becomes how to reduce this distance. Insofar as home day care is (usually) already proximate, grandparents' residential locations are not generally subject to public policy, and day-care centers are typically the farthest away, the focus swings to this last child-care setting. Three better alternative locations are

1. at natural transportation nodes,
2. close to home, and
3. close to work.

The first alternative obviously depends on the structure of a given metropolitan area. Given the diversity of workplaces and the fact that public transportation in Toronto is most fully utilized by suburban women who work downtown, placing day-care institutions at transportation nodes seems appropriate mainly for this particular category of employed mother. Even then, land-use conflicts would create difficulties at or near many transportation nodes. Finding appropriate, accessible locations there for day-care centers might be hard but not impossible. Fox (1978) suggests a variation: centrally located depots where children can be dropped off, to be sorted out and transported to their day-care locations, then picked up later.

Child-care locations near home are not as difficult. Churches and schools often have facilities that would require far less work to make them appropriate than it would take to build centers from scratch. More difficult but again not impossible are matters of organization, jurisdiction, financing, and zoning. Local schools, indeed, are being abandoned. Granted that this is happening in neighborhoods without great numbers of children, it is still not too much to expect that existing school buildings could be put to a variety of community uses, one of which is child care.[2] Indeed, a school need not be abandoned to be suitable for day care; rooms can be put to good day-care use as they become surplus for their original purposes.

Workplace day care, although not yet widespread, has been receiving increasing attention. At least one department of the U.S. government (Housing and Urban Development) has its own center, and the House of Representatives, the Senate, and the World Bank are about to follow (Weaver, 1984). In situations where employers sincerely want to attract certain categories of female employees, it has been shown that this is a highly effective measure. For example, nurses have been attracted to hospitals where nurses are in short supply by the provision of day-care services. In other situations, potential employees are not in as great demand, and employers are less motivated to experiment with something that requires space and, depending on the arrangement, at least a minimum measure of commitment and responsibility.

HEALTH-CARE TIMETABLING

Adaptation in provision of children's health care to recognize the social ecology of maternal employment could only provide benefits. Younger children need more frequent preventative medical attention and immunizations. Congenital problems require identification. Development requires monitoring. While prepaid medical insurance can remove some economic barriers to medical care, particularly if it is universal and comprehensive, logistical difficulties increasingly stand in the way of preventative medical care for young children. The services these children need are normally offered during standard working hours; pediatricians with evening hours for well-baby care are the exception rather than the rule. Clinics and emergency wards have recognized the need to offer immunization and other preventative services when children come their way under acute conditions. This reflects a need to catch up and repair neglected pediatrics, rather than being a viable long-run mechanism. If both parents work standard days and lack sufficient flexibility and if the timetabling of regular pediatric services discourages their use, then children are simply less likely to be seen and to get their shots. This is reflected in the recent resurgence of some of the formerly common but now preventable childhood diseases.

Flexibility in employment is helpful in this regard, but adaptation should not be the responsibility of users of medical services alone, many of whom are not in a position to be optimally flexible. One straightforward answer is a reorganization of the timetabling of pediatric services. Individual practitioners who work evenings should not be expected to work all day, too. The total number of potential patients need not be increased, only their appearance for preventative health care and the time of day this happens.[3] Group practices can and do cover the different times of day more flexibly.

Extended Maternal Leave: an Alternative

While my emphasis is on means to make maternal employment logistically more viable, alternative approaches to the problematique are not only possible but perhaps more desirable for some persons. There is no lack of empirical evidence of mothers' time-consuming obligations when their children are very young, of the importance of these years in children's development, and of the paucity of external supports. Career and economic demands very frequently supersede the difficulties of these years. Nonetheless, some women may prefer to be home during the early years but fear that they will be unable to return to the same job, the same caliber of job, or indeed any at all. In this situation, there should be the option for extended leave, with the job protected (provided the position remains). Shorter-term maternal leaves are more common, but address more the immediate medical and emotional needs after birth, rather than the longer-range logistical questions of the first few years. This is a virtual no-cost solution, considering that the employer gets back a worker with increased loyalty who needs minimal retraining.

Others go farther and argue that, when governments provide subsidies for child-care services for those who prefer continuous employment, equivalent funds should be paid for specified periods to those who prefer to stay home and take care of their own children. Sweden, for example, has a complex system that allows approximately nine months' subsidized parental leave, which can be split in any way desired between the two parents, over about the first five years of a child's life. Some of the Eastern European countries that pioneered various supports for employed mothers are now providing financial incentives for them to stay home for the first several years.[4]

Travel

Transportation considerations address the dynamic side of the problem. Not only are there many relevant aspects, but they vary according to what a given person needs or wants to do and where these activities are located (i.e., the essentially static side). For example, our analysis showed that means of travel can be understood only in terms of the activities they are supposed to facilitate and the kinds of people who do them, both alone and together. Among women, for example, family trips and work trips involve very different considerations at present. Transportation systems therefore may do some things very well, and for some people, but not other things, or for other people.

One typical approach to transit systems is to assess who their main users are and then to implement ways of serving them. In the current study, women — particularly but not exclusively suburbanites — with extensive job commitments in central locations were found to be main users of a centrally focused, relatively efficient subway system. Suburban buses are a helpful part of this system, to the extent that they feed into the subway system. While many employed women travel this way because it seems the best solution under a complex of circumstances, their experience of it, as part of the day's toughest transition involving little perceived choice, might be improved partly through increasing its effectiveness in cost and time and partly through response to the kind of situation these travelers undergo. The latter response might include a "softening" of the travel experience, as airlines try to do for a different segment of traveler. Public transit is certainly a utility and must meet utilitarian criteria, yet more attention to waiting areas, personnel attitudes, and colors, for example, might induce a greater measure of serenity into an otherwise tension-filled experience.

Monthly passes, which permit unlimited stops, starts, and transfers, promote more flexible linking of travel functions on the public-transit system and hence make the daily routine more flexible.

Some women with very little choice in travel take only suburban buses to work. While under many of the same pressures as other women, they also have to deal with slower, less frequent vehicles, often transferring from one to another. Intermediate-transit systems (e.g., smaller trolley-type trains on exclusive rights of way) can help speed up such trips, assuming the existence of a suitable number of nodes within suburbia and the ability to build such systems.[5] There are, however, no easy solutions to the demand for fast, frequent service to low-density areas without enormous cost. Shelters and benches recognize the experience of the suburban bus rider. In addition, I do not think it untoward to recognize the situation of this residual user of a large transit system—the one using only suburban buses—by making available a reduced-rate bus pass, for monthly trips only by suburban bus. It would be a second-class fare for essentially second-class service.

The fact that some segments of the population do not now use public transit is no reason for their needs to be ignored in transit planning. Public transportation not only fills a need in the lives of many employed women, but it provides an option to their husbands and to many other employed women, whose choice of travel by car would be less real and hence experienced with more tension without this option. Such a choice is extremely important in times of dangerous weather, fuel shortages, or national emergency. One major segment of nonuser was shown to be the family with children: the children themselves before they are well into school and any combination of parents and children. While there are logical reasons mothers prefer to travel by car with their children, is it beyond the imagination for public transportation to address their needs and preferences? This question is especially salient among housewives without a driver's license or access to a car during the working day. Are there not latent trips that simply do not now materialize, to people's detriment?[6]

Two nontransit-oriented solutions to the suburban problem must also be recognized. One is a greater emphasis on higher densities and integrated land uses within the suburbs, which would permit greater access to everyday needs without the formality and expense of vehicles or transit systems, but would help make public transit more feasible for other travel needs. Much evidence in the current study, some anecdotal, supports such an approach. The other involves an extension in time (i.e., through longer hours) of needed land uses and services, so that the one family car can be more efficiently used for noncommuting purposes within the outer reaches of the weekday.

Time, Space, and Collective Well-Being

Two threads running consistently through this analysis and discussion are time and space. Their structure and organization are essential to an understanding of the freedoms and constraints in everyday life. Those concerned with collective well-being, i.e., that built from the experiences of many individuals, must give more explicit attention to these dimensions in decisions that are now taken relatively independently by the various components of society. At present, planners consider only some aspects of spatial interrelationships, and virtually no one deals comprehensively with time. Yet the goal is at once simple and noble: expanding individual freedoms, which have been logistically restricted by the de facto organization of the community.

A vital step toward this goal is intensive study of the complex interaction of opening and closing hours in terms of who has what fixed time commitments and how well they mesh with the current and potential needs for other activities by significant sectors of the population. There are already several precedents for this type of knowledge, but these have not as yet proceeded beyond model-building. Our communities must indeed become laboratories for the cultivation of contexts that offer the potential for more pleasant and efficient lives.

Our daily routines are not molded by supreme engineers. They are a function of what we have to do, what we choose to do, and how well we are able to do these in the world that exists. The last of these, our community context, can be made to provide more opportunity and less constraint.

* * * *

At the least, we must recognize at the outset that the pattern and load of responsibilities put upon and taken by women have changed. The day when mother could and would do everything for herself, her children, and the household between nine and five on weekdays is now gone. The question is how the community can adapt to reflect and meet the altered needs of so many of its residents. Cultural lags are fixtures of history. Our recognition of the current lag, with its clear and present dysfunctions, requires us to cooperate and innovate in the design and implementation of solutions.

Notes

1 It is a legitimate question how much one should dare to generalize from data gathered in one location, Metropolitan Toronto. Every setting is in some way unique, and Toronto is unusual in its ethnic mix, its recent economic and developmental vitality, its relative social harmony, and its excellent public-transportation system. Nonetheless, virtually all our findings about the dynamics of time-use, which parallel studies elsewhere in the world, indicate the same results. Even a comparison of these daily-travel relationships with a sample in Orange County, California (Michelson, 1983), despite enormous differences in urban structure, climate, female participation in the full-time labor force, and access to automobiles, shows similarities with the Toronto data in the distribution and number of daily trips between men and women, in the total amount of daily travel time, and in weekday-weekend trade-offs in shopping. All in all, I feel that the phenomena behind the suggestions presented here transcend local idiosyncracies. What anyone chooses to do, though, should surely reflect the realities of the particular situation. Furthermore, my list is hardly exhaustive. If the results of the study suggest additional lines of action to any reader, so much the better. Ultimately, the success of any adaptive measure or combination of measures is an empirical question.

2 Senior-citizen use is also neither uncommon nor mutually exclusive with use for child care.

3 Professionals who enjoy a leisurely dinner out at night, thanks to an array of cooks and waiters providing them service, might understand appreciation for reciprocal evening services.

4 For some European initiatives in supporting maternal employment, see Kamerman (1980).

5 One is currently under construction in Metropolitan Toronto.

6 An older book, called *The Split-Level Trap,* comes to mind (Gordon, Gordon, and Gunther, 1961).

References

Aas, Dagfinn. "Designs for Large-Scale Time-Use Studies of the 24-Hour Day." In *It's about Time,* edited by Z. Staikov, ch. 1. Sofia: Jusautor, 1982.
Aldous, Joan, ed. *Two Paychecks.* Beverly Hills: Sage, 1982.
Altergott, Karen. "Traditions and Alternatives in Research Design: An Assessment of Time Utilization Studies." In *It's about Time,* edited by Z. Staikov, ch. 16. Sofia: Jusautor, 1982.
Asplund, Johan. *Teorier om Framtiden* [Theories about the Future]. Stockholm: Liber Förlag, 1979.
Barker, Roger. *Ecological Psychology.* Stanford: Stanford University Press, 1968.
Bayes, T., et al. *The Role of Women in Family Transportation Behavior.* Lexington: University of Kentucky, College of Home Economics, Department of Family Studies, 1982.
Becker, G. S. "A Theory of the Allocation of Time." *Economics Journal* vol. 75 (1965):493–517.
Belle, D., ed. *Lives in Stress: Women and Depression.* Beverly Hills: Sage, Focus Editions, 1982.
Benenson, Harold. "Women's Occupational and Family Achievement in the U.S. Class System: A Critique of the Dual Career Family Analysis." *British Journal of Sociology* vol. 35, no. 1 (March 1984):19–41.
Berk, R.A., and Berk, S.F. *Labor and Leisure at Home.* Beverly Hills: Sage, 1979.
Biderman, Albert, et al. *Historical Incidents of Extreme Overcrowding.* Washington, D.C.: Bureau of Social Science Research, Inc., 1963.
Bohen, H., and Viveros-Long, A. *Balancing Jobs and Family Life: Do Flexible Work Schedules Help?* Philadelphia: Temple University Press, 1981.
Bronfenbrenner, Urie. *The Ecology of Human Development.* Cambridge, Massachusetts: Harvard University Press, 1979.
Carlstein, Tommy; Parkes, Don; and Thrift, Nigel. *Timing Space and Spacing Time.* 3 vols. New York: Halstead Press, 1978.
Carlstein, Tommy, et al. "Individars Dygnsbanor i Några Hushållstyper" [Individual Routines within Several Household Types]. Lund, Sweden: Institute for Cultural Geography. University of Lund, 1968.
Carp, F.M. *Employed Women as a Transportation-deprived and Transit Dependent Group.* Berkeley: Metropolitan Transportation Commission, Document No. TM-4-1-74, 1974.
Catalano, Ralph. *Health, Welfare, and the Community.* Elmsford, New York: Pergamon Press, 1979.
Central Bureau of Statistics of Norway, *The Time-Budget Survey, 1980–81.* Norges Officielle Statistikk B378. Oslo: Kongsvinger, 1983.
Chapin, F. Stuart, Jr. *Human Activity Patterns in the City.* New York: Wiley Interscience, 1974.
Chumak, A., and Braaksma, J.P. "Implications of the Travel-Time Budget for Urban Transportation Modeling in Canada." *Transportation Research Record* vol. 794 (1981);9–27.
Clark, Susan. "Time-Use and the Status of Women." In *Cross National Time-Budget Analysis: A Workbook,* edited by Andrew Harvey, ch. 8. Draft manuscript. Halifax, Nova Scotia: Institute of Public Affairs, Dalhousie University, 1977.

Cochran, M.M., and Bronfenbrenner, Urie. "Child Rearing, Parenthood, and the World of Work." In *Work in America,* edited by Clark Kerr and J. M. Rosow, pp. 138-54. New York: Van Nostrand Reinhold, 1979.

Commission of Inquiry into Part-time Work. *Part-time Work in Canada,* Ottawa: Labour Canada, 1983.

Cullen, Ian. "The Treatment of Time in the Explanation of Spatial Behavior." In *Human Activity and Time Geography,* by T. Carlstein et al. New York: Halstead Press, 1978, pp. 27-38.

Cullen, Ian, and Phelps, E. "Patterns of Behavioral Responses to the Urban Environment" in *Public Policy in Temporal Perspective,* edited by W. Michelson, pp. 105-181. The Hague: Mouton, 1978.

Damm, D. "Analysis of Activity Schedules along the Dimension of Gender." In *Women's Travel Issues: Research Needs and Priorities,* edited by S. Rosenbloom, pp. 171-98. Washington, D.C.: U.S. Department of Transportation, 1978.

Derow, Ellan. "Married Women's Employment and Domestic Labor." Unpublished Ph.D. dissertation, University of Toronto, 1977.

Dumazedier, Joffre. *Sociology of Leisure,* trans. by M.A. McKenzie, New York: Elsevier, 1974.

Feinstein, K.W., ed. *Working Women and Families,* Beverly Hills: Sage, 1979.

Felson, Marcus. "Social Accounts Based on Map, Clock, and Calendar." In *Social Accounting Systems,* edited by F. Thomas Juster and Kenneth C. Land, pp. 219-39. New York: Academic Press, 1981.

Ferri, Elsa, and Robinson, Hilary. *Coping Alone.* New York: Humanities Press, 1976.

Financial Post. "Flextime Freedom Can Help Managers and Employees." February 18, 1984, p. 18.

Fox, M.B. "Time Allocation in Planning and Policymaking for Working Women and Their Households: A Social Indicator Study." Unpublished Ph.D. dissertation, University of Pennsylvania, 1978.

Fox, Mary Frank, and Hess-Biber, Sharlene. *Women at Work.* Palo Alto: Mayfield Publishing Company, 1984.

Fried, M.; Havens, J.; and Thall, M. *Travel Behavior—A Synthesized Theory.* Chestnut Hill, Massachusetts: Boston College, Laboratory of Psychosocial Studies, project 8-14, 1977.

Geerken, Michael, and Gove, Walter R. *At Home and at Work: The Family's Allocation of Labor.* Beverly Hills: Sage, 1983.

Giuliano, G. "Public Transportation and the Travel Needs of Women." *Traffic Quarterly* vol. 33, no. 4 (1979):607-16.

Gold, D., and Andres, D. "Comparisons of Adolescent Children with Employed and Nonemployed Mothers." *Merrill-Palmer Quarterly of Behavior and Development* vol. 24, no. 4 (1978):243-54.

———. "Developmental Comparisons Between 10-year-old Children with Employed and Nonemployed Mothers." *Child Development* vol. 49 (1978):75-84.

Goldberg, Roberta. "Maternal Time Use and Preschool Performance." Unpublished Ph.D. dissertation, University of Minnesota, 1977.

Gordon, R.E.; Gordon, K.K.; and Gunther, Max. *The Split-Level Trap.* New York: Random House, 1961.

Grønmo, Sigmund, and Lingsom, Susan. "Som i Norge" [As in Norway]. *Tidsskrift for Samfunnsforskning,* 1983, issue 24. Quoted in "Oförändrade Könsroller i Hemmen," by Ulla Nordenstam. Translated by W. Michelson. *Välfärds Bulletinen,* no. 1, 1984, p. 11.

Gutenschwager, G.A. "The Time Budget-Activity Systems Perspective in Urban Research and Planning." *Journal of the American Institute of Planners* vol. 39, no. 6 (November 1973): 378-87.

Hägerstrand, Torsten. "Geographic Measurements of Migration: Swedish Data." In *Human Displacements: Measurements and Methodological Aspects,* edited by J. Sutter, pp. 61-83. Monaco: Entretiens de Monaco en Sciences Humaines, 1963.

———. "What about People in Regional Science?" *Papers of the Regional Science Association* vol. 24 (1970), 7-21.

Hanson, Susan, and Hanson, Perry. "The Impact of Married Women's Employment on Household Travel Patterns: A Swedish Example." *Transportation* vol. 10, no. 2 (1981):165;n83.

Hansson, Robert O., et al. "Maternal Employment and Adolescent Sexual Behavior." *Journal of Youth and Adolescence* vol. 10 (February 1981):55-60.
Harper, Jan, and Richards, Lyn. *Mothers and Working Mothers.* New York: Penguin Books, 1979.
Harvey, Andrew S. "Time-Use Studies for National and Transnational Leisure Analysis." Halifax: Dalhousie University, Regional and Urban Studies Centre, 1983.
Hayghe, Howard. "Dual-Earner Families: Their Economics and Demographic Characteristics." In *Two Paychecks: Life in Dual-Earner Families,* edited by Joan Aldous, pp. 27-40. Beverly Hills: Sage, 1982.
Hemmens, G.C. *The Structure of Urban Activity Linkages.* Chapel Hill, N.C.: Center for Urban and Regional Studies, University of North Carolina, 1966.
Hodgson, Susan. "Childrearing Systems: The Influence of Shared Childrearing on the Development of Competence." In *The Child in the City,* edited by William Michelson et al., vol. 2, ch. 3. Toronto: University of Toronto Press, 1979.
Hoffman, Lois, "Effects of Maternal Employment on the Child — A Review of the Research." *Developmental Psychology,* vol. 10 (1974):204-28.
_____. "Maternal Employment: 1979." *American Psychologist* vol. 34 (1979):859-65.
_____, ed. *Working Mothers.* San Francisco: Jossey-Bass, 1974.
Hogan, M. Janice, et al. "Single Parenting: Transitioning Alone." In *Stress and the Family,* edited by Hamilton I. McCubbin and Charles R. Figley, vol. 1, pp. 116-132. New York:Brunner/Mazel, 1983.
Holmstrom, Lynda L. *The Two-Career Family.* Cambridge, Massachusetts: Schenkman, 1972.
Howell, Mary. "The Effects of Maternal Employment on the Child." *Pediatrics* vol. 52 no. 3 (September 1973):327-43.
_____. "Employed Mothers and Their Families." *Pediatrics* vol. 52 no. 2 (August 1973):252-63.
Johnson, Laura C. *Who Cares? A Report of the Project Child-care Survey of Parents and Their Child-care Arrangements.* Toronto: Community Day-care Coalition/Social Planning Council of Metropolitan Toronto, 1977.
Jovanis, Paul. "Telecommunications and Alternative Work Schedules: Options for Managing Transit Travel Demand." *Urban Affairs Quarterly* vol. 19, no. 2 (December 1983):167-89.
Kagan, Jerome. "Issues and Evidence in Day Care." In *The Child in the City: Today and Tomorrow,* edited by William Michelson, Saul V. Levine, and Ellen Michelson, pp. 216-40. Toronto: University of Toronto Press, 1979.
Kahn-Hut, R., et al., eds. *Women and Work: Problems and Perspectives.* New York: Oxford University Press, 1982.
Kamerman, Sheila B. *Parenting in an Unresponsive Society.* New York: The Free Press, 1980.
Kanter, R.M. *Work and Family in the United States.* New York: Russel Sage Foundation, 1977.
Koppelman, F.S., et al. "Role Influence in Transportation Decision Making." In *Women's Travel Issues: Research Needs and Priorities,* edited by S. Rosenbloom, pp. 309-53. Washington, D.C.: U.S. Department of Transportation, 1978.
Kriesberg, Louis. *Mothers in Poverty: A Study of Fatherless Families.* Chicago: Aldine, 1970.
Lawe, Charles, and Lawe, Barbara. "The Balancing Act: Coping Strategies for Emerging Family Lifestyles." In *Dual-Career Couples,* edited by Fran Pepitone-Rockwell, ch. 9. Beverly Hills: Sage, 1980.
Levine, E.P. "Travel Behavior and Transportation Needs of Women: A Case Study of San Diego, California." Master's thesis in city planning, San Diego State University, 1980.
Levine, J.A. *Who Will Raise the Children?* Philadelphia: Lippincott, 1976.
Madden, J.F. "Why Women Work Closer to Home." *Urban Studies* vol. 18 (1981):181-94.
Marsden, Dennis. *Mothers Alone: Poverty and the Fatherless Family.* Hammondsworth: Penguin, 1969.
Mårtensson, Solveig. "Childhood Interaction and Temporal Organization." *Economic Geography* vol. 53 (1977);99-125.
_____. *On the Formation of Biographies.* Lund, Sweden: Lund Studies in Geography no. 47, C.W.K. Gleerup, 1979.
Maslow, Abraham. *Motivation and Personality.* New York: Harper & Row, 1954.
Matsushima, C. "Time-Input and Household Work-Output Studies in Japan." In *It's about Time,* edited by Z. Staikov, pp. 188-208. Sofia: Jusautor, 1982.

McGinnis, R.G. "Influence of Employment and Children on Intrahousehold Travel Behavior." In *Women's Travel Issues: Research Needs and Priorities,* edited by S. Rosenbloom, pp. 75-103. Washington, D.C.: U.S. Department of Transportation, 1978.
Medrich, E.A., et al. *The Serious Business of Growing Up: A Study of Children's Lives Outside School.* Berkeley: University of California Press, 1982.
Meier, Gretl S. *Job Sharing: A New Pattern for Quality of Work and Life.* Kalamazoo: W.F. Upjohn Institute for Employment Research, 1979.
Melbin, Murray. "The Colonization of Time." In *Human Activity and Time Geography,* edited by T. Carlstein et al., pp. 100-113. London: Edward Arnold, 1978.
Meltz, Noah, et al. *Sharing the Work: An Analysis of the Issues in Worksharing and Job Sharing.* Toronto: University of Toronto Press, 1981.
Michelson, William. *Environmental Choice, Human Behavior, and Residential Satisfaction.* New York: Oxford University Press, 1977.
_____. *The Impact of Changing Women's Roles on Transportation Needs and Usage.* Springfield, Virginia: National Technical Information Service, 1983.
_____. *Man and His Urban Environment.* Reading, Massachusetts: Addison-Wesley, rev. ed. 1976.
_____. "Some Like It Hot: Social Participation and Environmental Use as Functions of the Season." *American Journal of Sociology* vol. 76 (1971):1072-83.
_____. "Time-Budgets and Time-Geography." In *Environmental Design Research: Methods and Applications,* edited by Robert Bechtel et al. New York: Van Nostrand, Reinhold, forthcoming 1985.
_____. "Urbanism as Ways of Living: The Changing Views of Planning Researchers." *Ekistics* vol. 40, no. 236 (1975):20-26.
Michelson, William, and Reed, Paul B. "The Time-Budget." In *Behavioral Research Methods in Environmental Design,* edited by William Michelson, ch. 5. Stroudsburg, Pa: Dowden, Hutchinson & Ross, 1975.
Michelson, William, et al., eds. *The Child in the City: Changes and Challenges.* Toronto: University of Toronto Press, 1979.
Miller, J., and Garrison, H.H. "Sex Roles: The Division of Labor at Home and in the Workplace." *Annual Review of Sociology* vol. 8, Palo Alto: Annual Reviews, Inc., 1982, pp. 237-62.
Mortimer, J.T. and London, J. "The Varying Linkages of Work and Family." In *Work and Family,* edited by Patricia Voydanoff, ch. 2. Palo Alto: Mayfield, 1984.
Niemi, Iiris, et al. *Use of Time in Finland.* Helsinki: Central Statistical Office of Finland, Study no. 65, 1981.
Nollen, Stanley D. *New Work Schedules in Practice.* New York: Van Nostrand Reinhold, 1982.
Nollen, Stanley D., et al. *Permanent Part-Time Employment,* New York: Praeger, 1978.
Nordenstam, Ulla. Oförändrade Könsroller i Hemmen [Unchanged Sex Roles in the Home]. *Välfärds Bulletinen* no. 1:1984, pp. 10-11.
Nye, F.I., and Hoffman, L.W. *The Employed Mother in America.* Chicago: Rand McNally, 1963.
Oakley, A., *The Sociology of Housework,* New York: Random House, 1974.
Ogburn, William. *On Culture and Social Change: Selected Papers.* Edited and with an Introduction by Otis Dudley Duncan. Chicago: University of Chicago Press, 1964.
Olmstead, B. "Job-Sharing: An Emerging Work Style." *International Labor Review* vol. 118 (May-June 1979):238-98.
Oppenheimer, Valerie K. *Work and the Family.* New York: Academic Press, 1982.
Palm, R., and Pred, A. "A Time-Geographic Perspective on Problems of Inequality for Women." Berkeley: Institute of Urban and Regional Development, University of California, Working Paper no. 236, 1974.
Pant, P.D., and Bullen, A.G.R. "Urban Activities, Travel, and Time: Relationships from National Time-Use Survey." *Transportation Research Record* vol. 750 (1980):1-6.
Parkes, Don, and Thrift, Nigel. *Times, Spaces, and Places.* New York: Wiley, 1980.
Patrushev, V.D. "Satisfaction with Free Time as a Social Category and an Indicator of Way of Life." In *It's About Time,* edited by Z. Staikov, ch. 17. Sofia: Jusautor, 1982.
Pickup, L. *Housewives' Mobility and Travel Patterns.* Crowthorne, Berkshire, England: Transport and Road Research Laboratory Report no. 971, 1981.

Portner, Joyce. "Work and Family: Achieving a Balance." In *Stress and Family* edited by Hamilton I. McCubbin and Charles R. Figley, vol. 1, pp. 163-77. New York: Brunner/Mazel, 1983.
Propper, A.M. "The Relationship of Maternal Employment to Adolescent Roles, Activities, and Parental Relationships." *Journal of Marriage and the Family* vol. 34 (1972):417-21.
Rapoport, Rhona, and Rapoport, Robert N. *Dual-Career Families Re-examined.* New York: Harper Colophon Books, 1976.
———. "The Next Generation in Dual-Earner Family Research." In *Two Paychecks,* edited by Joan Aldous, pp. 229-243. Beverly Hills: Sage, 1982.
Rapoport, Robert N., and Rapoport, Rhona. *Dual-Career Families.* New York: Penguin Books, 1971.
Reed, Paul B. "Lifestyle as an Element of Social Logic: Patterns of Activity, Social Characteristics, and Residential Choice." Unpublished Ph.D. dissertation, University of Toronto, 1976.
Renwick, Patricia; Lawler, Edward; and the *Psychology Today* staff. "What You Really Want from Your Job." *Psychology Today* vol. 11, no. 12 (May 1978):53-65.
Robinson, John P. *How Americans Use Time.* New York: Praeger, 1977.
Ronen, Simcha. *Flexible Working Hours.* New York: McGraw-Hill, 1981.
Ross, Catherine E.; Mirowsky, John; and Huber, Joan. "Dividing Work, Sharing Work, and In-Between: Marriage Patterns and Depression." *American Sociological Review* vol. 48 (Dec. 1983):809-823.
Rutter, Michael. "Socio-emotional Consequences of Day Care for Pre-school Children." *American Journal of Orthopsychiatry* vol. 51, no. 1 (Jan. 1981):4-28.
Schlesinger, Benjamin. *The One-Parent Family.* Toronto: University of Toronto Press, 4th ed. 1978.
Sen, L. "Travel Patterns and Behavior of Women in Urban Areas." In *Women's Travel Patterns: Research Needs and Priorities,* edited by S. Rosenbloom, pp. 417-36. Washington, D.C.: U.S. Department of Transportation, 1978.
Skinner, Denise. "Dual-Career Families: Strains of Sharing." In *Stress and the Family,* edited by Hamilton I. McCubbin and Charles R. Figley, vol. 1, pp. 90-101. New York: Brunner/Mazel, 1983.
———. "Dual-Career Family Stress and Coping: A Literature Review." In *Work and Family,* edited by Patricia Voydanoff, ch. 18. Palo Alto: Mayfield, 1984.
Skinner, L.E., and Borlaug, K.L. "Shopping Trips: Who Makes Them and When." In *Women's Travel Issues: Research Needs and Priorities,* edited by S. Rosenbloom, pp. 355-79. Washington, D.C.: U.S. Department of Transportation, 1978.
South Coast Shopper, The. Classified advertisement. October 14, 1980, p. 17.
Staikov, Zahari. "Modelling and Programming of Time-Budgets." *Society and Leisure* vol. 5, no. 1 (1973):31-47.
Staines, Graham, L., and Pleck, Joseph H. *The Impact of Work Schedules on the Family.* Ann Arbor: University of Michigan, Survey Research Center, Institute for Social Research, 1983.
Statistics Canada, Labour Force Survey Division. "Initial Results from the 1981 Survey of Child-Care Arrangements." Research Paper no. 31, Ottawa: Minister of Supply and Services Canada, 1982.
———. *The Labour Force: May, 1983.* Ottawa: Minister of Supply and Services Canada, 1983.
Stimpson, C., et al., eds. *Women and the American City.* Chicago: University of Chicago Press, 1981.
Stone, Philip J. "Women's Time Patterns in Eleven Countries." In *Public Policy in Temporal Perspective,* edited by William Michelson, pp. 113-50. The Hague: Mouton, 1978.
Studenmund, A.H.; Kerpelman, L.C.; and Ott, M. "Women's Travel Behavior and Attitudes: An Empirical Analysis." In *Women's Travel Issues: Research Needs and Priorities,* edited by S. Rosenbloom, pp. 355-79. Washington, D.C.: U.S. Department of Transportation, 1978.
Sullivan, Joyce. "Family-Support Systems Paychecks Can't Buy." In *Work and Family,* edited by Patricia Voydanoff, ch. 6. Palo Alto: Mayfield, 1984.
Szalai, Alexander, et al. *The Use of Time.* The Hague: Mouton, 1972.
U.S. Department of Commerce, Bureau of the Census. *Historical Statistics of the United States.* part 1, 1975.
———. *Statistical Abstract of the United States.* 103 ed., 1982-83.
Vanek, Joann. "Keeping Busy: Time Spent in Housework, United States, 1920-1970." Unpub-

lished Ph.D. dissertation, University of Michigan, Department of Sociology, 1973.
———. "Time Spent in Housework." *Scientific American* vol. 231, no. 5 (1974):116-120.
———. "Housewives as Workers." In *Work and Family,* edited by Patricia Voydanoff, ch. 6. Palo Alto: Mayfield, 1984.
Van Vliet, Willem. "Use, Evaluation, and Knowledge of City and Suburban Environments by Children of Employed and Non-Employed Mothers." Unpublished Ph.D. dissertation, University of Toronto, 1980.
Vincent, Clark. *Unmarried Mothers.* New York: The Free Press, 1961.
Walker, Katherine, and Woods, M.E. *Time Use: A Measure of Household Production of Family Goods and Services.* Washington, D.C.: Center for the Family of the American Home Economics Association, 1976.
Weaver, Peter. "Employers Committing to Child Care." *Los Angeles Times,* April 15, 1984, Part 4, p. 10.
Webster's New Collegiate Dictionary. Springfield, Massachusetts: G. & C. Merriam Company, 1981.
Weiss, Robert S. *Going It Alone: The Family Life and Social Situation of the Single Parent.* New York: Basic Books, 1979.
Yago, Glen. "The Sociology of Transportation." *Annual Review of Sociology* vol. 9 (1983):171-190.
Woods, M. "The Unsupervised Child of the Working Mother." *Developmental Psychology* vol. 6 (1972):14-25.
Ziegler, Suzanne, and Michelson, William. "Complementary Methods of Data Gathering in Literate, Urban Populations." *Human Organization* vol. 40 (1981):323-329.
Zimmerman, C. *Energy for Travel: Household Travel Patterns by Life Cycle Stage.* New Haven: Yale University, School of Forestry and Environmental Studies, 1980.

Appendix
The Survey Instrument

Family Time and Activity Study

University of Toronto

The Child in the City Programme

under contract to

Ministry of National Health and Welfare

Ottawa

Code # _____

Date _____

Address _____

_____

_____

Interviewer: _____

174 *Appendix: The Survey Instrument*

Sampling no. _____

Hello. I am an interviewer from The University of Toronto (SHOW BADGE). We are doing a survey under contract to the Ministry of National Health and Welfare. Could I take about two minutes of your time at the moment to ask just a few questions?

1. Do any children live here with you?

☐ No: We only need to talk further with families with children so we don't need to take any more of your time. Thank you.

☐ Yes: How old are they (boy or girl)? How old are you?

Person	Age	Activity
01		
02		
03		
04		
05		
06		
10		
11		
12		
13		

2. Who else lives with you here and what are their ages? (PROBE FOR HUSBAND OR WIFE IF NECESSARY) (PLACE INFORMATION IN BOX FOR #1)

3. What is your/his/her main activity during the weekday?

4. Are any of your children regularly looked after during the week, daytime or evening, by any of the following?

	Which child	Location (Exact address of intersection)
a. centre daycare? Y N		
b. daycare at someone else's home? Y N		
c. preschool programme(s)? Y N (i.e., before kindergarten)		
d. brothers or sisters? Y N		
e. grandparents? Y N		
f. other relatives? Y N		
g. other persons or babysitters? Y N		
h. lunch programs at school? Y N		
i. before or after school program? Y N		

IF THE FAMILY QUALIFIES FOR THE SAMPLE ACCORDING TO OPERABLE CRITERIA, PROCEED AS FOLLOWS.

Thank you very much. I don't want to take any more of your time right now. But I'd like very much--and it is very important for the accuracy of this survey--to come back at a time when everyone in your home aged 10 and over will be home for about 30 minutes and when I could talk with you/your wife (i.e., the female head of household) for about an hour or two afterwards.

University of Toronto researchers are working under contract to Canada's Ministry of Health and Welfare, as I mentioned, to understand the nature of the everyday lives of families with children in our changing cities. There are many things people have to do every day and getting them done can be easier or harder depending on many factors, like hours of work, size of family, where you live, what you have to do.

176   Appendix: The Survey Instrument

We would like to talk with you and to see what your family does in order to learn from you what you do to make the day come out right, what you find difficult now, and what you think would make most people's daily lives "smoother."

First we would like to talk to all of you about how you arrange your weekdays. Then we'd like to ask you a few more questions having to do with how you (i.e., female head of household) feel about your daily life, some possible causes of stress, and your opinions about and reactions to what we'll be talking about.

The purpose of this study is to get information which would help public and private agencies make sound decisions and policies affecting the facilities and servies that are available to families. This might have to do with childcare, or business working hours, or transportation, or perhaps other aspects of daily life.

We do not put your name on this questionnaire, and we will never in any way associate your name with the results or release any information which could identify your family. You are free to leave unanswered any question or questions you don't want to answer.

If these arrangements are acceptable, would you kindly so indicate by signing our "Consent Form?" The consent form will be separated from the actual interview, which will be kept confidential under University requirements.

When might we come (Tuesday-Saturday)? Can you arrange for everyone to be present (FILL OUT APPT. CARD)?

Time:
_____

Place:
_____

Telephone:
_____

Interviewer's
first name _____

CONSENT FORM

I understand and agree to the following aspects of the University of Toronto <u>Daily Time Project</u>:

1. There will be one visit by a University of Toronto researcher, lasting approximately 2 hours, to talk about factual aspects of my family's daily life and to discuss feelings about daily life, some possible causes of stress, and suggestions and reactions concerning the subject of daily life routines.

2. Confidentiality will be maintained, because my name will not be put on any form but this, and no information will be released which will identify individual families.

All family members present 18 years of age or older.

Name _____

Address _____
_____
_____

Telephone No. _____

Family Code No. _____

MAIN INTERVIEW
PHASE II

I'd like to repeat the purpose and nature of this interview and study for the other members of the family, so that you all understand why we're asking your cooperation. Then we'd appreciate all persons 18 and over who have not signed the consent form to do so. (READ DESCRIPTION FROM THE SECOND PARAGRAPH THROUGH THE CONSENT.)

(INTERVIEWER DISTRIBUTES TIME-BUDGET SHEETS TO MOTHER, FATHER--IF PRESENT--AND EACH CHILD PRESENT 10 YEARS OR OLDER.)

1. I'd like to get some idea of how each of you spent your time yesterday--beginning with when you got up and continuing through until you went to bed. As you can see from the sheets I've given you, I want you to fill in what you were doing, roughly how long it took, whether anyone was with you, where you were at the time, and whether you were doing anything else at the same time, as for example, talking with children, having an argument, eating a snack, or listening to the radio. Then can you check how you felt at the time, in terms of first how much choice you had as to whether or not to do what you were doing and second how tense or relaxed you were feeling, using the appropriate numbers. Travel from one place to another is an activity and we need to know how you went (e.g., bus, car, on foot, etc.)

Here are some examples as to how this could look, depending on what you did. Can you take a look at them? As you can see from the examples, we are interested in as much detail as you can remember, with a special concern for parent-child contact, including the whole range from fights to fun together and even routine things. Do you have any questions about the examples?

So let's begin with when everybody got up and fill it in until 8:30 or 9:00 a.m. or whenever people left for work or school. (INTERVIEWER WILL ASSIST THIS PROCESS UNTIL OR UNLESS IT IS EVIDENT THAT FAMILY MEMBERS CAN PROCEED ON THEIR OWN. DO CHECK WHAT EACH PERSON HAS DONE FOR COMPLETENESS INCLUDING TRAVEL & LOCATION.

INTERVIEWER ATTEND TO OBSERVATION CHECKLIST

Once you are at your job or school there's not need to give detail about your different activities, just that you were there, how you felt abot it, etc. I do want to know about anything that was not part of your job and about trips from or after work.

For anyone who was home during the day, I would like you to keep on filling in all the activities just as you started to--and for you people at work or school once you leave there again I would like the same detail about your activities.

Is everybody finished up to 6:00 p.m.? (IF NOT, WAIT UNTIL THEY ARE.) O.k. from then what were you doing until you went to bed? Please put down at the end what time you got up this morning.

Could you also check off answers to a few questions about how you feel about your daily routine.

CHECK FOR COMPLETENESS & APPROPRIATENESS INCLUDING WAKE-UP TIME

Well, that's all I need from you (father) and the children but since this is mainly a study of how mothers spend their time these days I have a few more questions that I'd like to ask you (mother), so perhaps we could move into the kitchen (other room) and give everybody a well-deserved rest after all their hard work on these time sheets.

1. RESPONDENTS MAY CONFER WITH EACH OTHER ABOUT DETAILS BUT ARE EXPECTED TO WORK INDEPENDENTLY AND WITHOUT THE NECESSITY TO SHARE INFORMATION.

2. IF ANYONE IS NOT HOME, ARRANGE TO LEAVE BLANK PAGES WITH INSTRUCTIONS THAT THEY BE FILLED OUT WITHIN 12 HOURS; ALSO ARRANGE A PICK-UP TIME. AN ALTERNATIVE IS A TELEPHONE INTERVIEW AT A FIXED TIME.

Appendix: The Survey Instrument

DATE: _____ PERSON NO. _____

TIME BEGAN	TIME ENDED	WHAT DID YOU DO? (Main Activity)	WHAT ELSE WERE YOU DOING AT THE SAME TIME?	WHO WAS WITH YOU?	WHERE WERE YOU? Room in house or nearest intersection	CHOICE	TENSE/RELAXED	ADDITIONAL INFORMATION (Item no., no. min. with whom)

CHOICE 1 2 3 4 5 6 7
none   some   free choice

TENSE/RELAXED 1 2 3 4 5 6 7
very tense   very relaxed

Interviewer only

Appendix: The Survey Instrument   181

Family Code no. _____

2. Here is a list that describes some of the ways people feel at different times. During the past few weeks, how often have you felt . . .

	Often	Sometimes	Never
a. on top of the world (terrific!)?	___	___	___
b. very lonely or remote from other people?	___	___	___
c. particularly excited or interested in something?	___	___	___
d. depressed or very unhappy?	___	___	___
e. pleased about having accomplished something?	___	___	___
f. bored?	___	___	___
g. proud because someone complimented you on something you had done?	___	___	___
h. so restless you couldn't sit long in a chair?	___	___	___
i. that things were going your way?	___	___	___
j. upset because someone criticized you?	___	___	___

3. Taking things all together, how would you say things are these days-- would you say you're:

☐ Very happy   ☐ Pretty happy   ☐ Not too happy

Appendix: The Survey Instrument

TIME: _____   Family Code no. _____

WHILE THE FAMILY MEMBERS FILL OUT THE TIME-BUDGET, NOTE INTERACTIONS BETWEEN THEM AND RECORD THEM, ACCORDING TO THE FOLLOWING NOTATION, WITH

S as the initiator and

O as the object of a communication

FOR THE "S," PLEASE PUT AN APPROPRIATE NUMBER:

1 = asks

2 = orders

3 = corrects

4 = anger or annoyance shown

5 = offers help

6 = supports, reassures, compliments

	Mother	Father	___	___	___	___	___	___
1.								
2.								
3.								
4.								
5.								
6.								
7.								
8.								
9.								
10.								
11.								
12.								
13.								
14.								
15.								
16.								
17.								
18.								
19.								
20.								

TIME: _____   Family Code no. _____

5. Now let's try to get some idea of how the day was for the baby (and/or younger children under 10 years old). (Directing questions to the mother) What time did the baby get up, etc.? (Use time budget as before for each baby or younger child.) THE CHILDREN SHOULD BE CONSULTED AS NECESSARY RATHER THAN MOTHER MAKING UNDUE GUESSES.

6. Now I am especially interested to find out if you or anyone else in the family did certain activities for or with your children yesterday that might not have been long enough to put on your sheets or which did not occur to you to mention. I am going to read you a list of reminders and you can tell me if and when you did these.

READ EACH ITEM BELOW ONE BY ONE AND FILL IN RESPONSES ON MOTHER'S TIME BUDGET WITH EACH POSITIVE RESPONSE, i.e., from <u>when</u> to <u>when</u> and <u>with whom</u> in Additional Information column.

CODE LIST

<u>Activities with Children</u>

1. Physical care (washing, feeding, diapering) of <u>babies</u> (up to 4 years)
2. Eating with baby
3. Physical care (washing, dressing, feeding) of children (4 years and up)
4. Eating with children
5. Supervision of school work without participation
6. Supervision of school work with participation
7. Reading of non-school books to children
8. Talking to/with children--mainly instructing or explaining, including about routines
9. Joking with children
10. Talking to/with children--mainly social
11. Listening to child (being audience)
12. Being affectionate with child, like hugging or kissing, of giving comfort, help, approval, permission, material goods, praise
13. Playing games, giving instruction
14. Joining in outdor games, walks
15. Waking child
16. Putting to bed--whole process or any part of it like getting child ready for bed or tucking child in
17. Watching T.V. with children
18. Travel to accompany children (including waiting for bus, chauffering)
19. Medical care or other health related activities
20. Supervision of meals
21. Intervening in children's fights
22. Keeping an eye on children in same room or checking child, keeping trace or whereabouts from a different room
23. Watching children
24. Gathering children
25. Making future plans, arrangements with child
26. Looking after child when sick
27. Losing temper
28. Fighting
29. Nagging
30. Giving child orders, disciplining child, or disapproving of something child has done

PERSON (Child under Age 10): _____

DATE: _____

TIME BEGAN	TIME ENDED	WHAT DID S/HE DO?	WHAT ELSE?	WHO WAS WITH HIM/HER?	WHERE WAS S/HE?

TIME: _____ Family Code no. _____

7. Overall how would you assess yesterday--as a good day or a bad day or neither good or bad?

```
    very                                          very
    good  _____ bad
              7    6    5    4    3    2    1
```

8. In general, do you feel you are just too busy to do everything you want to do?
    1. All of the time
    2. Much of the time
    3. Some of the time

9. What do you find you give up at times when you are just too busy, what doesn't get done? (PROBE IF NECESARY: Is there anything you have been putting off because you've had trouble fitting it in?)

_____

_____

_____

186   Appendix: The Survey Instrument

Family Code no. _____

Now I'd like to ask you to use the numbers on this card [HAND CARD B] to answer a few more questions about whether or not you have enough time to do what you want or need to.

You can use <u>any</u> number on the card from +10 to -10 in answering the questions. If you answer a +10 it means that you feel your situation is extreme and that you have much too much to do in the time you have. A +5 means you have somewhat too much to do in the time you have. A zero means you have just the right amount of time. A -5 means you have somewhat more time than you need to do what you have to do. And a -10 is the other extreme and means that you have much more time than you need to do what you have to do.

Is what I have said clear?

[IF NO, EXPLAIN AGAIN]

10. Could you choose a number to describe yesterday? Where did it fit on the scale from much too much to do, to much too little to do?

[PAUSE]

What about _____?
              b - g

_____ a. yesterday
_____ b. last weekend
_____ c. the last week
_____ d. the last month
_____ e. the last year
_____ f. an average year
_____ g. an average year
_____ h. your lifetime

11. What number represents the ideal situation for you? _____

12. Is there anything in particular which causes your having (too much/too little to do) in the time you have?

_____
_____
_____
_____

Family Code no. _____

13. What number would you choose to describe the relationship between what there is to do and what you have time to do:

		CARD B	CARD A
a.	at your job	_____	_____
b.	at home	_____	_____
c.	for or with your children	_____	_____
d.	for or with your husband	_____	_____
e.	for or with your friends	_____	_____
f.	for yourself	_____	_____
g.	regarding opportunities for your children outside the household	_____	_____
h.	regarding medical care for your children	_____	_____
i.	regarding medical care for yourself	_____	_____

IF RESPONSE IN FIRST COLUMN IS > +2 or < -2, ASK:

Does this cause you any concern, upset, or worry?

14. Do you have any special ways to save time, when you are busy or pressed?

15. What do you find the most difficult kinds of time pressure to deal with? KEEP ORDER OF ANSWERS CONSISTENT

   a. _____
   b. _____
   c. _____

   At what time of the day (and/or week) do they occur?

   a. _____
   b. _____
   c. _____

   What could be done, so that they wouldn't be so difficult?

   a. _____
   b. _____
   c. _____

16. Would you want to see opening times, closing times, working hours, etc. changed in any way you would find easier to cope with?

   PROBES: For example, the hours one can work. How would you change them? For example, the hours one can buy food. What would you change? In what way?

   What Change?   In What Way?

188   Appendix: The Survey Instrument

Family Code no. _____

17. Would you have the <u>location</u> of anything, in view of your daily life, changed? What? Where would you have it put?

What Relocated?   Where?

17a. Would you want any community services or facilities that aren't available to you now?

18. Now I'd like to ask you about your reactions to your children in different situations. In your opinion, does each child rate high, medium or low in the following?

3 = high   2 = medium   1 = low

child ____ child ____ child ____ child ____ child ____ child ____

		child	child	child	child	child	child
a.	sense of humour						
b.	school achievement						
c.	trying new experiences						
d.	happiness						
e.	independence						
f.	getting along with others						
g.	patience						
h.	ambition						

19. Let's assume that we all have times when we are pretty impatient or upset with our children; sometimes because of something our child has done, sometimes just because of the way we feel. I'd like to talk with you about these and other situations.

Do you have any times like these?

☐ NO (GO TO Q. 24)

☐ YES (CONTINUE WITH Q. 21)

20. Do you have any sense of when it is that you feel impatient or upset with your children? What is it that's happening?

Family Code no. _____

21. How do you think your behavior with the children changes when you are impatient or upset with them?

22. When you have a lot to do:

		CIRCLE ONE		
Are you:	a. more or less affectionate?	More	Same	Less
	b. more or less patient?	More	Same	Less
	c. more or less strict?	More	Same	Less
	d. more or less consistent?	More	Same	Less
Do you:	a. comfort children more or less?	More	Same	Less
	b. help children more or less?	More	Same	Less

As you can see, we have been talking about the nature of your day and that of your family. At this point, I'd like to turn to some straightforward questions that will help us understand this situation better.

23. We have already looked at your day, but a few more details about your housekeeping and employment activities are important. Do you have full-time, part-time, or no paid employment? How many hours a week?

   Full-time ☐ : hours _____
   Part-time ☐ : hours _____
   None   ☐

IF FULL- OR PART-TIME:

   a. What days and times do you work?
   b. Where is your work (nearest intersection)?
   c. What do you do there?

IF NOT SINGLE PARENT:

24. Is your husband currently employed full-time, part-time, or not at present? How many hours a week?

   Full-time ☐ : hours _____
   Part-time ☐ : hours _____
   None   ☐

IF SPOUSE WORKS FULL- OR PART-TIME:

   a. What days and times does your husband work?
   b. Where is his work (nearest intersection)?
   c. What does he do there?

Appendix: The Survey Instrument

Family Code no. _____

25. Who in your family has a driver's license?

- [ ] 01
- [ ] 02
- [ ] other adults
- [ ] children
- [ ] no one

26. How many cars do you have?

- [ ] 0
- [ ] 1
- [ ] 2
- [ ] 3 or more

Who is the main user of each?
_____
_____
_____

27. [IF EMPLOYED] How do you usually get to and from work (i.e., means of transportation)?

- [ ] auto (own car)
- [ ] auto (carpool)
- [ ] auto and T.T.C.
- [ ] bus or streetcar
- [ ] other (specify): _____
- [ ] subway
- [ ] bus or streetcar and subway
- [ ] on foot
- [ ] bicycle

27a. Do you usually stop for any errands along the way? IF SO, For what?

Appendix: The Survey Instrument   191

Family Code no. _____

28. [IF NOT SINGLE PARENT]   How does your spouse <u>usually</u> get to and from work?

- [ ] auto (own car)
- [ ] auto (carpool)
- [ ] auto and T.T.C.
- [ ] bus or streetcar
- [ ] other (specify): _____
- [ ] subway
- [ ] bus or streetcar and subway
- [ ] on foot
- [ ] bicycle

29. Who does which of the following family jobs mainly and who helps?

✓ = main person responsible   X = helps regularly   + = sometimes
(can be shared equally)

Item	Husband	Wife	Children	Others (specify)	No-one does it	At what time of the day and week is this usually done? (e.g., during lunch hour, to or from work, weekends, weekday nights, etc.)
Cooking						
Dishes						
Laundry						
Ironing						
Indoor cleaning						
Outdoor jobs						
Maintaining car (i.e., who takes car to mechanic)						
Repairs to house						
Planning family budget						
Paying bills, banking						
Caring for baby (i.e., or young children)						
Supervising schoolwork						
Taking children to medical care						
Taking children to dental care						
Grocery shopping						
Taking out garbage						

192   *Appendix: The Survey Instrument*

TIME: _____   Family Code no. _____

30. How many blocks (or miles) is it to the nearest: Do you usually use it?

	# Blocks (specify, in miles)	YES IF YES, Are location or hours factors in your using it? How?	NO If not, why not? Are location or hours factors in your not using it?
a. Bus, streetcar or subway stop			
b. Variety store/milk store			
c. Drug store			
d. Supermarket			
e. Hardware store			
f. Safe place for child to play other than private yard or balcony (specify)			
g. Bank, Credit Union, Trust Co.			
h. Community Centre			
i. Dry cleaner			
j. Fast food outlet or restaurant			
k. Laundromat			

Family Code no. _____

31. Do you normally have paid help or services from outside your family to clean, cook, do laundry, gardening, shoveling, or the like?

    ☐ YES   ☐ NO

    IF YES:

    Function(s) | Days and Hours Worked
    _____ | _____
    _____ | _____
    _____ | _____
    _____ | _____

    Are any of these mainly for the purpose of saving time? Which?

    ☐ YES   ☐ NO   IF YES: Which? _____

32. Do you use any outside commercial services or locations for needs like laundry, dry cleaning, entertaining others, etc.?

    Functions
    _____
    _____
    _____

    Are any of these mainly for the purpose of saving time? Which

    ☐ YES   ☐ NO   IF YES: Which? _____

33. How many rooms are there in your home? _____

34. How often per month do you eat your evening meal out? _____

35. How often do you bring prepared or takeout food home? _____ per month?

36. Have any of your children done the following within the past six months?

    a. Gone to a movie?   Y ____   IF SO, with whom?   _____ N ____
    b. Gone swimming?   Y ____   (list as many as apply) _____ N ____
    c. Gone skating?   Y ____   _____ N ____
    d. Gone to a museum?   Y ____   _____ N ____
    e. Gone out of Metro Toronto Y ____   _____ N ____
    f. Gone shopping for clothes Y ____   _____ N ____

Family Code no. _____

37. Now I'd like to ask you about last weekend. I'd like to chart how you spent Saturday and Sunday. Let's look at this form, which allows us to go through the whole day. Each person will get his or her own colour line. The day starts on the left. What time would the first of you get up? How long would you (he, she) remain at home? (START LINE ACCORDINGLY, KEEPING LINES APART, WITH THE PERSON NUMBER AT THE LEFT). What time would each person go to sleep? When would they wake up again? (PUT DOTS ON THE LINE TO SIGNIFY GOING TO SLEEP AND WAKING UP.)

SATURDAY

	AM 4	5	6	7	8	9	10	11	12 NOON	1	2	3	4	5	6	7	8	9	10	11	12 MIDNIGHT
Work place																					
Shopping or commercial place, including restaurants																					
Public office clinic, etc.																					
Outside, near home																					
At home																					
Place of worship																					
Recreation, etc.																					
Someone else's home																					
School, day care																					

37. (continued)

SUNDAY

	AM 1 2 3 4 5 6 7 8 9 10 11 12 NOON 1 2 3 4 5 6 7 8 9 10 11 12 MIDNIGHT AM 1 2 3 4 5 6 7 8 9
Work place	
Shopping or commercial place, including restaurants	
Public office, clinic, etc.	
Outside, near home	
At home	
Place of worship	
Recreation, etc.	
Someone else's home	
School, day care	

TIME: _____

Family Code no. _____

38. Now I'd like to ask you some questions about 7 situations in which people outside the household do things for you. The first is emergency baby-sitting for an hour or two.

	i. Who outside your household could you turn to to: RELATIONSHIP (e.g., family neighbour, friend professional, etc.) GO THROUGH (i) and (ii) FOR a) TO e)	ii. How often have you asked someone to a - g in the last month
a.	Do emergency babysitting for an hour or two	
b.	Do emergency babysitting for a weekend	
c.	Do an errand (e.g., like grocery shopping or pick up medicine)	
d.	Advise you about a problem with one of your children	
e.	Lend you money, when you are running low	
f.	Talk with about a personal problem? (Can you turn to your spouse for most problems?) Y ____ N ____	
g.	Get information about activities or services for children	

Family Code no. _____

[IF CHILDREN IN SCHOOL]

39. Do your children have to miss school in order to keep appointments with the doctor or some other service?

☐ YES   ☐ NO

[IF YES:] How often in the last month? _____

What kind of service? _____

[IF EMPLOYED:] Do you have to take time away from work to keep appointments (yours or your children's) with the doctor or another service?

☐ YES   ☐ NO

[IF YES:] How often in the last month? _____

What kind of service? _____

Do you lose pay? ☐ YES   ☐ NO

41. Is your choice of whether or not to see a doctor or a dentist, especially if you are not sick, affected by your doctor's or dentist's location or hours?

☐ YES   ☐ NO

Can you give me further comment about this situation?

42. If you or your children have a sudden illness and seek medical care, is your choice of where to go for help affected by your doctor's office hours?

☐ YES   ☐ NO

Can you comment? (PROBE)

Has this happened in the last year? ☐ YES   ☐ NO

[EMPLOYED WOMEN ONLY.
OTHERS GO TO Q. 55]

43. How much flexibility is there in your work schedule?

Much _____   Some _____   None _____

[IF MUCH OR SOME] What is is about your job that lets you be flexible?

_____ rules of employer   _____ workload   _____ other, (specify)

_____
_____
_____

Family Code no. _____

[IF SOME OR NONE]   What is it about your job that makes it hard to be flexible?

_____ rules of employer   _____ workload   _____ other, (specify)

_____
_____
_____

44. [IF CHILDREN GO TO SCHOOL]
How many days this month has each child missed school because of illness?
_____

45. If your child is ill and requires an adult at home what do you usually do?
_____
_____
_____

[PROBE IF NECESSARY:]   Have either you or your husband stayed home with a sick child in the last six months?

_____ husband   _____ wife   _____ both   _____ neither

46. [IF CHILDREN GO TO SCHOOL]
What do you and your children do about professional development days?
_____
_____
_____

47. Do you and your children have any arrangements during their summer school holiday different from the rest of the year? (SPECIFY)
_____
_____
_____

Appendix: The Survey Instrument   199

Family Code no. _____

48. a. What do you think is different in your children's day because you have a job?

a. _____
b. _____
c. _____
d. _____
e. _____
f. _____

48. b. Do any special behaviours of your children appear only at certain times of the day or when you (or your husband) are doing certain activities? Please be as specific as possible. (NOTE BEHAVIOUR, TIME AND PERSONS)

	Behaviour	Time	Persons
a.			
b.			
c.			
d.			
e.			
f.			

49. If your children have to get in touch with you at work, how easy or difficult is it for them to reach you?

_____ very easy
_____ somewhat easy
_____ not so easy
_____ not at all easy
_____ impossible

50. How often do you feel a conflict between being a mother and "working?"

_____ very often
_____ quite often
_____ some of the time
_____ seldom or never

200 Appendix: The Survey Instrument

Family Code no. _____

51. How satisfied or dissatisfied are you with your balance between work and family?

    _____ very satisfied
    _____ somewhat satisfied
    _____ somewhat dissatisfied
    _____ very dissatisfied

52. What advice would you give a young mother just starting outside paid employment?

53. In the case of yourself and your family, what kinds of things did you consider when you decided to go out to work full-time (or part-time--whichever is applicable)?

54. How content would you say you are today with that choice?

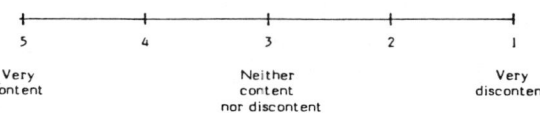

5	4	3	2	1
Very Content		Neither content nor discontent		Very discontent

55. [IF A FULL-TIME HOMEMAKER]

    a. What advice would you give a young mother who is staying at home with her children?

    b. In the case of yourself and your family, what kinds of things did you consider when you decided to stay home with your child(ren)?

    c. How content would you say you are today with that choice?

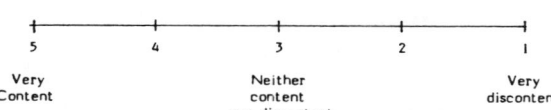

5	4	3	2	1
Very Content		Neither content nor discontent		Very discontent

[ALL RESPONDENTS]

Now I would like to ask just a few questions about stresses and strains you may be experiencing. [USE CARD A]

Family Code no. _____

56. How much concern, upset or worry has <u>ill health</u> been causing you in the last month--your own or others?

    0   none
    1   a small amount
    2   a moderate amount
    3   quite a bit
    4   a great deal

57. How much concern, upset or worry has either <u>employment or unemployment</u> been causing you in the last month--your own or others' employment or unemployment?

    0   none
    1   a small amount
    2   a moderate amount
    3   quite a bit
    4   a great deal

58. How much concern, upset or worry has <u>education</u> been causing you in the last month--your own or others' education?

    0   none
    1   a small amount
    2   a moderate amount
    3   quite a bit
    4   a great deal

59. How much concern, upset or worry has your <u>marriage</u> (relationship with _____ _____) been causing you in the past month?

    0   none
    1   a small amount
    2   a moderate amount
    3   quite a bit
    4   a great deal

Family Code no. _____

60. How much concern, upset or worry has <u>being a parent</u> been causing you in the last month?

    0   none
    1   a small amount
    2   a moderate amount
    3   quite a bit
    4   a great deal

61. How much concern, upset or worry has <u>money</u> been causing you in the last month?

    0   none
    1   a small amount
    2   a moderate amount
    3   quite a bit
    4   a great deal

[USE CARD WITH CATEGORIES OF INCOME]

62. a. Which letter corresponds with your own individual income before taxes from employment? _____

    b. Which letter corresponds with your spouse's income before taxes from employment? _____

    c. Which letter corresponds with your gross family income before taxes? _____

[IF MORE THAN 1 INCOME IN FAMILY OR SINGLE PARENT WHO HAS JOB, ASK Q. 63.
IF ONE INCOME IN TWO PARENT FAMILY, ASK Q. 64.]

63. If you were unable to continue your job, or stopped working from choice, what would the financial consequences be?

(If necessary to get specific behaviours)
What would you do in that case?

Is there any regular payment you might have to discontinue?

64. If you were suddenly to bring a second income into the family, what do you think you would do with it?

65. Beyond what you've said, what other advice would you give us for making daily life easier to manage?

66. What request would you make to governments or others in the community to help make daily life easier to manage?

Appendix: The Survey Instrument 203

Family Code no. _____

67. Would you be interested in hearing the results of this study in about six months together with other persons who have helped--and saying what you think about these results?

☐ YES   ☐ NO

How should we contact you?

68. Is there anything you want to tell us about this experience of being interviewed; anything you think we ought to know?

TIME: _____

That finishes our interview. We'd like to contact just a small percentage of families with whom we're speaking in July to repeat a few of the questions whose answers may differ then. But except for that possibility, this is all we ask of you, and we're extremely grateful for your help. Thank you!

204   Appendix: The Survey Instrument

Family Code no. _____

FOR INTERVIEWER ONLY

On this page, please indicate briefly anything about this respondent (or family) or the responses which you obtained which you think would help us to understand or interpret the data (especially material that is not picked up directly by the interview schedule but which became obvious to you).

Please note housing type: 1. Single family

2. Semi-detached

3. Row

4. Walk-up apartment

5. Elevator (up to four floors)

6. Elevator (five or more floors)

7. Other: _____

day of week reported in time-budget: _____

weather and approximate high temperature on time-budget day:

_____

_____

Index

Aas, Dagfinn, 32, 165
Achievement, 112, 114
Affection, 73, 114
Age, of children, 78
Ahrentzen, Sherry, 143
Aldous, Joan, 165, 167, 169
Altergott, Karen, 26, 165
Ambition, 112, 114
Analysis, strategies for, 28-31
Andres, D., 102, 166
Asplund, Johan, 12, 165
Automobiles. *See* Travel, mode of

Baby sitting, *See* Child care institutions and practices
Barker, Roger, 18, 165
Bayes, T., 48, 165
Bechtel, Robert, 168
Becker, G. S., 9, 165
Behavior settings, 18
Belle, D., 83, 90, 165
Benenson, H., 35, 165
Berk, Richard A., 15, 26, 45, 74, 165
Berk, S. F., 15, 26, 45, 74, 165
Biderman, A., 85, 165
Bohen, H., 137, 165
Borlaug, K. L., 121, 169
Braaksma, J. P., 48, 165
Bronfenbrenner, Urie, 6, 35, 165, 166
Bullen, A. G. R., 48, 168
Burke, Kenneth, 12

Canada Health Survey, 26, 85
Capp, Andy, 46
Carlstein, Tommy, 9, 18, 142, 165, 168
Carp, F. M., 122, 165
Catalano, Ralph, 6, 165
Central Bureau of Statistics of Norway, 44, 62, 165
Chapin, F. Stuart, Jr., 9, 11, 165
Child care institutions and practices, 4, 64, 101, 109-10, 110-14, 117-20, 133-35, 147, 158-60. *See also* Household work; Contact, parent-child
Child development, 104
Child in the City Programme, The, University of Toronto, xv, 16, 31
Child-raising practices, 114-15, 148
Children: age of, 78, 104-8; and housework, 63-64, 70-71, 83, 92, 103, 108-10; collective response to, 158-60, implications of maternal employment, 101-15; contact with, *see* Contact, parent-child
Choice, 87, 132-33, 162
Chronogeography, 9
Chumak, A., 48, 165
Clark, Susan, 165
Cochran, M. M., 35, 166
Comfort, giving of, 115
Commission of Inquiry into Part-time Work, 136, 157, 166
Community, 8-10, 116-44, 155-64
Commuting. *See* Travel
Competence, 73
Conflicts, personal, 83-85
Consistency, 115
Constraints. *See* Choice
Contact, parent-child, 20, 47-49, 52-53, 55, 56-57, 63, 70, 78, 90, 94, 103, 107, 136, 147-48, 151-52
Control, 98, 100, 136
Cooperation, 113
Cost of living, 35
Cullen, Ian, 9, 16, 19, 166
Cultural lag, 2, 63

Damm, D., 121, 166
Day care centers. *See* Child care institutions and practices
Delinquency, 102
Dennis the Menace, 61
Dental care, 69

Index

Department of Commerce (U.S.), Bureau of the Census, 2, 36, 169
Department of Transportation (U.S.), Urban Mass Transportation Administration, xvi
Depression, 74, 99
Derow, Ellan, 45, 47, 48, 62, 64, 166
Discussion sessions, with respondents, 30
Division of labor, within households, 60–71, 82, 90, 155
Driver's license, 128–29
Dumazedier, J., 32, 166
Duncan, Otis Dudley, 168

Eating, 54–55, 80, 95–96
Education, 86
Employment: concerns about, 86, 100. See also Employment status; Maternal employment
Employment status, 35–36
Ethnicity, 59
Excursions, 53, 95, 130, 147–48
Extroversion, 102

Family, 7–8
Family size, 78
Fathers. See Husbands
Fatigue, 73
Fear, 102
Feinstein, K. W., 166
Felson, Marcus, 10, 166
Ferri, Elsa, 166
Figley, Charles R., 167, 168, 169
Financial Post, The, 137, 166
Flexibility: in employment, 117, 136–43, 156–58; personal, 73
Flextime (flexitime), 137, 157
Flextimer, 137
Food. See Eating; Prepared food
Forth, Sally, 49
Fox, Marion Barg, 45, 47, 159, 166
Fox, Mary Frank, 34, 35, 166
Fried, M., 166

Garrison, H. H., 168
Geerkin, Michael, 27, 59, 62, 65, 70, 73, 166
Gender differentiation, 4, 71, 102, 108–11
Gershuny, J., 59
Giuliano, Genevieve, 121, 166
Gold, D., 102, 166
Goldberg, Roberta, 20, 22, 166
Gordon, K. K., 164, 166
Gordon, R. E., 164, 166
Gove, Walter, 27, 59, 62, 65, 70, 73, 166
Grandparents, 119
Grønmo, Sigmund, 63, 166
Guilt, 73
Gunther, Max, 164, 166
Gutenschwager, G., 9, 166

Hagarty, Linda, v, 31
Hanson, Perry, 48, 121, 166
Hanson, Susan, 48, 121, 166
Hansson, Robert O., 102, 166
Happiness, 26, 85, 98, 113
Harassment, 73
Harper, Jan, 65, 145
Harvard Graduate School of Education, 83
Harvey, Andrew, 44, 165, 167
Hassle, 1, 90
Havens, J., 166
Hayge, Howard, 2, 34–36, 38–39, 167
Health, 86. See also Medical care
Helpfulness, 115
Hemmens, George, 15, 167
Hesse-Biber, Sharlene, 34, 35, 166
Hierarchy of values, 33
Hodgson, Susan, 31, 102, 167
Hoffman, Lois, 73, 101, 102, 104, 167, 168
Hogan, M. Janice, 90, 167
Holmstrom, L. L., 35, 73, 167
Home day care. See Child care institutions and practices
Homework, 103, 107
Hospital for Sick Children Foundation, 28
Household help, paid, 64–65, 71
Household work, 4, 5, 15, 27, 44–47, 51, 52, 54–55, 60–71, 77, 78, 80–81, 83, 90–93, 103, 108–10, 122, 130, 137–38, 155
Housing costs, 35
Howard, Greg, 48
Howell, M., 35, 48, 64, 73, 102, 103, 167
Huber, J., 34, 35, 60, 74, 169
Husbands, 56, 60–71, 74, 81, 85, 97, 108
Hägerstrand, Torsten, 9, 10, 166

Identity, 73
Income, 39–42, 59, 78, 86, 89–90, 100, 127–28
Independence, personal, 102, 113
Inhibition, 102
Interests, 7

Job sharing, 156–57
Johnson, Laura, 28, 167
Jovanis, Paul, 137, 167
Juster, F. Thomas, 166

Kagan, Jerome, 102, 167
Kahn-Hut, Rachel, 167
Kamerman, Sheila, 35, 65, 70, 73, 90, 164, 167
Kanter, R. M., 33, 167
Kerpelman, L. L., 48, 169
Ketcham, Hank, 61
Koppelman, F. S., 121, 167
Kriesberg, Louis, 90, 167

Land, Kenneth C., 166
Land-use, 117, 142–43, 162–63

Latch-key child care, 102, 111
Lawe, Barbara, 73, 167
Lawe, Charles, 73, 167
Lawler, Edward, 122, 169
Leisure, 32, 43-44, 51, 55-66, 94, 107, 130, 146, 152
Levine, E. P., 121, 167
Levine, J. A., 167
Levine, Saul V., 167
Life concerns, 86-87, 100
Lingsom, Susan, 63, 166
London, J., 2, 34, 35, 73, 168

Madden, J. A., 121, 167
Marriage, concern about, 86
Marsden, Dennis, 90, 167
Maslow, Abraham, 33, 167
Maternal employment: and household tasks, 4, 44-47, 50-59, 60-71; and its community context, 116-44; and personal outcomes, 5-6, 72-88; and summer vacations, 145-53; and time-use, 43-59; child care and, 4, 47-48, 50-71, 117-20, 133-35; equity in, 3-4; expenses in connection with, 36; external settings and, 4, 116-44, 154-64; factors leading to, 32-42; implications for children, 101-15; in perspective, 1-13; incidence of, 2, 34; policy and practice, 154-64; time devoted to, 66, 81, 94, 149-51. *See also* Part-time employment
Maternal leave, 160-61
Matsushima, C., 44-45, 47-48, 62, 167
McCubbin, H. I., 167-69
McGinnis, R. G., 48, 167
McKenzie, M. A., 166
Medical care, 69, 142-43, 160
Medrich, Elliott, 103, 111, 167
Meier, Gretl S., 157, 168
Melbin, Murray, 13, 168
Meltz, Noah, 157, 168
Michelson, Ellen, 167
Michelson, William, xv, 7, 9, 19, 28-29, 31, 85, 145, 163, 167-170
Miller, J., 168
Ministry of National Health and Welfare (Canada), 16, 31
Mirowsky, John, 34, 35, 60, 74, 169
Mortimer, J. T., 2, 34, 35, 73, 168
Motivation, 102
Multiple Classification Analysis, 59
Mutual aid, 91-93, 144
Mårtensson, Solveig, 10, 118, 120, 142

Naiditch, Linda, 31
Networks. *See* Mutual aid
Niemi, Iiris, 44, 62, 168
Nollen, Stanley D., 137, 157, 168
Nordenstam, Ulla, 63, 168

Normative conflict/agreement, 74, 84, 85
Nye, F. I., 168

Oakley, A., 168
Obligatory activity, 53-54, 59, 81, 94, 145-46, 152
Observational methodology, 22
Ogburn, William, 2, 63, 168
Olmstead, B., 157, 168
Oppenheimer, Valerie K., 34, 36, 168
Ott, M., 48, 169
Outcomes, personal, 5-6, 72-88, 111-14, 131-35, 152-53
Overload, 114-15

Palm, R., 10, 121, 168
Pant, P. D., 48, 168
Parent-child contact. *See* Contact, parent-child
Parenting, concern about, 86
Parkes, Don, 9, 165, 168
Part-time employment, 50, 53, 117, 136, 156-57
Patience, 113, 114
Patrushev, V. D., 16, 19, 168
Pediatric care. *See* Medical care
Personal time, 77, 78
Phelps, Elizabeth, 16, 19, 166
Pickup, L., 48, 121, 168
Play. *See* Leisure
Pleck, J., 44, 63, 73, 136-37, 169
Portner, Joyce, 48, 73, 168
Poverty, 89-90, 94-95
Pred, A., 10, 121, 168
Prepared food, 95-96
Preschools. *See* Child care institutions and practices
Problematique, 3; on maternal employment, 3-6
Propper, A. M., 64, 168
Psycho-social disorders, 73
Psychology Today, 122, 169
Public transit. *See* Travel, mode of

Quality time, 20, 48-49, 52-53, 106

Rapoport, Rhona, 10, 35, 169
Rapoport, Robert N., 10, 35, 169
Recreation. *See* Leisure
Reed, Paul B., 9, 19, 168, 169
Renwick, Patricia, 122, 169
Response rates, 26
Responsibilities, within households, 69-71, 91-93
Richards, Lyn, 65, 145, 166
Rivers, Catherine, xix
Robinson, Hilary, 166
Robinson, John P., 44, 169

Role responsibilities, 32-33
Ronen, Simcha, 137, 169
Roper Poll, 35
Rosenbloom, Sandra, 167, 169
Ross, Catherine, 34, 35, 60, 74, 169
Routine, daily. *See* Time-use
Roy, Caroline, 59
Rutter, Michael, 48, 73, 74, 87, 101, 169

Sampling, 24-26, 28
Satisfaction, 73, 83-85, 98, 119
Schedules, of work, 63, 136-43
Schlessinger, Benjamin, 89, 90, 169
School, 107
Screening, within sampling, 28
Self-actualization, 33
Self-conceptions, 26, 85, 98-100
Self-confidence, 73
Self-esteem, 72-73, 102
Sen, L., 48, 121, 169
Sex roles. *See* Gender differentiation
Shift work. *See* Schedules, of work
Shopping, 51, 56, 67, 69, 106, 111, 121, 129-30, 142
Single parenthood, 2, 35, 89-100
Skinner, Denise, 73, 103, 169
Skinner, Louise, 121, 169
Sleep, 43-44, 51, 54, 66, 80, 106-7, 147, 152
Smythe, Reggie, 46
Social activity, 67, 80, 94, 98, 100, 106-7, 111, 129, 147-48, 152
Social ecology, 6-13; *see also* Program in Social Ecology
Socio-economic status, 78, 90
South Coast Shopper, The, 32, 169
Staggered hours, 136-37
Staikov, Z., 8, 165, 167, 169
Staines, G. L., 44, 63, 73, 136, 137, 169
Statistics Canada, 2, 37-39, 169
Stimpson, Catherine, 169
Stone, P., 43, 44, 62, 169
Strictness, 114
Structural conditions, 7
Studenmund, A. H., 48, 121, 169
Subjective measurement, of everyday life, 27, 72-88, 116-44
Sullivan, Joyce, 137, 169
Systems, 7-8
Summer vacation, 145-53
Superwoman, 73
Survey methodology, 22, 23-31
Survey Research Center, University of Michigan, 19
Sutter, J., 166
Szalai, Alexander, v, 15, 43-45, 47-48, 169

Television viewing, 51-52, 80, 103, 106-7
Tension, 81-83, 85, 87, 97, 98, 131-35
Thall, M., 166
Thrift, Nigel, 9, 165, 168
Time-budget, The, 14-23, 63-64
Time-geography, 9
Time-pressure, 9, 26-27, 75-81, 85, 86, 87, 96-97, 98, 116-44, 152-53
Time-use, 9, 43-59, 90, 93-96, 104-11, 148-52. *See also* Time-budget; Time-Pressure
Timetabling, 117, 142-43, 162-63
Toronto Transit Commission (TTC), 129, 143
Trade-offs, 9, 67-68
Transitions, in daily life, 81, 132
Travel, 4, 48-50, 51, 66, 79, 83, 93-96, 103, 106-7, 110, 117, 120-35, 146, 161-62; accompanying persons, 123-24; and child care, 133-35, 159-60; mode of, 125-33; to work, 133-35
Two-person career, 63

Unemployment, 39
Urban Mass Transportation Administration. *See* Department of Transportation (U.S.)

Vanek, J., 44, 62, 64, 65, 121, 169
Van Vliet, Willem, 64, 102-3, 169
Vincent, Clark, 89, 170
Visiting. *See* Social activity
Viveros-Long, A., 137, 165
Voydanoff, Patricia, 168, 169

Walker, K., 47, 62, 64, 170
Weaver, Peter, 159, 170
Webster's New Collegiate Dictionary, 2, 170
Weekends, 56-57, 67
Weiss, Robert, 90-91, 97, 170
Woods, M., 47, 62, 64, 102, 170
Work, 32-33; *see also* Maternal employment; Employment, concerns about
Worry, 97

Yago, Glenn, 120, 170

Zero-sum game, 8
Ziegler, Suzanne, 31, 170
Zimmerman, C., 121, 170

HD 6055.2 .C22 T676 1985
Michelson, William M., 1940-

From sun to sun

DE 3 '85

DE 17 '85

OC 01 '86